I0457317

The Great Excitingly Holy John The Baptist

MESSENGER

Stanley E. Kornafel

AUTHOR

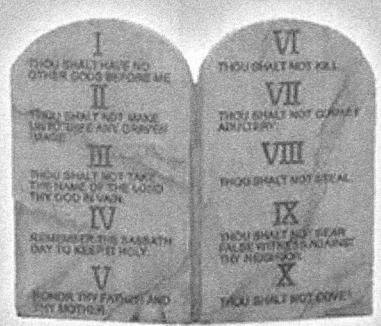

Copyright © 2023 by Stanley E. Kornafel

All rights reserved. No part of this book may be reproduced in any form or by any electronic or mechanical means, including information storage and retrieval systems, without permission in writing from the publisher, except by reviewers, who may quote brief passages in a review.

This publication contains the opinions and ideas of its author. It is intended to provide helpful and informative material on the subjects addressed in the publication. The author and publisher specifically disclaim all responsibility for any liability, loss or risk, personal or otherwise, which is incurred as a consequence, directly or indirectly, of the use and application of any of the contents of this book.

WORKBOOK PRESS LLC
187 E Warm Springs Rd,
Suite B285, Las Vegas, NV 89119, USA

Website: https://workbookpress.com/
Hotline: 1-888-818-4856
Email: admin@workbookpress.com

Ordering Information:
Quantity sales. Special discounts are available on quantity purchases by corporations, associations, and others.
For details, contact the publisher at the address above.

Library of Congress Control Number: 2015946355

ISBN-13: 978-1-957618-71-5 (Paperback Version)

978-1-957618-72-2 (Digital Version)

REV. DATE: 04/17/2023

The Great Excitingly Holy John the Baptist

APPRECIATIONS

This book is dedicated with much respect and thanks to all persons of the Hebrew Faith and Christian faith who provided help by assisting with information but, also to those who didn't wish to be bothered thinking such matter was trivial.

ACKNOWLEDGMENTS

The author wishes to express his gratitude for some much enjoyment he received as the following freely provided help via information: Reconstructional Rabinical College, Chicago plus Ohev Shalom, Swarthmore, Pa. and Congregate Beth El Men., in Broomall, Pa.

.

TABLE OF CONTENTS

PREFACE

Why are there so many questions regarding the man? Looking for specific nswers? Maybe, looking for some direction or guidance? Does the book answer all and every question? Since the author was not alive during that period of history all he could do was rely on information from what was recorded in writing by those that were actually there during that time period. many different sources were found that provided opinions while others only offered matter full of omissions or twisted statements for explanations leaving such to be construed in uncertainty. Also, it was found that people in the modern era omitted or twisted factual matter then offered unsupported opinion about not only the person but others including some of the prophets falsely making what was true to be what was not intended.

Of course, since those sources were not even born during those times, and or had no names of any witnesses such was not considered as credible, therefore those sources could not be used. So, it was where such raised the question being, how is that those of the Catholic, Christian and Jewish religious faiths, don't connect the dots while comparing the facts? So, anything not factually in written form supported was discounted. Such was done because if not, it would have been merely duplicating short statements of assumed false opinions or fiction.

In the intent of putting only true factual matter into the writing a decision of where to get information had to be made. Such matter had to be relied upon. Searching in discussion of different faiths, as well as reading from many sources, it was concluded that there was no sense in going to resources not of the original Christian and Jewish religions. But even some of them were also discounted as having either omission of paragraphs or chapters. ad such been used there would have been too much distraction or discord. Being critical was necessary to prevent confusion.

So, with all of those matters considered it was determined to use a late Nineteenth Century Catholic Family Bible. Since being taken from the original material matters it was accepted to be depended on for accuracy where all citing and quotation that were stated or shown were taken from that Bible. However, for those persons that do not care about or whether such is true there is no need for any explanation. For if truth is not important then the question is, why even bother to read anything?

Noted should be that there is no Hollywood or dream land romance or fantasy to be found in the contents. Written as close to presenting truth as much as possible was the factor for determining the result. Wherefore it is that there are enough periods of affection, love, trust and life's hardships to be found in what people at the time went through. Without adding any fantasy or fiction such is portrayed. To the author, an absence of truth is being without life. Ask an Ameba.

But there are those places where information was lacking, so along with his opinions and questioned matters Stan put some realistic assumptions as answers. For those that make statements of untruth, omissions of fact or twisted matter that looks like something factual when in fact it is not, perhaps the contents will stimulate the need for genuine research to find the truth.

Perhaps reading this book will provide many answers to those of faith. But to the others may it provoke a lot of real controversy. Either way, such will no doubt provide a little time for relaxing thought, that is, until one comprehends the depth of what he or she is reading.

Maintained was writing from objective viewpoints. So, when challenged by what he discovered the author made suggestions. Also, opinions as well as useful questions were provided. Such was done especially where there appeared no written matter provided any genuine answers. After all the author was not interested in theories.

Then too there are matters which, due to lack of any available information, denied any possible fair addressing. Amazing it was as to what he found, as how much people don't know. In those cases, such were left with questions asked. A stirring of the mind! Wow, answers only causing the growing of curiosity!

And so it is, from Stan, the author, he says, watch out! There may be some discoveries made which may allow there being some fun time of curiosity even to the point of reading amusement, while learning and receiving some knowledge.

Yet it is for sure, the information provided herein is bound to ignite much controversy. So, enjoy reading it in entirety.

And please do not skip over matter with assumptions, but read in detail. And do so with as much challenging enjoyment as he found writing it.

Sincerely,

Stan

INTRODUCTION

What a simple holy life! Was the man a Herald, or just teacher? Or, was he the genuine Holy Messenger of God who had actually been foretold by the ancient prophets? While a fascinating ancient read for the general public it may also provide some challenging substance for the academic! Generous descriptive information frequently allows drifting into the living means of the ancient world's population. Then as the fascinating drama of John's to be parents unravels a mindset of the time periods life style and peoples character abounds. Although their future son was foretold, the unknowing parents coping with frustration realizing their age seem to lose hope for any children.

However, no matter how exciting the matters of his birth which sends a message, how many truly listened and then, who even understood? Then as John the Baptist pursued his mission while challenging their-mindset he becomes a thorn in the religious and civil authorities' sides as the world around him slides into turmoil. Saluting John's purpose, a king invites all of the authorities to the ruler's birthday party.

What people in general have to say about the Baptist always generates interesting conversations. But rather than read with focus they already know, rather assume which always lead to skipping around or over. However, this book was not written by skipping through the research. Rather much investigating reading was performed which necessitated focus. Then added were the detail conversations with theologians from various universities of many religious sects and ancient history professors.

What people in general have to say about the Baptist always generates interesting conversations. But rather than read with focus they already know, rather assume which always lead to skipping around or over. However, this book was not written by skipping through the research. Rather much investigating reading was performed which necessitated focus. Then added were the detail conversations with theologians from various universities of many religious sects and ancient history professors.And where did it all end but, in a book of factual matter revealing matter that most people never knew or had taken too lightly with wrong assumptions. Such depth of ancient historical matter will truly cause readers to think about what they read in the past as much aswhat they by passed.

Not only a book to enjoy the story but also having educational appreciation due to its learning value. With all of the years gone by although the learning institutions will appreciate its content readers will enjoy the interwoven stories that make up the content.

PART I
History, People, Their Things and Parents

Chapter 1.
Do Not Older Persons Safe Guard Antiques Handed Down?

Ages in time, B.C. it was before the year of our Lord Jesus Christ There was no such thing as running tap water through pipes, only that running in creeks, streams and rivers. Pencils as well as pens such as fountain and ballpoint were only in the distant future. Then to there were no mass-produced books since the printing press was but a dream. Yet the people of those times treasured their values of religious faiths and traditions. So much so were such matters of importance that they handed the matters down from generation to generation. Only through means that were available which

What is it about those matters that cause people to be fascinated? Why do some of the situations raise the curiosity of some people but not all? Such information may be found written about and even discussed in the schools along with the religion's institutions. Yet with all of the historical documents and items found by archeologists there are those that give no value to any of the findings. But even today, do not people hand down important items to their kin?

Do not older persons safe guard antiques handed down to them, especially note books or family records? Realizing the simplistic life style, along with the complex hardship of the times would certainly help in understanding the substance of the subject matter. But then, if not of any religious faith, why would such a reader be reading it? For sure, there is no Hollywood here. Can people truly relate to the ancient times? It is highly doubtful. Yet perhaps there are more of those that can where such thinking is possible. Surely the homeless in this country, as well as those in other countries living out of tents or occupying caves can relate. Are there not those running from the various warring factions, that may be even better to understand? But mostly, perhaps this writing may present some sort of assembled picture. Maybe such can reveal not only the character of the man but the truly exciting story of John as well as his purpose.

What was considered yesterday as essentials are those things people today actually take for granted. Yet items such as cars, heaters, air conditioners, washing machines, fans, shower rooms, flushing toilets, perfumed soaps and cleaners were not even imagined back then. Yet even back then keeping healthy by staying clean was an essential. But, it too was also only a dream.

Then void of any such thing as freezers, refrigerators and electric or gas stoves, surviving meant having sufficient food to eat, which were huge challenges. Back then just having food to sustain them for the next day had to be the primary concern. Needless to say, so was clothing to wear and foot wear. Then there was the all-important matter of having a roof over one's head. Only the government along with military had any form of jobs with income. Now it was that mass production as well as mass farming hadn't been invented yet. So, with that matter combined, what jobs were there? Then too there was the coping with warring parties, thieves and hunger. Along with all of that, the people had to cope with the unexpected hindering forces of nature.

Yet with all of that mentioned, it seems that people overlook the biggest matter which was technology that was not around until the beginning of the eighteenth century. Up until that time vocal communication was only enabled in the person to person. Telegraphing means hadn't been invented nor had the telephone system. Thus, people were restricted to speaking to each other when only in each other's presence. Such it was that such life was being normal even for the well to do. And with all of those things taken into consideration if all was lost, what remained?

Perhaps with nothing material left, it was their religious faith in believing in God the Creator that carried them. Even today with all of the theories and progress mankind has demonstrated, the fact is that mankind is not able to create any form or thing from nothing.]Truthful fact is that man still absolutely needs things, materials or equipment all ready existing to put together to make something else. Man cannot truly create as cannot create from absolute nothing. Invent yes, rearrange or add to, for sure people can do all of those things. But the fact in truth remains that to create from nothing, mankind cannot do.

There was no such thing as stores to sell books or manuscripts, so any such thing as a literary work was not even heard of. Especially it was since there was no way of marketing or the most important matter of selling it. Furthermore, any form of writing was only done by learned men. During that period of history any education beyond the home was a rarity. Knowledge from education was only provided to those in families already having the knowledge. Also, there was the means of the high-ranking military or being in the upper elite.

Surviving the day by the common person was the primary importance. Being able to read was something only thought of. Then also due to the daily hardships it wasn't something desired to learn. Why would they have wanted to learn when they couldn't apply it? What for would they want to read when they couldn't use what would have been read? Perhaps such thinking was because it was not a necessity for proving food on the table.

Who would have wanted to waste time trying to learn to read when there wasn't anything to read that would improve their lives? Life during that period was either about being a member of the labor, soldiers, farmers or store owners. Of course, there were the other groups that needed to be able to read. Such was the ranking military, political and religious groups. Also, writing of any kind was laborious which demanded time. It wasn't a matter of simply grabbing some paper and pen or pencil then sitting down writing. Rather such was done only by certain abled persons that either had the time to take or where their position required it.

Such things as computers, telephone and electronic message sending devices were not even thought of at the time. Most important though is that there were no such thing as developed writing instruments. Then too, there was no such thing as writing paper. Especially such that is readily available today. Thus, if any matter found its way to being necessarily inscribed it was for sure it not only had to be truthful but also important.

Wherefore it was that for matter to be recorded it had to have been deemed necessary to the point where others should know about the matter.

Now considering all those things people had to cope with, is it any wonder that communication in those times was way beyond trying? Difficult would be the only true absolute way of describing communication during that period. Such meant that only by one person to another person on the spot or to another group could true communication be had. People were without any means of duplicating and stores to sell. Therefore, it was that there was no means to make any money off of what would be written. So, of what was written then comparatively by also others saying the same, why would they have written if the substance were not true?

Back then people only had means that would have prohibited spending on such materials anyway. With the major entertainment being struggling to provide food for the day who could afford paying for a luxury such as a written document? But then weren't most of the people back then also illiterate? So why would anyone then has even thought of writing things? Of course, if they could not read they most assuredly could not write. Most especially those that could, if such things were not true would they have written? Fiction and novels of humor or other are stories of nothing more than making believe. And considering the time period, who had time for make believe? So, it is now that one must take into consideration the serious matters of this book. Then, and only then, could the following question be answered!

And the question is, during that time period who would have had any time to waste even giving any thought to writing material that wasn't true? Then to, during those hard times who would want to put in the labor to write about things from the imagination? Most highly important to be considered is the matter that such would not have been able to be produced in volume.

A very big and major fact is that being void of volume, there is no profit. So, what person would have wasted their time? Then also why would more than one person write about the same matters if they were not true? So, it was when people desired to communicate with someone it was either a person directly to a person or persons to a group of people. Such vocal contact was the only communication means available. As a result of those times of hardship only highly significantly important matters were the only things written down. So it was that if information was not verbally passed on or not written, such matter simply got lost.

With all the modern conveniences of the day people are in a box. Even when picking up a book, people fail to realize that back in those times there was no means of reproduction. Also, neither was there any form of duplication such as carbon paper or copy machines. Such meant that all writings were done by hand. So, if there was any form of duplication to be written it would have to down by copying each page by hand. Keeping that in mind, it would have meant actually manually writing another page of the same matter.

It was still, no less a monumental task a feather along with the worst or cheapest paper. Then after completing the page copy the same matter onto another page. Such meant to write one word, then one line, then one page, then after a few, was made a tablet or book. Being so importantly busy today is considered as watching the television, sitting around the commuter or sending messages over the hand devices. Yet back in ancient times there was no such technology. There were no such things as telephones, cars, instant A good test to appreciate such would be to use an ink well with a clothes, instant foods or instant beverages, high schools and technical training centers. Then too, people only had financial means that would have prohibited spending on such material items.

Why is it so important to take those matters into consideration? Because, such things have a direct relevancy to the ways of the people during that time period! And it is that time period of which the book is about. Perhaps with all that being said, the major entertainment must have been to provide food. With meals for the day, being of primary concern, who could afford paying for an expensive luxury? For sure written documents would have been highly expensive, beyond the availability of the average person. Then again is asked, weren't most persons illiterate?

What the author finds most fascinating are the opinions he has often heard from some people. Over time he has heard such things mentioned as the bible is a printed fairy tale or simply another comic book. But aren't comic book stories or printed fairy tales' fiction? Are they not written by one person or two knowing the content is not true or didn't really happen? For whatever reason it was that such people had made a choice of refusing to believe. Of course, those same people refused to allow any discussion. Even about the Old Testament it is the same attitude prevails.

What person would take the time, encountering all the hardships mentioned above to write about a myth or other made-up fantasy? Especially, when not receiving any form of notoriety or high financial reward for the effort? Such would be likened to a person clearing the field of stones, rocks and tree stumps, then plowing a field only to plant plastic flowers. Why all the work if there is nothing to be gained? Just perhaps, there is more in life with truth and values than in self and materialism.

People may wish to think twice before considering the Old Testament as some fable. Most assuredly such thinking can only be considered as nothing other than childish. Highly noticed of those people is how important it is to them that they keep a closed mind, along with having the last say. Yet, even when having put the matters as stated above leaving no monetary reason for the scriptures, all such people would do is change the subject or refuse to answer. After all of any attempts at having a discussion it would be absolutely necessary for their having their way.

Either it came down to getting the last word. Such was by covering up the truth by asserting their initial statement or changing the subject. So, then the question, what is truth? Perhaps the best answer is the question of, what use is thought and discussion if truth is not the target? What results is nothing less than chaos. Untruth is nothing more than gray matter of incorporated deceit and fiction. And what can be built on half or in between measures? Also, where there are two faces of what is, which is not?

Then there is the sad part of watching such antics, as seeing those around such persons simply scratching their heads in wonderment as if there is no answer. Of course, there is no answer! As when people are asserting that which is true to be fable, It is only what they want to believe while refusing to accept truth. Self-righteous persons are always right in their minds even if they are wrong. But then that is the nature of the world. With all of those matters combined, such should not only be taken in context but also fully considered. Then it can be realized how it is no wonder that the significant importance of the Baptist was never reached. Also, what is missing is the true high level he should have been given, yet simply by many as not even considered. Yet, the very contents of the books of the Old Testament speak.

It is them along with being coordinated with the gospels in the New Testament that give facts of substance. Not to stop there, it is also helpful to consider other books written about other persons directly and indirectly which puts forth sufficient matter to support his importance. How awesomely inspiring it is where people have written about other persons of notoriety that touched on John's influence. Even in the writings about Jesus Christ it can be seen where persons have skipped right over John, or went around him. Also, others show little respect for what he did.

It was almost to them where depicted; he was someone that had been just another commoner. Yet it is that John was known of the many prophets of old ancient time. And how many of the Old Testament prophets were of ages before Isaias? What is a real shame is what is not known of how many prophets had passed on prophesies or written information regarding things that were to come. Then it is where the same information had gotten destroyed or lost. Perhaps there was a fire, flood or other natural catastrophewhere such valuable words could have been saved, but were estroyed. Then also there were the untold wars, where such matters of untold value were purposely destroyed. Also, there were those several about his time, with many of them being younger actually came after him.

Yet, it is there were many highly significant things that Isaias spoke or foretold which came about. And because of such, he is one of the persons which most people are familiar with. Amazing how most people don't read such matters in detail, but skip around. They try to find matters they are familiar with or which appeals to them.

However, it is necessary to look beyond as opposed to the immediate or what pleases the eye. That is, it is necessary to consider all writings, then being able to combine them. More combinations a person can find the better it is of having a more realistic result. Such compared matter then provides that which is more complete, as well as true. Those matters that are even merely similar add meat. Especially when combined, such allows better assessment to the main matter being read. Not just a few that merely appeals to one's feelings or one's assumptions should be read, but also those in proximity.   Each prophet had their own say. Along with manners of describing the situation, the difference was that some had only a few words. Then perhaps, taken by the single phrase such words would only amount to very little. Yet every little bit of such words taken along with a few from other sources, together amounts to a whole lot of one big time truth. How easy it is to discard that which does not appear to make sense or fails to provide a conclusion.

Now it is that one truth combined with one or more truths actually strengthens the support of the smallest truth no matter how insignificant it may appear. And what does all of this aforementioned matter have to do with John the Baptist? It all has everything to do with him and his family since they were about that time period. Depicted are the whys and what fore's of the events that took place. Plus, there are the descriptive words of what took place and how. And so, it is for those interested in the truth, this book presents such along with the author's commentaries and opinions plus where none could be reasonably made such matter is left questioned.

 Yet it is that these notations were put, not to take up space, but were inserted to present highly possible realistic explanations or reasoning as well as giving others a base to build on How could words of the Baptist have been so powerful in truth that his presence caused so much havoc? Why did his mission frustrate others so much they sought his death?Since the Bible and Koran both acknowledge him, with his great significance to as well as around the people, how did John come to be lost over the ages? Tis a shame, that with all of the Bibles of different faiths and religious books of different religions, John has become nothing more than a lost figure.

However now in the modern era these are times of education and progress. Yet to most people it is that they can't even remember the man's name. Then along with forgetting his name it can be reasonably assumed how they forgot his purpose. Surely it must have been that they never realized his true level of importance, especially of what he did, along with why. And if one does not understand the why, along with what his purpose was, why could all significance of John then not have been realized?

So, without that comprehension how does such not leave an absence of reason to remember him? Eventually to them he would only be just another man that was about in the period's history. Now it was during those times where it was of very strict Jewish religious beliefs. Such it was that being ruled in the faith was not if people felt like it. For such was not a matter of choice. Rather back then it was either they were of the group and believed or they didn't. Now it is, as the bible shows, Elizabeth and Zackary were very much about the Jewish faith.

Of such strong measures was the faith in those days, that death by stoning as a means of punishment in those days for adultery. Then to as it applied to prostitution how would such matters not have caused grave concern between them? Especially where compliance was enforced by strictly harsh penalties, how was such a woman's situation not precarious? In the least, who was fooling who? Perhaps such may have even been the question of the day.

`For sure their situation was not the kind of thing they needed to be harassed about. Especially they being of an older age how would such often pressing words from other people not have caused much anxiety? Would there have been those false assumptions from people talking which creates real problems? Who would believe them? Who could they turn to? Meanwhile, it is that along with the Old Testament there just happens to be the New Testament.

Now it was that since Zachary and Elizabeth were many years way ahead of the birth of Christ, why are they not found in the Old Testament? Then also since those two along with John's birth had been at the time before Jesus Christ, why are the three of them not in the least discussed at the end of the Old Testament? Yet for sure if one does not believe in one, the other avails only a limitation. And for those that don't believe in either, there is no need for discussion. After all, it is that what is written in the new confirms what was written in the old. Yet also it is visa versa here applies. However, for those that do, the old must be taken as fact, since it was the Lord God's word expressed through his prophets. And so it is that much respect is held to those facts.

Then there are those matters that are derived from comparisons along with use of imagination of matter. And it is, that such matter may have been lost over time. Considering the time period of which the book was written along with the span of time too much history has happened. Why was all this aforementioned matter put? Because, it was felt to be most important, being matters of the mind.

Comprehension of the living ways as well as the mental and religious conditions that existed during the ancient time period is significant to the understanding of how people acted. No persons of the present time period, especially in the developed countries, could ever realistically imagine the ancient time period. Feelings of living in the conditions presented to the people during that time period along with their daily mind set and emotions can only be suspect. It wasn't just the luxuries they didn't have, but there were no such things as modern conveniences. For people to read about specific persons and events from the past is a challenge.

Reading about matters during those times without comprehending the conditions that existed would not do the reading of such material any true real-life justice. There was no real peace as wars or warring parties never ceased. Abraham brought order but even then, there were factions, until Moses who brought unity. Then oppression, wars and the Romans. Although they brought order it was in a form of bondage bringing their statues and emblems. And with all of that the Hebrew religious leaders even then found a way of division. Leaving the people in disarray, some while losing their faith turned to worshiping Abraham. It is not just the buildings construction and the transportation modes that are important to consider. It is also the material things they didn't have which is highly essential. But to fully understand it is what must be taken into account is all of those things.

Choosing to skip over what is not being of interest or what may seem to be unimportant could have negative thoughts during the further reading. It is the real combination of matter and events that allows for the comprehension of the true mental attitudes and mind sets of the times. Why? Because they never had such, they could not have known to miss such. Yet they lived with what they had or able to do. Sometimes it may have been trying to hold on to the day because everything was going well. And then maybe it was rushing the day hoping it would get over quickly because thing had just been so topsy-turvy. But for sure it

The Great Excitignly Holy John the Baptist

had to have been one day at a time.

Even for the well to do class it was necessary not to delay matters of importance, therefore it is also essential for the readers not to delay. To omit or deny the reading of certain parts merely for convenience or because of assumption could eliminate the true understanding of what it is that is presented. To understand just how great John the Baptist was, it is necessary to comprehend how truly amazingly holy the man was. And for sure it is the man was very much a holy person of a special breed.

And so, as it was with him a fiery heart, the light of the word within a cloud of the spirit, let us return to those thrilling days of ancient times when the great, exciting holy, John the Baptist spread the word.

PART II. THE PRIEST

Chapter 2.

According to St. Luke, John's Mother Elizabeth Was up in Years.

A little thought for the mind. It was that although John, who was sent by God, even before he was born, was by the prophets amidst controversy. Perhaps here would be a good place to present the controversy. It was that Jesus Christ had not even been born as well as neither had John the Baptist. Now since it was that Christ yet hadn't been born along with John preceding him did not that present a different matter of times? Then since Zachary and Elizabeth even preceded John, would their times not have put them also in a different matter of time periods?

Now it is fact that the married couple preceded John. Then also it is that John being their son followed them. Also, it was that John was born some time, though shortly, before Christ. Do that matter not present fact that the three had to have preceded the Christ? So, with such factual matter having being established, how is it that the married couples' time is not found in the Old Testament? Also, since John's birth was before the Christ how is it that his birth is not found in the Old Testament? Why are the three in the least not mentioned in the Old Testament?

And so, it began! According to St. Luke, John's mother Elizabeth was up in years. She was in fact way beyond her child bearing time. Also, she was considered barren since never ever having had any children. Such is recorded in Luke: 1: 7, wherein it states, "but they had no son, for Elizabeth was barren; and they were both advanced in years". Now as most married women would surely do after some time, she must have even started praying to conceive a child. Also, it was where her husband, who was older than she, was also way past his child producing years. Would not both of them have prayed for a boy? But slowly it was that time slid by as well as so did their years. Perhaps realizing time was passing their prayers soon took on a different twist.

The Great Excitignly Holy John the Baptist

Maybe during their young years, it was hoping and praying for a specific child such as a male child. But, then as time passed would they not have altered their thinking as hoping and wishing for any child? With the years going by would the hopeful parents being desperate, not be expressing their prayers for a girl or a boy? Then once reaching her older age would she not have acted as others? Considering those factors, would she not have probably given up? Or even hoped not to have any children?

Surely people back then during those ancient times were just as intelligent as people of today. Maybe it wasn't so much of what people thought. Back then, were people lacking of comprehension or learning ability? No, rather it was that there was the big void of having no tools. What can be built without the proper tools? And not having machinery what kind of tools could they have had back then? Imagine sleeping on a bed without springs or a firmly supported mattress. Or, how about cooking without a stove having any readily available controls?

Then there is the really big item. Imagine never having running hot or cold water. Even better, think of not having any kind of running water! It was either, the creek, a stream or the well, and that was the extent of it. But to the couple getting up in years perhaps those were small problems. As for both of them, was it her or was it her husband that had a physical problem? There were no means of scientifically medical testing at that time. Therefore, since there was no way of knowing what could they do? Or perhaps, better asked is what remained for them but prayer?

Why, are those matters mentioned so much as even repeated in different ways? Such is necessary to understand that even with all of those problems the people had to cope with being dominated. Not just ruled along with being kept held under thumb, but dominated. Only when understanding all those factors coming together can one then truly understand why the people were praying for a Messiah. When people of the day are questioned in discussion they mention that they understand.

Yet when questioned about specific things all of a sudden it becomes clear they only know what they only wanted to read. It became apparent that they didn't read in detail, nor did they take into consideration what was not depicted in the written matter. Anyway, with time passing the two must have acted just like other people. Maybe being up in years the two likely got set in their ways. Slowly, they must have come to grips with the fact of life. Eventually Elizabeth and Zachary must have finally realized most likely that they were not blest as not going to have any children.

Sure, there was always hope. But for them had life slowly turned into nothing more than a daily drudgery routine? What remained for them to look forward to? For sure they still had to face each other every day, regardless of how either may have felt. Yet both were aware that as each day that went by all would be the same. Another day going by only meant that there would be less of a chance for the woman to conceive. This was not some trivial item that could have been forgotten as a pimple. Rather it was a most important matter to the couple. So much it was where they both wanted a family.

People have a way of looking down their noses at others having difficult personal problems. And surely during those years of growing past their time, the two must have received their fair share of such things. Were there the mean looks of contempt? Then some days it may have even gotten ugly. Maybe some days they even had the enjoyment of hearing some undeserved slurs. Oh, how such little things to others can cause some big pain.

Would such have been received even from their so-called friends? Would such not have caused unneeded anxiety, especially when dragged to their abode? And then there were the neighbors, along with those at the market place where everyone was aware of her position. Certainly, such people must have reminded the two. Maybe not when together but one way or another every time either was seen. Tis a shame, but it is that people are so selfish in their ways of not giving consideration to others. Oh, how the busy bodies of the world can make a day go sour.

Without even trying while attempting to be nice it may have been a wrong word.. On some days or by some people it could have been the correct word but at a bad time or in a bad tone. Wow, and then to add to all the gossip there was her husband having aposition in the synagogue/temple.

Not one of the common people of the neighborhood, her husband Zachary was a priest. Then to, as was the custom he was even older than she. Oh, how the rumors must have circulated. And then there was the gossip. Oh yes, the necessary gossip, by people talking. And how they can talk, especially about what they don't know about. It probably got thicker by the years. For sure there was plenty of material to build on. Then there were the added expressed thoughts generated by the erroneous assumptions provided by the imagination. It wouldn't have taken much for a person that loved to spread rumors to initiate some gossip.

And then there was the often-nasty vocal garbage started by someone that had a hatred of the couple. Perhaps it was there was some bitterness that was from being jealous or simply spiteful. After all she was married to a highly respected priest. A person can almost taste the gossip that must have gone around from time to time. Why not, is it not the way people are? Maybe only a few words spoken not intended as anything other than a little talk. But as some women may have been jealous of Elizabeth, especially her having life so easy, would the talk not have gained momentum? Or maybe, there was some man carrying around some anxiety. Perhaps the man was mad because he felt he could have been a priest, but for one reason or another was denied. Then along with Elizabeth being good looking, maybe such gossip could have even reached the ugly stage. Yet it could have been someone over hearing only a little or some parts of a conversation.

And then there are those mistakes of a few words void of their true meaning. What remains are the people guessing or having false assumptions. Then when the same person repeats the matter including their own added nonsense what happens? Does not the next listener take it all in as truth? Some days may have actually been easier than others. But for sure it was that there was a day here and there that even led into a couple of days in a row where such frustration turned into anger against each other. Such may have been especially difficult for Elizabeth.

When one or the other may have been able to realize who may have started one of the gossips, their dwelling may have turned into a real nightmare. Especially it may have been with their coming to realize it was someone they respected. With his many years as a priest, he would have enjoyed all the privileges of the temple. And for sure it was that most people in the area were aware of such.

The Great Excitignly Holy John the Baptist

So along with that, the couple was healthy yet not having any children. As it was they were pretty well off that is compared to others. Such information would have made it easy for any growing of gossip. Also, it is that the next person would have gotten to hear the built-up matter. Then thinking it to be true, that person then passes it on to someone else with his or her added word or two. Oh, what sadness there must have been from time-to-time hearing some of the spoken garbage from a friend or two? Such may be truly considered when taking into the accounts of the day of John being named.

So it was that Elizabeth minded her position as a wife. Most important was where she maintained her respect for her marriage partner. Then to, Zachary respected his wife Elizabeth. With him though would not such have been a special form of respect? He was fully aware of how much she desperately wanted a child. Surely, she prayed as well as he also prayed. Yet what must have been really frustrating was for him praying for the same while in the holy area of the temple. Surely, she must have daily kept after him to do so. Especially on those days while knowing that her husband would be in the altar area..

Aware of knowing the place he was to be in, would she not have reminded him? But how could he answer to his wife when there not having realized any results? All he could do, the man did so as to keep her trust. How much did he admit that he did so, as well as did often? A person could almost feel the unmentioned sorrow each was carrying. And yet it was probable that they didn't bother to complain to each other since they were both aware of how the other felt. Each could have felt for the other where emotions probably flowed like running water.

Of course, even that may not have been enough to keep her from having doubts about him. Especially, such thoughts may have been strung out when she may have been having a blue day or feeling hurt from one of the rumors. But no matter what doubts there may have been of one of the other, they never raised the issue to any arguing. Leaving the matter up to their creator they knew it was beyond there doing. So it was that the days passed. Now as it was, it just so happened, when it was to be just another day. Like any other day it was where even more so since it was one of the week days. So, it was the usual routine of endurance for Zachary and Elizabeth.

The Great Excitignly Holy John the Baptist

No special occasion or a weekend, rather it was simply another weekday. Probably it was where both at the time in their lives all healthy were not expecting anything out of the ordinary or anticipating anything different to occur. Perhaps that day even maybe some thoughts may have been where each would get through the day with ease. Yet with the constant thought of no child, she was probably just dragging herself around going through the motions. Then with her husband being despondent such emotions only made the going tougher. Some mornings being so depressing they may have even been more than a challenge.

Then it may have been for Zachary each day had become more and more burdensome. He must have felt as if he was carrying some sort of a metal cactus in his gut. Was it nerves, tension, ulcers or mental self-punishment? And with him constantly dwelling on his inability to produce a child, would some mornings not have been where he didn't even want to get up? How would such a heavy burden not destroy a person's personality? Then to, would it not affect his mind keeping him off balance?

Would holding such misery inside not cause him to be unable to have any further interest in life? Should he have grown miserable, even almost intolerable? And then, how would such a depressing attitude not rub off on his wife? Such must have been extremely difficult for Elizabeth. How would she not having been actually feeling the same way? Also, there was his realizing of his failure to fully succeed. After all there was the issue of his priesthood. It was that he was also constantly carrying the thought of him having been passed over for being a high priest. Fact was that his ambition of reaching the highest office as a high priest had not been realized.

Of course, his wife was fully aware of the fact, but she didn't try to hold it against him. Most likely her kindness didn't even help with his professional situation. However, her understanding must have at least made conversations somewhat pleasant. Such meant a great deal especially since she knew how his setbacks deeply affected her husband What sadly depressing days there must have been that she had to cope with! Elizabeth couldn't very well talk to him about his priestly duties. Especially such it was since there was not to be any advancing. Then to she couldn't very well speak to him about things regarding expecting a child.

The Great Excitignly Holy John the Baptist

Oh my, how some mornings must have been a real chore? What held them together? It may have been that stress could have reached the level where it was the main course at the time for breakfast. With Zachary not being able to father a child such realization probably festered. With him carrying his hurting deep down inside it burned at him every day. Perhaps there were never any tears shown by him on the outside. Yet on the inside there were probably bucketfuls. At least some sadness had to have burned every day between the two. And sometimes it may have been where there was actual misery. Could it have been even that awful type of misery, such may have been that carries actual pain? Such a low attitude may have resulted where it was almost from time to time that such mood may have been dense enough to be cut with a knife.

A person could almost hear him tear at himself. Those days really feeling low, perhaps he would break out under his breath ranting to his Lord, why he has no child. Then his wife upon hearing his cries couldn't hold back her built-up sadness. How would she not break down with her insides all built up with depression? Would Elizabeth not have been despondent? And perhaps with her it may have even been more so, as carrying the feeling of being robbed of motherhood. Would their having seen neighbors or others with children not further their anxiety?

Yet the older couple must have truly loved each other, as well as had respect for each other. Maybe they even made the most of every day as they did things just to keep busy. Attempts at keeping the mind out of the rut could have been a priority. But then to, most days had most likely gotten into a monotonous routine. During those days when nothing out of the ordinary was ever expected or planned how would the days not have been difficult? A person could almost feel the letdown feelings that emanated from the couple. Perhaps there were those days when even neither could help each other as they trudged through a day.

Who thinks about good things when swimming in a depressed atmosphere? Sure, maybe they eventually even came to grips with realizing their being passed over for a family. But since no one could really help what good was the realizing? Watching, with maybe a little tear in her eye, Elizabeth saw her husband exit their doorway in his priestly garb. Would she have felt a little pride seeing him clothed with white linen on his head then also the rest of him covered in white linen? Then with the sun's rays hitting his outfit, would it have caused her a moment of reflection? It was one of those days of her feeling her warm love for him.

As the sunlight glittered through, reflecting off his white garb it caused her to reflect on their younger days. Having had many years of love they were able to share, it could have been any day.Even though the Lord had not given the opportunity to raise children, they did have each other. Such in itself was really a tremendous blessing of which both had come to realize. So many men and women traverse the world alone or, if not alone, they have appalling conditions to contend with. Yet unable to turn off her feelings she still may have smiled while in a blasé' state of mind.

As he passed through the doorway, did it hold her captive in thought? They had gone through so many hard times, maybe her mind drifted into thinking about one or another. Then having suffered so many setbacks the couple probably quit talking about them. Or maybe, they kind of smiled at each other realizing what they had overcome together. But either way, it was that he never gave up on her. And then her being appreciative of that matter it may have allowed Elizabeth's mind to drift. Why would she not have slumped into a state of good recollections? Recalling their younger years, maybe she even reminisced.

Thinking about a night they had when they had been married only a short time perhaps it lifted her mood. Her husband wanted to travel the world in any way that they could. Yet, Elizabeth knew somehow in her gut, that they had to stay where they were and enjoy each other for as long as the Lord would allow. While laying around some time maybe optimistic words were spoken by each describing their thoughts trying to cheer each other up. How many children they would be having must have been a part of every conversation. Such simply had to be the focal point. Perhaps, such was even where they agreed to how many boys and or girls they would have.

A large family was not only thought of, but was most highly desired by both. Yet little did either of them know that having a large family was not what the Lord intended for them. But, in fact, a greater glory was to be theirs. However, coming to grips with such a life matter didn't make their lacking go away. Also, the two's attitude also may have slid into a pattern where they were simply biding their time.Surely with nothing to expect along with not being able to plan for a child, such must have really left the two stressed out. Such feelings must have been especially hard with each feeling inadequate.

Would not any ordinary person encountering such conditions be stressed with planning for a child that never comes to fruition? However, over time Elizabeth being the woman that she was came to realize just how deep the love between she and Zach was. Maybe along with being so much in love they also had a strong faith.

So strong was their love and faith that perhaps they felt they could overcome all obstacles. Yet it would have only taken a small incident to cause a loss of optimism or loss of respect of the other. Yet with all of the good people around along with all of their good intentions there was no one to help. No one could offer any suggestions on how to try harder or offer any new or different alternatives. Eventually Elizabeth and Zachary came to understand that there was no one to help.

Maybe they helped each other come to grips with those things. Such supporting each other may have provided some ease for them to have at least some direction. Surely, it must have been where they found it more important to carry on every day, with at least making their days productive and happy ones. No matter how or how much they tried though, coming to grips with such a life matter didn't make the situation go away. Also, the two's attitude also may have slid into a pattern where they were simply biding their time. Surely, with nothing to expect along with not being able to plan for a child talk was empty. Maybe it had reached the point where the issue had left the two stressed out.

With each feeling inadequate, yet with all of the good people that were around along with all of their good intentions, there was no one to help. No one could offer any suggestions on how to try harder. Also, there was no one to offer any new or different alternatives. Nor could any of their friends offer any suggestions as how they could help themselves or who to see. Now it was that since the priests as well as other holy people couldn't help, nor offer any praying assistance, who was left to come to their rescue? Though the couple was up in their older years, with all their life experience, it was that the two may have eventually found themselves caught in a rut of helplessness.

The Great Excitignly Holy John the Baptist

There was no one anywhere that could provide any type of remedy. Oh, how the couple must have suffered especially on those days where the feelings of loneliness and isolation had taken over the atmosphere. Yet instead of falling into an easy shell of frustrating depression, Elizabeth must have shown her strength. She made sure they did not remain in a rut of helplessness for long. Whatever it was, perhaps she must have believed that the Lord wanted only happiness for them in whatever form it was to arrive. Quite possibly she may have felt that even with all hope gone for having any children the peace which the Lord God had given truly surpassed all human understanding. With men having their down days, Zach certainly had more than his share of those days. His wife would have had to have been strong especially with her having her days. Perhaps she was able to receive some acknowledgement of unspoken gratitude from him.

Maybe there were those days when he may not have had a good night's sleep. Perhaps the subject matter wouldn't stop ringing in his mind where he found himself really thankful for her support. Respectful of his wife, he may have started his day coping with going through his time of anxiety. Then she was there showing her best intended actions. For sure, as close as they were, he must have known in his heart of her anxiety. Then to, he also was aware of her love of him, as she provided her daily verbal support.

Perhaps it wasn't just the verbal matters, but her not letting herself down by keeping up with her daily chores that wives normally do. If she didn't keep herself together mentally and emotionally who would? Certainly not her husband, for she was fully aware that he was emotionally drained. Feeling so inadequate his hurt inside must have run deep. Then to face his partner, his wife with his anxiety, her supporting role was paramount.

If she didn't emotionally support him, he may have fallen into a real state of suicide depression. Then what would she have been left with? So, it may have been that during that time in their lives, for the two maybe it was not just another day of passing the time but one of getting over the challenge they both endured. However, for Zachary, although it began as one of those usual boring days something would be different.

It was just another weekday just like any other. Such it was where he being a priest was to officiate according to his office's practice. And such was a most sacred custom moment of much tradition. So, having already been chosen by his peers, it was his turn of duty.

With all of the responsibility of the office, for that day it was for him to be inside the temple, to conduct an offering. This wasn't some single prayer or other that the common people could do. Rather his position would be at the holy place. Yet, it was not in the most holy of holies. But at least he knew he had a purpose of responsibility. He had a duty which was that he was there to worship his Lord God for his people.

CHAPTER 3

But Actually, Maybe Zach Preferred Him Being Alone.

Not having the position of a high priest, he was forbidden to enter the most holy of places, which was the holy of holies. But as a priest he could at least enter into the holy place which preceded the holy of holies. Such would be similar to a vestibule in a house. And it was such was the holy place where the altar was located. Not only was it that it was his turn, but it was the day where he had the privilege of being all alone at the altar. And since there was only one entrance there was only one way to get inside. This all meant that once inside it was all about him.

Of course, this wasn't the day for one of the big kind of red-carpet ceremonies. Such major ones were only performed on weekend, holydays or for special occasions. Of course, during those services, the high priests as well as others participated. But actually, maybe Zach preferred him being alone since he could offer his special prayers for his wife to have a child. Either way, his service for the day was probably that purpose of sacrificial prayer on behalf of the whole people. There it was his duty probably to offer some leavened bread along with burning incense as an offering for peace.

During other services there would have been unleavened bread along with crackers and oil. Then to there were usually two services performed. One would have been held in the morning probably being the one where the public attended. It would have been at that service where they presented their gifts to be offered. Most likely it was held in the morning and the other service in the afternoon could have been the same.

But it was that particular day where for him it was to be different even though there was nothing special scheduled. With none of the public bringing anything or having reason to attend, for Zach it would have been the simple bread and incense offering. No doubt he must have taken advantage of the situation. After all, being able to offer at the same time his prayer along with one for his wife, it was a special time. This was his day alone of obligated responsibility with no one to assist him Oh, sure there were many other priests around that could have performed the ceremony but it was by policy where that day, it was his turn.

So it was that those other priests had other responsibilities to take care of, however their duties were outside of the altar room as not inside with him. They were still inside the temple but outside of the holy altar area. Guarding the entrance way was one of their duties at the time as for them they had their responsibility along with other levities to prevent any entrance by anyone. It was an absolute strict custom that no one was permitted any entrance to the ceremony if not scheduled. Such was the holy custom that it guaranteed Zach a time fully alone able to pray to his Lord God.

It is essential to take into consideration the strong religious faith the people had during that time period. There was much strife as well as much suffering from oppression. Also, it is most important to remember that no one up to that time had ever seen their Lord God. Meanwhile it was that other people of the world during that time period were worshiping the planets, or stars while other peoples were doing such things as sacrificing to stuffed figures of animals while in other counties or tribes the people were actually killing one of their own then offering parts of if not the whole dead person as a sacrifice. Plus, in other places, who knows what other people did that didn't know of or about the true Lord God?

Yet it was at the time that the Jews did have the factual matter of the true God. Of course, it was all about that matter which was relayed through Moses and the prophets. Although such information was handed down to them during the time periods that passed, again it was that none of the Jews had ever seen God. Yet it was they rejoiced because at least they had the words of Moses to rely on. Plus, they also had the commandments which were given them through Moses directly by God the Creator.

So it was that the people knowing those things kept them in their hearts. Such trusting is what was taught. Then having the stone tablets which were material things that were actually seen it allowed for their growing of a strong faith. Now it was that daily during the time of sacrifice people were always there. Always it was people were within the temple walls conducting business. Also there probably were those that were there for socializing as well as partaking in the religious ceremony through their prayers. With the temple covering a large area, the people being within the walls of the temple were contained in the yard or plaza. Yet it was that none of the common people were ever permitted inside the two holy spots.

Meanwhile in performance of his duty, Zachary's was not a single simple act procedure. Some of the simple things as done in the modern times such as lighting a candle or singing some hymns depicted peoples' involvement. But back then there was no such actual doing by the people as it was all about the priest. It was that during the time of Zachary where his action at the altar was a most highly sacred moment. No people of ordinary means could carry out the offering as only men could rise to the position of a priest. No matter how great a woman was or her authority they were never permitted to be priests. Even the type of clothing to be worn by a priest was regulated. So also, was that which was to be offered. Then also so it was that each item to be offered had a specific way of being offered along. Also, along with the how was for what purpose.

Requiring much veneration from him, his position also demanded knowledge of the scriptures. Such holy matters were only performed by certain persons that had put in their time as well as were specially qualified. Then too even qualified persons with sufficient interest still had to be approved by the high priests. Demanding most respect, the whole scene drew much reverence for what was being done. Such reverence had to be shown especially since it was all being performed for who else, but praise to their Lord God. Also, it was that the duty had to be done with the purpose of why! Steady growing emotions of Zachary along with his thoughts must have greatly intensified as he would have gone through the motions. Did heartfelt sincerity occupy his total being? Even to the point where his personal childless burden was removed? Would such focus have been to the extent of being taken over, in a most heart piercing manner?

Most assuredly the atmosphere inside was always freshly clean to start.

The Great Excitignly Holy John the Baptist

Yet the air would soon become slowly filled with rising smoke. As the burning incense consumed the air one could almost sense the solemn emotion of Zachary. While moving around in a state of holy feelings did his emotions take over? Having performed this duty over and over for such a long time had it become a bore to him? Or was it such a special moment to him knowing how he could offer personal prayers for him and his wife? Then too, surely he was aware of the people outside the altar area which would have been praying. And it is that there were always many, many people doing such.

So perhaps he also felt that his prayers along with those of the many people outside would be heard. And then, maybe even they would have been answered. Such things about the people are found in the written record of Luke Chapter one. There it is where he states about the multitude of people being outside in prayer during the time of service. Important here is to comprehend the intent of the word, multitude. Why? Because it indicates a large number, as not being several or simply a few. So highly significant is the word multitude that its usage must be taken into consideration with the small type of service. Such combination clearly indicates the faith of the people as such was not a ceremony having special interests nor was it a holy day. Rather it was the simple daily service performed thru their custom.

For years he and his wife had been praying for a child. Possibly it may have started out in hopes for a boy. But then as time passed, with no new life perhaps their prayers were probably reduced to times of begging. By then it would have made no difference to them. Whether a boy or girl it made no difference as in desperate frustration they most likely prayed for either. Just after such a long time it was they may have prayed that any child would be welcomed. They may have even pleaded so hard their prayers had turned into moments of begging. Why not, as she was the wife of a priest? Such it could have been her thinking especially had she grown impatient.

Had her heart grown hard thinking of why should she have been left out? Was such her thought, or was it the fact that they had lived such a sheltered life where maybe she was lonely? Such was the home front where her husband wanted terribly to have a son, yet it was that she had not been providing. There may have even been days of total boredom. Would not such miserable days have fed the fires of lonely anxiety?

The Great Excitignly Holy John the Baptist

Such times may have been, especially when Zach had no duties to perform along with there being nothing going on in the market place. Perhaps such difficult times were actually for a purpose. Maybe the couple had been selected by the creator that knew of their strong faith. Perhaps God allowed it to enable such a trying marriage, for the purpose of actually preparing them for the hard times ahead. For perhaps it was that raising John the Baptist would not have been an easy chore. Just maybe there was a reason beyond the human understanding.

What if due to the neighborhood, along with John's holiness the Lord God would have required parents of much character? Could not their years of hardship been intended from above? There were no televisions, computers, radios, telephones or vehicles so what would they have done for amusement? Then with no child being in their midst it must have created days of absolute boredom. Would such times not have magnified any feelings of empty loneliness? Then also would not such feeling have intensified any anxiety?

How easy it could be to say they had or did something. But it must be strongly considered how they were up in years. Such was by then were a time where it was way past their child producing years. How could other people have understood their situation? Unless having experienced the same marital depriving how could anyone comprehend the depth of the woman's depression. And then too would not the same apply to a man? Then since the two were combined in the same residence occupying the same bed, would not such anxiety or depression be magnified? Yet, if never having experienced such hurtful matters, how could anyone be truly able to relate? However, it must have been that there were days which could have had at least provided some pleasant moments.

Now, with Zachary being all alone, isolated from all the people, would not his mind have wondered, recalling all those things? Surely the years of bearing those thoughts must have really exploded in his mind. For at least a few moments, would he not have contemplated on of one of those times when he and his wife dreamed of their children to be had? Meanwhile, filling the air around him was the burning incense where it mixed with the air which probably but slowly permeated his nostrils. After years of practice with the odor coming to mean so much its strong presence must have quickly removed any doubt as to why he considering his years of service. Then combined with the intensity of his praying, maybe it overwhelmed the man's mind to the point where it took his pride to new levels.As the action of the minutes slid by, while performing his duties, there could have even been felt some mild excitement. Such feelings could have really blossomed, especially with him being aware that the other priests were outside.

Such would have put any man in a similar position to enjoy a feeling of peaceful contentment. Also, not to be over looked is the fact that there was the crowd of people that were outside. Regardless whether they were shop keepers or shoppers or those socializing, all were aware what was going on inside. Plus, they knew what the usually normal amount of time the service took. So it was that the people were outside along with the other Levites and Pharisees. Then too, there were the other priests along with the Levites in attendance being in the hallway that ran from the entrance to the holy place. But they were there with specific duties of keeping the people out. Where ever those priests were, for sure there would have been some located at the entranceways. Their full responsibility for the time was the ensuring absolutely that no one entered.

It was that one day, that one-time special occasion for him when the priest in his daily performance was assured of being all alone. Not only was no one assisting, but no one was even permitted to be in the same immediate area to even watch. It was his time to be alone with his Lord God. As with any human organization there's always the other matter. There's those occasional other some ones that abuse their office. Whether it would be for monetary gain, greed or power some people just have to have more. Then too, those persons with such on their minds don't care how they get it or reach their goal.

Whether it is stealing or doing something criminal that could even ruin another person's character it is their ambition that only matters. As long as success is realized regardless of what damage they cause to others, that's all that matters. And because of those matters there came about the split of religious factions. Whether it was the actions of one person or several such actions resulted in a separation. Over time it was that the priests while continuing the same custom became the Sadducees. But as for the conservatives it was that they had to be different. It was that they pressed for more prayer, but also required more giving. Less and less became their mode of making offerings which was costly.

The Great Excitignly Holy John the Baptist

After all, of what was offered whether an animal or the incense, it was still a matter of cost.

So it was that their group became known as the Pharisees. Yet with all of the discord both groups remained believing in the same one Lord God. So it was that meanwhile amid all the controversy Zachary remained a priest true to his belief. Would it not have been that he too may have had many opportunities of temptation? Many opportunities had to have been presented for other things. With him being a man like the others is such not the way of the world? And then why not? Would he also have not experienced those moments for greed or power that people get? Yet, Zach lived as he believed. It was that he kept his self being above such things.

Then being the good person that Zachary was, he tried his best to be one of holiness, while doing what was right. Such must be assumed as true since there is no written matter anywhere that would suggest otherwise. So, it was where his character was so strong that even though he had not reached the highest office, it was that he was truly respected. Just a person of simple means not being known for any abuse, greed or seeking of any power.

The man did his best at what he could do. Yet being a priest/rabbi of such esteem, he did have a post that was above most others. Able to enter the holy place where others could not, must have allowed his having a great feeling of at least some accomplishment. Here it was where the man was in a position for demonstrating his faith. Plus, for him, it was a time where it was extra special. It was the only day, time and place where he could actually leave all his collected baggage of anxieties or depressed feelings outside. Even many others that were religious persons were denied entry. Those being of a lower religious level would never have been allowed to enter. Then knowing that women were never allowed to be priests could have also added to his good feeling. However, knowing his wife's feelings perhaps it also cast a shadow over him

Maybe it was instead that he felt bad as her not having been blest with any children. Also, there may have been the feelings of being restricted from ever being a priest. How much could she have taken; he may have wondered? Certainly, those thoughts may have also come across his mind as he prayed. How much mixed-up feelings could he have had from day to day. Are any of those matters shown in the Koran or other religious books? It must be asked, why not? So, it was for him, not just a job or duty but a privilege. Then such duty along with its responsibility mixed with his family's situation must have overburdened him mentally. Perhaps even higher levels of hardship may have come from the skeptical expressions made by his peers.

And oh, how superiors or persons of higher ranking can be so selfish or arrogant. But then such it is where people not knowing and understanding can be so hurtful. Perhaps they may not have intended any type of hurting of feelings. But even the best of words spoken in a cynical tone or at the wrong time or in combination can be devastating. Then to there are those that have the comical attitude. Regardless of the day, or time such persons often find it being able to express how everything is a joke or funny. How would their slurs not be hurtful? Especially when it was during a person's time of having much personal difficulties? So, there is a question here that is asked. When one considers the above, how would those persons not suffer when receiving such words? Perhaps even knowing there was no wrong intended?

Then to be cooped up with the married partner that may have incurred a similar matter. Maybe at times it may have even been worse. Having been in a situation perhaps a person had fallen among a few that had rubbed it in, enjoying their mental abuse. What a day such may have been.

Tribulations of the couple there surely must have been. Yet it is where none of those little things they may have encountered are mentioned. Such matter is considered as would have been noted by someone even if only one or two things. But there being no record of anything they may have endured, simply does not make sense. Maybe such matters were noted, but lost in a storm or flood. Then also maybe they were destroyed in a conflict or an earthly eruption of some sort. Of course, such missing matter calls for people to use some common sense.

With a little thought such areas of missing matter can be filled in. Maybe not with exactness trying to put them like to other people, but with a little effort of some thinking, such thought along with the use of imagination could at least provide some relevant closeness.

The Great Excitignly Holy John the Baptist

Is such matter really important? Maybe by itself probably such matter is not. But when considering how people in general think, then about the couple's situation, how is one to relate if such matters are not taken into consideration? All of this is important especially since it has direct bearing on both of them with what occurred in the near future.

CHAPTER 4.

A Person Could Almost Feel His Attitude of Confidence Building.

Now it was, that usual day of nothing would be a particular day. It was that day where inside at the altar Zachary was offering the incense. Such was the time for the means of sacrificial prayer. Does the Koran really state, that he was working inside the Temple? Not only is the word "working" error as applied in its use, but the phrase is demeaning. Such is not only wrong but especially out of place. While omitting any indication of what was being, worked at, it is so vague that the word becomes useless.

First is the question of whoever wrote the phrase? Where is a name and witness? Then is asked where were they at the time period of Elizabeth and Zachary? Were they even around during the time period of history? Such must be questioned because it was that the event was during a time B.C. or before Christ. Did not the Koran come about until a much later time? And a hundred of years afterward is much, much later time. Even it was that centuries in time had passed.

Now it is that the gospels of the bible were written by people that were physically there and present during that time period. But if not during those specific days they knew other persons who were. Or maybe not immediately thereafter, but having contact with people that were about the time of the older couple. So, what does that all mean? It significantly means that those persons doing the writing could have gotten their information directly from the very people they were writing about. Also, it is they could have received their information directly from others that were there, who may have seen or heard during that time period.

Not to forget is most important, that it is they could have spoken to people who actually knew the people being written about. But for whoever was available that had the information which was provided those doing the gathering, it had to be taken at the time. They just couldn't wait until some other time or year as such matters of importance couldn't wait. Since there were no such things as tape recorders or tablets of note paper any information received would have been written to preserve it. Such would have been done especially if the matter was deemed essential. In those days memory was the most valuable tool available. Now it is that Zachary was a priest, where he was performing his duty at the place of the holy altar. He was not just some visitor or a hired hand, somewhere wondering around in the temple catching the sights.

Specifically, as recorded he was at the most holy place of the temple. Then what is most highly significant is that he was not working such as gardening or planting flowers. Why was usage of the word "work" put if not solely intended as a misleading term? But most especially it is that the phrase doesn't specify what type of work it was. Also, it is such is misleading because the word, work by itself, is void of what form of work was being done. To do such can only be taken as a means to require use of the imagination. There is no doubt that such things are terrific when reading fiction or fantasy.

When researching or, even simply reading of factual matters from history things may be taken differently. Such matters left to the imagination leaves a lot to be desired. Also, it is that leaving out of, or omissions of known fact of specifically what work was done, is somewhat deceitful. It is that such an act allows the twisting of fact into what is not. Basically, the leaving out of descriptive parts leaves too much to guessing. And guessing then reduces all to a being theory, which in no way can be considered as fact. Then being not fact, it cannot be a truth.

Generally, people truly consider the word when used by itself as labor. Therefore, the word is usually attached to some form of physical exercise or also it is taken as a form of manual labor. An example could be where such could have been taken as digging a whole, cutting wood or polishing some things. For Zachary, it is for certain, that such was not the case. As there is no imagination needed when reading Luke's description, in his section of the Bible.

Fact is, as reported, Zachary was practicing his priestly duty of offering at the altar. It was an act incorporating only the most holy reverence. This holy performance was done in the room that was before the inner sanctuary. Wherefore it is that such place was known as the Holy of Holies. It was that the Holy of Holies was where the Arc of the Covenant would have been from time to time. Whereas, since it was the most sacred highest place of holiness inside the building, it demanded veneration and not work. Wherefore it is that the fulfilling by any priest, such as Zachary, of his holy duty cannot at any time be considered as work. To even think or categorize such holy means as work could only come from people absent of any respect for the Lord God. Such thinking could be taken as heinously disrespectful at best.

Now it is to another matter where the person of Zachary must not be confused with Zacharias, as they were two different people. It is that Zacharias was one of a group of the last of the Old Testament prophets. Shown by the written records of the past, it is that he was not the man married to Elizabeth. The fact is that Zachary was the only husband of Elizabeth. Any reference to the contrary of him being the husband is totally in error and wrong. It is that such is proven by the repeated mentioning of the couple in those ancient writings. Since they are depicted in various as well as several times is sufficient proof that establishes the couple as Elizabeth and Zachary.

Things done by Zachary were at the altar of incense where also found in the room would have been the golden lamp stand along with a table. Had there been other forms of offerings such would have been done at the table of the loaves of proposition. One must consider the sanctity of the two sections along with the sacred actions performed. Sanctity of the event in the holy place prevented any time where people would socialize or engage in meals. Motions performed by a priest such as Zachary while at the altar, was all about the offering of prayers. Praying was before as well as during the burning of incense which was for the intentions of peace as well as of the people. Such a holy time could not be considered in any manner a form of work intensely respectful, the sacred ceremony was a matter of worshiping the Lord God for his people. Therefore, to consider such a time in any way such as work is almost blasphemous, simply attempting to deceitfully twist it into something of which it is not.

Worshiping by a priest, whether of the Jewish or Christian religious societies is of the most holy sacredness. It is not only the what, that was done but the holy intention of the event. So much so is the sacredness that it cannot even be remotely considered in any other fashion or category other than holy worship. So, it was that up to that time of day it had just been another day of going through his normal life's routine. Perhaps Zachary even left his abode in the morning feeling all low. Yet it was where he was aware that at least he had something to look forward to. Confidently he knew how he could lose himself, once at the altar. For a person of his conviction such was a big matter. For it was, that once inside his place at the altar, most negative thoughts relative to his personal life, possibly were able to be put out of his mind. Such would occur especially when once his service began.

So passionately it was how he must have gone through the motions of the ritual. Understanding how practice makes perfect perhaps it would have been that Zach having so many years of practice would have moved with skill full precision. Though all movements would have been with intense holiness they would also have been done in a fashion liken to a boxer. Plus, his moves were probably made particularly easy that day since there were no expectations of occurrences out of the ordinary.

Preparation with prayers was done right from the start, then they intensified when along with the burning of the incense. Praying as he watched the smoke rise maybe he got caught up in the moment as he intensely offered his prayers. Maybe Zach may have even been emotionally overwhelmed. What the priest was doing, perhaps it is in today's world people might consider such procedure as high school stuff or superstition yet, back then there was no such thing as high school. His area would have been quiet plus there was no one else around.

Would such a situation have allowed the man's confidence to have soared to a high level? Perhaps it may have been a special feeling that would have heated any man's ego. And then along with Zachary being a man holding the office of a priest, why not a little ego? Especially it could have been him realizing the situation. Surely, he was fully aware that during that particular hourly time the whole altar area was totally occupied by him.

Such exclusivity it was that no one else was in the room, but himself, he was all alone. Just maybe even a warmness of extra holiness could have overwhelmed him. Fully into what he was doing, maybe he even experienced a couple of joyous moments feeling of being really close to his Lord God. A person could almost sense his humbleness as he moved around with certainty. This was not the same as during a consecration of a male child where several priests would attend. Nor was it a day of a special celebration where even the high priest as well as the people attended. No, this was not a day of one of those special occasions.

Rather it was a day of a different time. It was the usual regular type of ceremony of which was practiced even more than once in a day. Being just one of the normal weekdays it was the one day that he really looked forward to.Here it was on that particular day where Zachary had the full responsibility of solely performing the total duty of the service. However, the big plus for him was that it was all by his lonesome. But, had he any idea of what was about to transpire would he have been even more respectful? Only a person that has ever had a holy experience of duty could fully appreciate his mental activity. So it was that during the service he was performing, Zach may have reflected on his position.

No, he wasn't thinking about his home life's problems, rather it was his concern was his immediate position. There it was where at the time all the other priests, as well as the people were not allowed in the same closed in area. Then too, raising the security of the situation it was where there was only one entrance. That meant there was only one way to get in. Wow! A person could almost feel his attitude of confidence building. Surely, it was known to all that the service was to be nothing out of the ordinary. To everyone else in the temple, especially it being the usual daily routine as done with other priests, it would only take the normal amount of time. But to that particular priest, at that particular time the situation at hand would be different.

There was not to be any extra service to be performed therefore it would only be the normal service of usual duration. Along with everyone else outside, as well as denied any entry how would his focus not have gotten a boost? Not only was it that entrance to the altar room was restricted but there were the Levities and priests guarding to prevent any person's entry. Then to, there were the scribes along with other lower religious persons guarding the main entrance to the hallway. So it was that even if someone was found in one of the other rooms that needed attention there was plenty of authority abounding that could have provided any assistance, food or beverage needed.

The Great Excitignly Holy John the Baptist

Even in such an emergency the priest performing at the altar would not have been disturbed. In fact, he would not even have own about it until after the service. Perhaps it was just the right day at just the right time. Then too, just maybe, it was that Zachary was in the right place at the right time. But for sure it was not coincidence of what was to take place. Had he overcome his lowly feelings with sincere prayer, or had they been replaced with ego? His emotions at first may have even been totally flat, as earlier feeling a bit of being rejected. Being healthy, maybe everything seemed as if it was all going according to the usual manner of performing his duties. But perhaps, finding such in repetition, earlier he may have felt that life was becoming boring.

When he left his residence maybe he was feeling the same low way as usual. Then also his wife may also have been feeling in her low state. And being his better half would she not have had to put up with his negative attitude? There was no move to the television to watch some half hour serial. Nor was there a telephone where she could have called one of her friends. Gee, and then to think that there was no radio where she may have wanted to listen to some good classical music. After all, what had she to look forward to, other than just another day of being lonely? And with none of those advantages along with not having any children how empty the residence would have seemed.

No activity plus no other family members living with them, oh how alone Elizabeth must have felt. Of course, it would be extremely difficult for anyone, who has not directly experienced any long periods of loneliness to comprehend what she must have gone through. With her husband not around, as well as having no children, for the rest of the day there wasn't much to look forward to. Oh sure, there was the preparing of food that would keep her, what? What would such chore do, keep her amused? Maybe there was even the time of being entertained, especially if she had a small accident such as spilling something. Or maybe there was a little forgetfulness as left the rolls in too long. Such may have been boredom in today's times, but back then perhaps it was a moment of excitement. Then there may have been the mending or washing the clothes to keep her busy. But being of the normal daily routine, how much of that could fill a day?

No matter what was done, nor how often, all was probably done along with at least some wondering being done when her husband would return. What a tedious and often boring life they must have had. Especially knowing their prayers for having children had never been answered. And those things must have bothered both of them day after day. Those were difficult feelings which could have only grown year after year. Such could have been where disappointment may even have turned to often feelings of depression. Then too, on some days maybe could there have been anger against their God?

Then, what about Zach's attitude? Was he not carrying a load of bitterness? But, on that particular day things as well as time were to be different. Unknown to her, it was that her husband's usual attitude during the service had changed. Whatever it was that happened, perhaps that day he was feeling his old self of pride. But then along with all of the good stuff, there are those days where the not planned for things just seem to happen. No matter how well things are planned or thought of being as the usual something happens. Even when they start off seeming to be going as expected, are there not those days when things just seem a little, not so well? Perhaps a finger can't be put on it. Also, maybe an explanation of words just can't be found. Yet there may have been the feeling that something just wasn't right. But who pays attention to such feelings?

When things may seem that all is going as usual with nothing different happing, does the unexpected happen? Is it not during those times of normal feelings, when all of a sudden the unwanted, unexpected occurs? Would not such thought be applied to those also having lived in the ancient times? But at least they didn't have to worry about being run over by some crazy behind the wheel. Such may happen where some person gets mentally wiped out on alcohol or drugs. Then also it could be a person being on some drug while being immersed in depression going around in a killing spree. Such, would be where they were running over people because they felt that they were having a bad day. For sure it was not the same for the old couple. Totally in the dark as unknowing what was to occur that day but it was to be where that particular day in the life of Elizabeth and Zachary it would never be forgotten. No matter what their life was like before that time it was a different day of which very few experience.

From that particular day, their life would never be the same again. Their home life would never experience any more being tedious. Nor would the couple realize any more days of boredom. Actually, their lives would be so turned upside down it would never even be close as the quiet life they had experienced. But how could they have known what was about to happen? He was not one for using a crystal ball to see the future. Then also she was not one of cards or tea leaves. So, with all of that, along with the fact that no one had ever warned them of things that were to come about, the couple had no idea as to what was in store for them that day. No storms or visitors plus there were no relatives expected that would have required special readiness. So, to them it was just another boring day of going through the motions. Maybe it was a day to relax and take advantage of the good weather. Then with having something quick for dinner it could be an enjoyable evening for both. Would she tell him about how she spent the day, and then would he describe to her what happened in the plaza? What if anything could she have been thinking about as the hours passed?

What if, it could, it might then there are the ifs' ands and buts. The unforeseen, unexpected or not planned and how does such affect people when unknowing?

Zachary was one of the human species that was unable to foretell the future. His life schedule was similar to everyone else during the period and as such his day must have started like all the others.

PART III.

His Service Includes a Surprise

Chapter 5

Suddenly, Zachary Must Have Been in the Least Stunned!

Wow! To Zachary's surprise, there he was all alone when it happened. Without any warning or advanced notice there he was fulfilling his duty along with his responsibility when what appears but an angel. Now, it is recorded in Luke's part of the Bible that there was only one angel. Furthermore, it is the angel did not say such things as we or u, but in fact even gave his name.

Suddenly, Zachary must have been in the least stunned there he was looking at the person's sudden appearance. Surely alarmed, how could he not have been frightened? It was not moments of wonder or amazement of a little thing that happened. Rather it was an ongoing situation of Zachary trying to cope with what was happening. There was only one entrance, yet out of nowhere the figure of a person appears.

There it was, not only coping with the unexpected but being confronted with an unknown being. Such instance is recorded in Luke chapter 1:11, where in it is written, and there appeared to him an angel of the Lord, standing at the right of the altar of incense. How would it not have been that Zach would have been terrified? What means did the being that was facing him use to manage for getting inside? Where did he come from?

And then, how could his appearance have been so instantaneous as not being announced? It was one moment where Zach was there by himself with no one around doing whatever it was his duty. Suddenly in another moment of fear, just like that, there was a person standing alongside of him. Who wouldn't have been instantly shaken up?

Does the Koran state that Zachary went to visit Maryam? Really, so what could such type of an emergency be that Zachary would have stopped the religious ceremony to go see her? Then too, who was the woman? Does the book suggest why or for what purpose Zach would have gone to see her? Should he have done so, what would the other priests have done? Would not they, the ones not participating in the service have been able to do so?   But where is there any mention of them? Does the Koran indicate how she was able to seclude herself away from everyone else? Since this is not shown, consideration how is such not just more mind games?

It is in fact, even by history standards that there was a separate section in the Temple constructed specifically for women. Why is there no mention of the separate room for women in the temple? Why is there no mention of the other women that were there? There was only two places' women could have been. Since she was not in the altar area with Zach, she would have had to have been in the room for women or in the plaza or main yard. If not, where else would the woman have been?

Why does it not show how she was of any importance that she would have been able to go where only priests, were permitted? So why are there no specifics mentioned of where she was? Also, why does the book not mention anything about what the other women were doing? Why not, or what the men were doing? So, it is asked, why is so much information missing or omitted which leaves the matter as a Hollywood unfinished script. Then also she would have only been there for a short period of time.

So why is there no reason provided as to why she had need of any food? Also, the question is asked, for what purpose would she have needed any food? Such is asked especially when there was plenty of food to be found outside in the plaza of the temple. Any eating that would have been done would have been outside in the main yard with the other people. Perhaps a lot of this nonsense is cleared by the information in the aforementioned chapter.

Now it was a rule that even the high priests wouldn't eat inside the service area. So why is there no showing of how a woman was given an exception? Is there any statement as to why the secretive woman would have been elsewhere other than in the plaza or room for women? Highly significant here is that during the day of the ceremony there is no such person as Maryam mentioned being involved in the situation, in any of the books of the bible. Why is it that her name is nowhere found with regards to the ceremony or the occurrence in any of the gospels? Perhaps not at the temple during that day but at least one of the apostles may have been in the area close to that time period. Yet, it is that the person that wrote such regarding a Maryam was not only not here during that time period but hadn't even been born yet. Therefore, the fact is that the matter must be combined with the fact that such a person was not even around until centuries after Zachary.

Wherefore if copying from the Bible then leaving out parts who would know? And then if only reading while believing without comparing it becomes what? So, now it is to return to the factual written record of the apostle that was around during that period. Recall that Zachary had no one with him, when he entered. Also, it was that no one was scheduled to arrive. So, to him it would have been the simple routine of making the offering for peace then leaving. Also, since Zach was the only person in the confined altar area, someone would have had to have interrupted his service to advise him that someone wanted to see him. Important here to remember is that there were no such things as talking over a wire. Such meant that there was no intercom.

Where in the Koran does it mention that Zach was interrupted by any person? Surely for such a thing to happen it would have been highly contrary. Had such an occurrence really happened, there would have been much turmoil about her. For sure the woman as well as others knew about the restricted areas. Furthermore, the woman would not have done such as she would have provoked a physical confrontation. Having to deal with the scribes or other priests, she would have been physically removed.

Then also such could have aused herself harm since she would have violated heir traditions. With all of that, why is such matter not found written in the record of at least one of the bibles? Such contrary commotion would have been recorded by several persons. But as it is such was not recorded by anyone during that period of time. However, along with those points remains a most important question. Would Zachary, being a learned priest, have been so disrespectful that he would have stopped the service for just anyone? Of course not, especially not for a woman of no consequence. Then even if he was notified of the woman, most assuredly he would have advised one of the other priests or would have had one of the scribes make the errand. Then to simply go anywhere when already being occupied by the visiting angel, such would not have hapned. or sure common or regular people just wouldn't do such a thing, let alone a priest.

Lastly it is questioned why is there no mention about all of the other women that were also around? Plus, where does the Koran depict about the scribes and other priests that were security but not part of the service? Why does the book not show any reason as to why they could not have been able to provide what was wanted? Especially with there being a number of them available, that is if there was such a woman? For sure with them guarding the entrance ways they also would have known about the woman.

Wherefore, it is that these matters establish only a state of total self-contradiction. Such a sacred service it was that priests performed was most holy, where other persons were not permitted around let alone in the same services area. And if scheduled to be there such a person would have been inside with the priest. Furthermore, it was a hard fast rule that no one would even consider entering the area, especially when a priest was in the midst of performing the offerings.

Then there is the big item which is that had there been such a person, surely she would have been able to have been given food by any number of several other persons. Why is because it stands to reason as there were simply too many other people around along with the guards, other priests and scribes. Important to remember is the large volume of people that were there, not performing the service. Then there are the other factual matters of it being that Zachary's wife name was Elizabeth.

Now it was where he had no communication with the outside plus there was no attendant helping him. Also, there was no such person as Maryam or any other person assigned to him. Furthermore, if there was a Maryam with her being a woman she would have been fully and physically restricted. She would have had to remain in the same isolated section, which was in the same designated area as the other women. Either that or in the plaza but for sure there was no other choice. Plus, if found outside the designated areas she would have been physically removed.

The Great Excitignly Holy John the Baptist

There's just too much missing matter, all of which leaves nothing more than a mess of mom-bob jumbo. Anyway, for sure it was that wherever she may have been Zachary would not have known such. Then too, even if he was advised, for sure others would also have known, but still it remains that he would never have stopped his service to his Lord God. Never would he have stopped simply to bring some food to some strange woman. Also, if there was such a woman and she was sickly, again it is that other persons would certainly have known it. If she was even close to the service area with all of the security around someone would have seen her.

During those times there was such a thing as having respect for sacred places, as well as the sacred services going on at those places. And the truth is that Zachary, the priest was not playing the dice game or having a time of it burning trash. Also, important that must be considered is that there were the other priests and scribes along with the guards that were also in the temple area. And it is that they would not have allowed her getting even close to the room's entrance, no matter who she was. Such was the rule which was so big that it was under penalty of death for any unauthorized person to enter the altar area. Such was the rule that there were signs posted which stated such.

Returning to the service it was that the priest did have a visitor but it was no female. As a matter of fact, it wasn't even by a human. At first, maybe Zachary may have thought that with all of the people outside in prayer surely someone must have seen the unexpected angel. Then also there were the numerous members of the priest order along with scribes being on guard at the only entrance to the altar room. This is repeated here because it is of so much importance. It was that such were special moments of a sacred time where absolutely no one was allowed entry. During the time of Zachary being inside, it was that all of the other priests were outside of the room.

They all had the duty to prevent any strangers from entering. Perhaps persons may have been allowed entrance before the service started. Or even after, but never would anyone be permitted entrance any time during the actual performing of the service. And such was especially true about women. Persons would have been allowed entrance had they been so scheduled.

The Great Excitignly Holy John the Baptist

But there is no record of any one being scheduled for that particular service. So it was that once the service started any entry would have been absolutely prohibited. So, how was it, Zach must have asked himself, that a person had really gained entrance? Most especially, he must have asked himself, when the entire entranceway was blocked? Also, it is that there is absolutely no record of any Levite guards detaining anyone. Nor is there any written record of the priests chasing anyone.

Anyway, it must be considered just how scared Zachary could have been. Surely fear must have struck hard. He must have thought to himself, that with all the guards around, why didn't they stop the intruder? After all, they had never before allowed any such thing to happen. An important matter here to be considered is that up until that time, Zachary had never seen an angel. Nor is it in any records of him even knowing anyone that had any experience with an angel. So, it must be taken that at first glance, he must have been stunned almost speechless.

Then to, nowhere is it recorded where any of the other priests ever mentioned having seen any such beings as angels. A well-known fact about people is, that when put upon by a stranger they get defensive. Also, where a person may encounter someone new, where they are not supposed to be, does not a natural reaction take place?Then where such is the first time when unexpectedly a total stranger appears close is not the reaction one of apprehension? Then add to that where the person was not announced how would the reaction not be one of being scared? So, with all of those matters, then combined with his being up in age, how would Zach not have been terrified? Even so scared out of his wits that maybe even his legs may have been shaking! Perhaps even his teeth were chattering.

When given thought to his reaction, it stands to reason that he was scared. Otherwise, why would the angel have begun his introduction in the manner of which he did? So it happened, as recorded in St. Luke in chapter 1:13- 14, where the angel began not only to talk but spoke with authority. As stated in the written record, the angel stated, "do not be afraid Zachary". Now, since when are greetings made with such alarm, unless it was addressing something on the person that was showing?

It was the angel didn't start by saying hello or good day. Nor was

Zach asked for some water or bread. Rather it must be taken that they were words which clearly indicate that they were to calm the man down. From those few words it can only be assumed that Zachary was probably bodily, visibly shaking. Then as the record shows, the angel continued where he stated, "for thy petition has been heard, and thy wife Elizabeth shall bear a son and thou shalt call his name John, and thou shalt have joy and gladness and many will rejoice at his birth."

Wow! Maybe as other men would have done, he too might have been happy. Upon hearing such statements, perhaps any priest would have liked to experience a sudden feeling of joy. But, not so with him, for it was that Zach was fully aware of him and his wife being way beyond the natural child bearing years. So, it was really, he must have thought, who was kidding who? And who was this clown anyway, Zach may have thought? Probably he couldn't imagine anyone coming in then disturbing him with such arrogance.

Being human that he was, Zach was probably full of all of the normal feelings of ego, cynical Ness and impatience. Also, it may have been that at the moment he became closed minded. Immediately at first Zach may have thought to himself that the person wasn't real. Maybe it was some type of illusion, he may have imagined. Perhaps the old man may even have thought that his old mind was playing tricks. Why not? After all, it was evident to him that the person didn't know Zachary's age. Yet at the same time, there must have also been some confusion.

It would have been remembered that the entity did state that he knew the name of the priest. Such Zach must have kept on thinking, especially with him being past the good years of producing children. So, wouldn't those matters alone have made anyone skeptical? Then why not, wouldn't Zachary by then, feeling of some sort of pressure, feel the same way? For sure he himself knew his own age, as well as his wife's age. But the visitor, of who Zach did not know, what would he know? Also, would not have Zach been readily concerned? Knowing his wife was up in years why wouldn't he have been concerned? It seems by the contents of the written matter that Zach really failed to comprehend the situation.

Evidently it was that the priest failed to recognize that the entity was not human, but in fact from heaven. Surely he would have had deep concern for the laborious action of his wife at her age. With all of the thoughts going through his mind would he not have thought how such child bearing at her age could have caused damage to his wife, even death? Then also there must have been his realizing of the pain she would receive. As such matters may have been considered most surely they would have been a grave concern to him.

Most important to be remembered here is that there was no immediate family being in the close by area of the couple. Also being of a major concern had to be that if his wife was hurt, how would he be able to handle the child while caring for her? If she was to end up critically hurt, then what? What if she was disabled where she couldn't fully walk? Or, what if her brain was damaged where she couldn't make decisions? Such matters may have also flashed though his mind. What would he be able to do in his old age? Then to, how would he manage? So many negatives all at once must have run through his mind. Yet he had to face the situation at hand.

Wow! Who or what was this person standing before him? And just who did the person think he was, saying such things? Especially with Zachary being a priest, should not the person have watched his tongue? Would not the priest have thought such to himself? But did Zach really hear what had been said? Was he listening or too busy assuming things? Could it have been that he didn't understand the full impact of what had been told to him? Then to maybe in his low state of mind, perhaps he really wasn't paying attention!

Maybe, he may have thought to himself that it was his imagination playing tricks. Perhaps wanting a child so much it was that upon hearing such statements, he may have even been offended. For sure at first Zach had to have felt something. Would he not have taken such a statement as an insult? Then to, perhaps it may have seemed that he was having a wishful dream. Maybe the priest was even so positive in his thinking he could think that the entity was not real. After all, Zach had not been advised or told before hand of having any visitors. Nor were they any special appointments being scheduled with offerings.

So just where did this person come from? And then how was he able to speak such things? Also important was, how did that person come to know of the petition? Certainly, such would not have been one that Zach would have broadcasted to everybody. So how did the person know of that which he had been making for a child? Why was he embarrassing Zachary with his stating of his wife to bear a son? Would such not have gotten anyone in a similar situation angry?

Then with all of that, the angel even added what may also have been taken as injury. Surely, when the angel stated how the child would be a male child by mentioning his name, it must have sent the priest back on his heels. What is this sorcery that is happening, Zachary must have thought? Who needs those kinds of insults? Would such thought have crossed his mind? Then being aware of his duty being stopped he may have thought, why now, especially since interrupting the performing of his holy service? Could not the person have waited outside till the service was over? All keyed up, would not have Zach considered all of those thoughts?

Now it is most important to fully understand what was said next. So critical for understanding John's purpose it is to fully comprehend the depth of the statement. Yet the full phrase is either downplayed as trivial or overlooked. Is it because of people's rush to enjoy the other statements? Or maybe it is that the people really don't want to know what was stated? Also, maybe it is they find it easier in refusing to accept truth. It is the nature of man to be contrary to truth. Even when such matter may have been put in writing it is ignored. Yet it is factual that the matter is part of the written record of what the angel spoke.

As depicted in the written matter of Luke 1:15- 17, it states, "for he shall be great before the Lord, he shall drink no wine or strong drink, and be filled with the Holy Spirit even from his mother's womb, and he shall bring back to the Lord their God many of the children of Israel". Most important here is of the statements being highly significant as they ring of what some of the prophets had stated so many, many years before. Who would know from whom Luke received his information? Was it from a friend of Zachary, a relative or associate? For sure Luke had no cause to invent such matter.

Also, is it not possible that he may have gotten the story from a Zachary relative himself? Very similar and almost identical are the words that had been predicted in the prophets foretelling of John. But Zachary was certainly not thinking of what the prophets may have said. Then also neither would Luke have been thinking such things. Not caring who may have said what before his time, it was that Zach had the instant problem at hand.

Experiencing such an entirely new kind of situation was one thing. But occurring in the most holy place for the priest it had to have been nothing less than overwhelming. Oh, sure in the past he probably had to cope with some jeering especially when first becoming a priest. Then to there may have even been some teasing by his peers. But this was a kind of situation which he had never encountered before.

Therefore, not having any experience in dealing with a situation similar to what he had been presented, how would he not have been stymied? Perhaps he found himself fully stressed out. Such it may have been that he may have even felt lost. Then also what must be highly considered is his position. Since the angel had interrupted his service would Zach not have become at least irate? Then with all of the slurs would he not even been totally livid? All the while showing his arrogant side Zach must have displayed his being scared.

Perhaps the tired old man may have been so scared he may have even been trembling. Such it was he may have been shaking, especially upon having heard such unexpectedly strong words. Then also it was hearing such from a total stranger of who he had never met. Wow! Certainly, it was not the kind of time or day he was expecting to have. Maybe in all earnest he wanted to reply, but perhaps his teeth were chattering so bad the priest couldn't get the words out. Then, added to that was while being all alone, it was he had no means of protection. But then being of the holy order he would not have carried such weapons.

For sure it was that at the moment the man had no ideas as to what to expect next. But recorded by Luke in his chapter 1:17 it is written, "and he shall himself go before Him in the spirit and power of Elias, to turn the hearts of fathers to their children, and the incredulous to the wisdom of the just". Then continuing it states the full purpose of John where it is written; "to prepare for the Lord a perfect people".

Noted here, as critically essential it is that the angel did not say or even indicate that it was Elias that was coming. No, rather it was that that angel Gabriel clearly stated, "in the spirit and power of Elias". What those words did was to make absolutely clear, without any ifs, ands or buts, just how holy John was. Such clarity manifests that John was not a man of flesh but of spirit born in flesh. Furthermore, it is that the written matter stated that the angel in authority confirmed what Isaias had spoken. Highly significant also, is that another prophet had spoken of the matter. Such is shown in what the prophet Malachiah had foretold. It was at the time when the prophet was responding to the corruption of the Jews. Malachiah recorded such matter in his chapter 3: 1, where it is as written, "behold, I send my angel, and he shall prepare the way before my face, and presently the Lord whom you seek and the angel of the Testament whom you desire shall come to the temple".

What seems to be missing or erroneously assumed is that God did not control people as puppets. There were warnings or choices given to which people acted or didn't. And what is so significant with that is that He would not be so specific as to state such things as by how many yards or feet. So also, He would not have stated on which day they would have come to the temple. Wherefore it is highly significant here that what is written does not, nor even indicate, anything about someone coming ages or years before the Lord. Such is fact since the phrase specifically states, "before my face". Now it is that such wording can only mean being close by or near or doing yet exactly within the same present time.

There can be no other assumption or explanation as before someone's face means exactly that which is being in the same presence. If other meaning was intended, surely the Lord is intelligent enough where He would have so stated. Therefore, it can, even in only the least, be taken that it was all about John and his being the preceding messenger of as well as at the same time as Christ. Substantially significant to support this was the stating of the word "Testament". So how does that word add support to John's mission?

It provides the final clue which was that Christ is the Testament as being the New Testament. Now it is that there are people around who attempt to put on some act. They speak as if they have some form of authority which would provide them a right to declare that the true prophets ended at a certain time period. Then there are those that attempt to claim only certain prophets are the last of the breed. Yet those same persons that are ready to put a dividing line refuse to answer when asked why, when both sides of any proposed line are stating similar matters?

The Great Excitignly Holy John the Baptist

Surely if Luke and Matthew can be considered as credible along with Isaias then, why should Malachiah be disregarded? Why should he not be given the same latitude of respect? Simply because there are irrelevant differences is not credible reasoning. Such matters are frivolous leaving no reason to eliminate the person. Especially it is when based solely on simple foolish opinions. Such words since not supported by any facts are and remain only theory which in fact means nothing more than drawn out assumptions.

Highly substantially significant is to be noted that which is important to be remembered which is what the angel Gabriel did not say. And it is, that the angel did not say or even infer that Elias would be the one going before the Lord God. Now it is from the written record, where the angel stated, "and he shall himself go before Him in the spirit and power of Elias, to turn the hearts of fathers to their children and the incredulous to the wisdom of the just to prepare for the Lord a perfect people".

There are strong words that could have been spoken, but were not. Also, it is fully correct that the angel did not state or indicate that Elias would be the one arriving. And it is that those words where altered, twisted or replaced with something else is not the truth. Rather they are nothing less than lies as well as a misleading deceit. Fact is that had God intended for the person of Elias himself to go forward in His wisdom He would have stated so. For sure it is most certain that the Lord God would have specified exactly that. But the fact is that He did not say such, nor did the Lord God indicate such through his angel.

So, there it is, one entity of the spirit being the angel Gabriel. Then there were the two entities of man being Elias and Malachiah. All three said or stated or foretold in prophesying, specifically, yet basically the same thing all in the same fundamental words. With the words being of the witnesses of three separate entities there is nothing to be disputed, nor is there left anything remaining that could be confused. Especially since the words of the three being of different times the truth of what they said speaks for itself.

Wherefore the truth is that John would be going in the power of Elias. And it is that the word, "of" clearly evidences what was intended as well as what should he learned. Such intention was that John was of the power similar to Elias. Whether similar, the same or even close to, but not Elias. Fact of the entire matter is that had the angel intended to alert the priest that Elias would have been born again but to Elizabeth for sure it is that the angel would have stated exactly that.But he did not, as was only stated "in the power of". Established by the very proof is that the man's name that was to go before the Lord Jesus was also foretold. As stated such it was that the name of the messenger was to be John, and not Elias. Now, most assuredly it is, going in the power of one is not the same nor can be confused as being the person of the power. Thus, the phrase was used to alert the fact that John would be of the same holiness as Elias.

Any other way of putting the matter would simply be an untrue distortion. And such is realized as being of unsupported fact or simply put it would be a lie. Also credibly notable are the words that Isaias spoke which clearly identified the mission of John the Baptist. Such are taken from Isaias, chapter 40; 3. There it is recorded that he stated, "the voice of one crying in the desert". Here it was put for simple understanding of nothing less of John's duty which was that of a messenger. And it is where John's ministry was reported as found, which was in the desert.

People allow themselves to get all wrapped up in the words of one crying in the desert. There are too many people who use the word wondering as if the Baptist was wondering around loose of mind. But such is far from the truth, as John had direction as well as a good mind which is evidenced by what followed. They falsely assume that with such they are able to know everything. Yet with closed minds people refuse to understandably connect the words, voice of one crying. Wherefore it is, that those very words are what John's whole purpose was all about. The man was to be the speaker, the announcer or the messenger.

It's multiple-choice time as each of them all apply especially since the Baptist was about the desert. Then if that wasn't enough it is even foretold what John would say. Continuing in the written record, it is shown in chapter 40; 3 to 5, where Isaias stated, "prepare ye the way of the Lord, make straight in the wilderness the paths of our God". Taken by itself the part of the sentence could apply to everyone. However, to fully comprehend what was intended by those words it is necessary to accept the matters of the preceding paragraph. But then if the preceding matter is refused to be understood or believed then the rest remains only words where such would not nor could require any clear definition.

Attempts are made to twist it to mean that the Lord Jesus would be making the paths straight, which is entirely false. Actually, to consider such would be nothing less than fantasy as would suggest that God would have nothing better to do than spend time flattening out the land. It is that the paths were to be made straight for Him their Lord God. Then continuing in the same chapter, it is stated what the result of the Lord's presence was to be.

And such result is defined where it is stated, "every valley shall be exalted, and every mountain and hill shall be made low, and the crooked shall become straight, and the rough ways plain, And the glory of the lord shall be revealed, and all flesh together shall see that the mouth of the Lord hath spoken". Perhaps it is too hard for people to understand what and how. Then too maybe such people are in too much of a hurry as looking. But not taking the minute to focus, if they don't take the time to think about what all together indicates, what remains? How could they understand the significance of the few words that mean so much? Also, those with closed minds or being self righteous, perhaps it is they falsely assume they know. Or maybe they are those of the highly educated that think they know everything. Then as being only mortal, how could they know everything about everything?

Yet it is that most refuse to consider those matters. They falsely assume because that is what they choose to believe, that they mean very little. But what if in fact they are the intended meanings? Are they not a part of the everything? Also, there are those that stop or refuse to go beyond the Old Testament. When people refuse to look beyond what a person knows into the past how does such not keep a person from knowing of anything, especially when there is a connection to be made? How is falsely assuming that their knowledge is all that matters is nothing more than turning away self education? Such is similar to those that refuse to turn the page in a book assuming they know what lies ahead.

Is such not the same as those feeling they know what the ending is about? Of course, some reread when they hear from others who have read the ending. Then also there are the others where even upon hearing they refuse to look or reread. Oh, sure they may make good guesses on the persons' actions. But what value is that when they fail to know the why and who is affected? Then also they fail to understand what was realized? Is it false pride or closed mind? Yet those persons fail to realize the joy of having known the truth. So much it is that people lose by false assumptions and self indulgence. What hath it profited them to read only to a certain point, then falsely assuming the rest?

Or when people fail to read to the end, how is the continuity then not broken? Even in sports, such can be seen where people leave only minutes early assuming the ending. Then the next day they come to find out that the losing team in the last minute turned the insurmountable score to their favor. It's all about continuity. So also, it is to be considered are those that press for the stoppage of prophets after a certain time period. How is such not making it some sort of a game.

Just because a person feels good about what one prophet states, but not about another, is no reason to discount the prophet not cared for. Also, where a prophet didn't state what a person was expecting to read or not shown at their thought of time, then what? Is that any genuine reason to discount the prophet? Plus, there are those persons that state how certain prophets were not prophets simply because they don't agree with what the prophets inferred. Yet such persons that make such statements were not there at the time. Also, they were not even born during the time of profits. Not actually experiencing the time of the said prophet lacks continuity and without such remarks become nothing less than guessing. So, who are they to judge whether the person was a profit?

What stands out with all of those that object to so many things? It is that they never provide any credible type of proof or valid reasoning. Factual matter that can be shown as attested to that would back up their statements, would surely be proof. But when requiring answers to questions that demand valid reasoning, all of a sudden the excuses are presented for not answering. Talking or writing with many words is one thing, but the doing so void of credible supporting facts is just that, it's all talk of words, talk and more talk. Excuses and rhetoric are not substance of viability nor are they matters of proof. But eventually even a ventriloquist runs out of breath. Is not such as those who assert their selves as authority yet provide no proof for their talking?

Now it is, there are those that believe in the New Testament. But,i it because they were raised among others that do? So many people refuse to read the Old Testament because they assume in their minds that it is not necessary. Or state how those persons in the old were guessers or they give other excuses. Yet it is they do not know about the why. Other than what they hear, they know little which in fact limits their true knowledge. They are almost like those that discount prophets that they don't like because of personality.

So it is that only the present matter is believed without really knowing the full details of the Old. Tis a shame since it is that the matters of the old led up to the New Testament. Here it is again, that word, "continuity". Regardless of how one feels about it the New is actually part of the Old Testament as being continuous in matter. No, it is not continuous with the same Lord but is surely continuous as being about Him, being the Lord God.

Do those having closed minds fail to comprehend just how much they are missing? How would they ever be able to understand the full connections of the old with the new? Maybe such opinions are because of the reverse or stoppage of thinking. Here it is those persons don't read the Old Testament feeling that they don't have to, as to them it is foolish to read what is unnecessary. But if they were to understand that they are not of the spirit world, maybe they would comprehend that they don't know everything. And so, is it here a falsity? Since such persons don't know everything, how could they hardly be able to determine what is unnecessary?

In daily life are there not persons that can be heard speaking to another stating their apology? Are apologies not made daily for the making of wrong assumptions? Unfortunately, it is always a matter of convenience for people. It is they would rather accept the word of one person or matter from someone they don't know, taking the easy way of wrong assumption, rather than pursue what could possibly be correct or right. Then it happens where even when several persons speak contrary, it is that written matter proves the verbal in error. Yet it is the way of the world, because words are easily believed.

Those that look at all choices while comparing every detail may realize truth. And it is the truth is what may be correct or right, not that which is only assumed. However, for those who close the mind to choices what do they have left, other than follow the one way without really knowing. But since it is the easier method, even with thinking, that is what is done.Now also, there are those of the same groups that cannot nderstand why they refuse to accept the spiritual yet also refuse to discuss. Of course, such presents a large if not a monumental problem for them.

If there is no belief in the spiritual, then there can be no belief in a creator and God. But don't ask them how all living matter started when it is fact that nothing comes from nothing. Also, it is that from rock nothing starts by itself. Yet there is no answer only excuses. However, it is that they do believe in the scientific theories. Fully in assumption those people believe in the theories which are nothing more than unproven opinions. Also, they are only predetermined opinions drawing conclusion, yet still not proven fact.

Such is the theory of the beginning of everything from the big bang. Amazing how many excuses are given as the same people refuse to provide credible answer. Why can they not give a credible answer as to how there could be a bang with nothing to make it happen? A bang is a thing and all things require something which is matter. Scientific fact is where there is no matter there is nothing. And nothing plus nothing still equals nothing. Why is because pure nothing is a void. Yet fully knowing that the result was nothing but rock, people have no answer to the fact that nothing comes from rock. Also, the same refuse to answer as to how along with what was the cause of the bang. Substantially significant absolute fact, is that absolute nothing, absolutely cannot produce anything. Even air is something as made up of ingredients.

And it is that before the big bang there was only an empty void of absolute nothing, not even air. A big nothing, it was being there was no substance of any matter. So it is, that when pressed on what caused life after the bang, again all goes quiet with no answers. Yet it is people take the easy road falsely assuming the theory is something to believe in. Well then that leaves the only thing remaining which is that of talking to an ameba. But at least amebas like rocks don't tell fibs or lies. Oh yes then there's the water. Now it really gets interesting as people easily assert that the water came from the rock. Really, then which piece of rock was it that created the water? Or they change things around. Interesting it is how people can make up things such as to suggest how the rock came from the water. Yet, when asked which came first the fun really starts.

Regardless of what people chose to offer they are still left with the question of, how did the matter get there in the first place? But not only do people not have any new answer but only return to the same old theories. Such it is remaining that either one believes in a creator or the rest is all comic book stuff. Here the following is presented in order to ask questions. It has been established that Jesus Christ is the start of the New Testament. Also, it is the time period referred to as A.D. Is it not trueing then, that what came before him was of the B.C. time as well as the Old Testament? Is not that the same as comparing a wound or sore with a scar?

So, with that being said, since Elizabeth and Zachary were born before the time of Jesus Christ, how is it that they are not in the Old Testament? Especially, such is asked since their growing years were also before Christ. Such matter would not have been brought up, except that the period of time in question was not one of days. Rather it was that the couple was many, many years around before Christ was even born. Such was their life span of time that the greater portion of their life was in the Old Testament. This matter is easily determined because they were in their older years even beyond child bearing way, before their son was even conceived. What this all means is that they actually only spent a minimum of years in the New Testament before having passed away. Now besides all that, there is John their son.

And is it not the written record of more than one, where the Baptist was also born before the arrival of Christ? True it is, that John was only born some six or seven months before Jesus. Still, it is where he came before Christ. So, should he not in the least be mentioned in the Old Testament? Perhaps there are many thoughts on this subject. And maybe leaving it all to being trivial is the easier way. But the easier way is not necessarily the better method. However, the author feels it should be more about not making it convenient. Why? Because maybe, it might cause some form of thoughtful educational controversy.

Oh sure, how easy it is, as just write it off as not important. How convenient it is for people to say such things. Then too, there are those that mention such things as prophets not being of any importance.

The Great Excitignly Holy John the Baptist

Along with history even the news of the day shows others use direct or manipulative force on people to force them to believe matters which are not true. But force is their only means. Such is because they want others to repeat what they want them to believe.

And without the use of force the lapse would probably cause people to think. Then if able to think they could then draw some of their own interesting conclusions. Unfortunately, it is always easier for people to look the other way or listen to the person with the loudest voice rather than the quiet one speaking truth. Since the time of Adam and Eve, such has been, as well as is the way of the world. Yet, after all of the force along with all of the manipulation to coerce people, there still remains the truth of the ancient written records.

Amazing what helter smelter preconceived minds or erroneous assumptions can cause. A person may even understand such but stil retains the same attitude. A perfect example is fully shown by the actions of Zachary. But then since he too was also a human being, why should any difference have been expected?

So, there he was also a human being of the male species. Up in years the elderly man had been put under unexpected severe strain even reaching the panic stage. So why should he have mentally been any different from any other person? Who would have acted any differently? What else could have been expected from the down to earth man, who was really sad feeling low as having no children along with being aware of his late years? Plus, aware of his wife's age along with her anxiety why would his self confidence not have dwindled?

CHAPTER 6

So, With No Means to Publish In Volume, Why Take Notes?

Now it is that there are religions started by people who were not there during the ancient times. Such it is that they may enjoy the falsity of a twist or omission of matters. Also, other persons not happy with the old simply generate a religion of their own, with their own deity or person as the subject. Then there are those that take from what was written by others decades and centuries before only to remove or alter and leave out various parts. But that is all about attempting to make that appear to be of something which it is not.

Yet it is such information during the ancient period must be taken as true. Why true? Because the matter is attested to then being in written form and credible being fact when so stated by more than one person. However, what is most important is that those persons were there back then or who knew those that were. Plus, it is that they are several and not just one person doing the saying. Significant it is that all those matters together, brings around the question of money.

So, with no means to publish in volume why take notes? Then, why would any of them back then have even bothered to have written such matters if it such matters were not true, when in fact there was no money to be made for writing the material. It is fact as recorded in written form that the Baptist did speak similar words as so foretold by the prophets. Not only was there simply one recording but there were others. Did not three separate persons put forth written information about the same matters?

It is that four different people of the then ancient time period wrote in their own words what they knew. There were the four apostles of Luke, Matthew, Mark and John that each separately attested to the Baptist! Yet, even with four separate witnesses confirming about John, people would rather omit phrases or insert their own words. It is absolutely amazingly fascinating how people would easily believe what Hollywood or the government puts. Believing what is fantasy or fiction is easy compared to what is recorded in factual historical testimony.

Why not, after all the fiction doesn't need any explanation or research. Taking such liberty to alter, change or omit what was written is as easy as fiction being the needing only the using of an eraser. Often it appears as if those that do so, assert themselves as some form of authority. Of course, what is amusing, is that those very same people that take it upon themselves to change or omit parts of what is written, are in fact of no authority to do so.

Why do they lack any authority? Those persons are void of authority because they were not there during the ancient time period. Also, they didn't know anyone from that time period where they could have gotten first hand information. Since such persons were not present then, or don't know anyone from the time period as well as do not have any named witnesses, they are without the knowledge, and without such are without authority. Such are only persons improvising with wrong assumptions or basing their work on guessing.

Whether guessing or assuming such does not rise to fact, nor are such words fact by itself. Also on the other hand, it is that where written information is presented in detail but not denied with proof by others it remains written fact. Therefore, such written matter is the only matter that is to be relied upon. Have other writings been found from the same time period regarding the same matters that produce contrary material? No. Wherefore it is that it can only remain that the original written words are the only truth of factual matter that can be relied upon.

Forms of hindsight guessing or assumption void of credible facts of proof do not change truth. Also, especially sad it is that people don't respect the writings of those that were back there during those times. Now it is that those persons which are fully denied of any authority to make changes is supported by the fact that those persons were not living or present at the time of the ancient time period. Why, because such persons failing to be there during those ancient times, along with having no person that they knew from that time, removes any credibility. Failing to provide supported fact only results in a theory. Plus, such persons or other attempting to change what is written flatly fails since not credibly shown why.

The Great Excitignly Holy John the Baptist

Interesting is that those persons provide no credible reason for their interest to change words or eliminate the written words of the prophets. Also, the putting up of statements as if the person is in the know completely falls short since not having any good reasonable cause. It is that without a cause of purpose what for would be such action be other than for self? Yet, it still remains most important, to be questioned is whether such a person was ever there during the time period or had an acquaintance from that period.

What all of this amounts to is that if their arguments are not factually supported then they remain opinions which are mere unproven theories or fantasy. Yet because of having some sort of an office of authority in a learning institution or religious entity such theory is taken as some sort of fact, even though it is not. However, any authority regardless of where or how high the person ranks need validity. Void of such does not replace actual credible written fact of intent and meaning. Nor can such authority be substituted for the original written words.

Therefore, it is the most essential fact remaining which is, that the written record remains what it is, the truth. Why? Because it is that supported written facts not contested during the same time period are not subject to being altered or changed. Plus, it is that what is permanent fact is that the written record of its time by itself always speaks for itself.

Fascinating it is looking on the internet or listening to people as the voice of their self-appointed righteous opinions. Attempting to disregard the apostles they do simply because they disagree with what they wrote. Yet all is shown void of any viable purpose. Since those same persons fail or refuse to back up their words with credible purpose also void of true facts such can only be to satisfy the person's interest. One person may say the apostles were disorganized as having no committee or other formal organization behind them but provide no material on what type of committee.

Then other people fail to give credit of the times along with the newness of what was involved. Also, it is where others say they contradict each other. Yet such persons refuse to provide any credibly specific showing of how. Then there are those who even offer their closed minds stating how the apostles were taken in by foolish fantasy. Of course, those same persons also refuse to provide any justifiable cause for such thinking.

The Great Excitignly Holy John the Baptist

Also, it is that those same persons refuse to put any factual matter to support their opinions or assumptions. Or they refuse to answer when shown how one compliments the other.

And it is that opinion not based on factually supported matter remains only a bunch of opinion. Such is nothing more that speaking hollow words. So, the only thing that remains for them is for them to disregard what others say by omitting some of the prophets or what they wrote. Omitting persons or matter simply because a person doesn't wish to recognize them or such written matter, is what? Even children throw temper tantrums when not getting their way. But it is that the way remains.

How is omitting or changing original matter nothing less than making false statements? Then, simultaneously not allowing the explaining of the truth, what is that? Such is nothing more than fantasy which produces nothing but more non-truth. But then it is as the saying goes, if a person keeps repeating a lie, people will believe it. But the best are the ones who claim everything was made up. Yet when they are asked for what purpose would several persons make up something replies are only suggestive.

Now, when pressed where there was no profitable motive, suddenly all is quiet as there is no answer. When put that there was no financial gain, such persons are unable to provide any viable reason. Finally, when asked if they thought the apostles wrote because they had nothing else to do or just for the fun of it? Especially since there was no way of printing to make a profit why would they have done such? With no such things as distribution as well as void of book stores for what purpose would they have made the effort of the writings?

It is easy for people to draw on assumption that the apostles were paid. Then when responding with the truth of there being no duplication methods they choose not to discuss the matter. Want proof? Any person that wishes to prove such simply make up a story. Then try to get someone to write the story while advising them that there would be no compensation. Also let those people find others that would spend time writing for nothing when not being a part of the action they would be writing about.

How convenient it is for people to make assertions then force their way while refusing to look or consider any of the other shown alternatives. By starting something with an attitude, as if they being all knowing is the easy part. But then by doing so do they not show closed mind, or matters of self only ways? But all assertions or words backed by use of force does not make the matters correct. Rather it is like a band aid covering up a permanent sore. Refusing to look or listen, it is all about their own way or no way. Yet such does not remove truth that was written. Truth is such as found in the written records of the Old Testament.

So, then what remains after elimination or omission if not only parts? And where a person starts eliminating prophets or omitting the phrase or words, then what remains? Simply to satisfy their way of thinking, then what comes next? What remains where the elimination of others or omitting what they all had to say is done?

It creates confusion allowing distorted thinking or even the quitting of thinking. Such omission or elimination is simply a way of forcing ones thinking of misleading matter or untruths. Any refusal to offer factual support, or give credible supported matter for eliminating words of or the prophets is just another form of putting up a false front. Then also there are those who claim the apostles were always high on wine. What foolishness are such words when void of all thinking. Who can write what they saw or remember in such detail and clarity if they are under the influence of alcohol or other mind drugs? Then is it not those same persons that make such statements while refusing to read, look, compare and discuss not all about their self?

What it comes down to is they only want to hear themselves speak of what they want. But such is nothing less than being of self. Gee, might as well try having a conversation with a rock. But at least the rock knows where it came from. Why is it that those people insist on being accepted as well as having their way while refusing to talk about the supporting facts of the matters in discussion? Some organizations or bands even resort to violence to physically force their way of self thinking. Such brain washing may be effective as forcing people to conform in practice, but it doesn't replace the truth. It still remains that those that relinquish themselves to such bad people haven't really changed their thinking, as there is no thinking. And those that physically force their way merely over rule the peoples' physical being.

But the true factual written matter still remains. Such fact it is that with all their force they can't change the original written matter. Why is it that such people refuse to even allow any thought? Position, greed or power, which is it? One only has to take their pick or maybe a combination. Closing all doors to the matter that maybe the apostles were telling what they remembered in truth by use of force is not that only physical? With those persons, it is all about power and not about what is truth. For sure everything that was written in the ancient period had to be taken from memory. Why, because in those times there were no such things as tape recorders.

Furthermore, it is that during that time period there were no such things as memo pads and ink pens. Nor were there any such things as pencils and portable sharpeners. So, being without means to record exactly every syllable spoken at every specific minute, what other means was there? If they couldn't rely on their memory how did they keep their information? What then, did they make it up? But then is asked which ones made up the story? And if more than one speaks of similar then why if not the truth?

There were no book stores or movie theatres during the time. So, for what purpose would they write such? Now, if it wasn't of great importance to hand it down for others to know, why then make the effort? Thinking in the big way one must consider that there was no Hollywood, movie theatres or publishers to publish books. So why would the apostles have written their information if it wasn't truth? But then since the apostles are no longer alive anyone can say anything they feel like. Of course, that also means everyone can believe or disbelieve whatever they want to.

What is really nice to hear is how people are able to twist or omit matter solely because they want to. All is done simply so that they can believe what is most convenient or disregard what is not in their interests. Even if not the truth, a lie or misleading for the sake of convenience does not replace truth. Wherefore it is that the omission of fact or twisting fact into fiction is nothing more than fakery or lying. So, when such is done what is gained if not to demonstrate physical power? Also, it is that perhaps if people took the time to try to understand the hardships or the then time period, thinking might be more serious. But that would require making an effort. And it is such would take time along with facing facts.

The Great Excitignly Holy John the Baptist

Of course, they won't allow that to happen because if shown how wrong they were it would be a personal setback to their ego. But with everybody wanting everything instantly, it is easier to have excuses for not taking the time. Then to, it would be trying to get their memory into the written matter. As normal, it is easier to take the path of the guessing or false assumption way. Such would mean that readers of the matter would appreciate what was provided and given, especially since all was done free of charge. Then with at least some true understanding people may look at the written words differently. Perhaps with a more sincere effort they may even get some true comprehension of what they were researching.

Now it was that the apostles were simple, poor and uneducated or minimally taught people trying to do what was right. A reader may have to look three or four times to understand an individual's efforts. But, if they do, they would actually realize how without knowing it, that the apostles complemented each other. How would such be realized? Can anyone during the course of a normal day remember every specific detail of the day? Then to, can anyone recall every specific word in every specific sentence spoken by someone else over the course of a day? And with that being said, rather than in false assumption knocking them, perhaps people just might read a little more. Further it may be, that people may read more of the same matters with more intensity.

Reading at the same time what others stated in detail about the same matters or same speeches does such not establish credibility? Also, and just as important, it may provide a good means of clarity. Therefore, it is that such combining of thoughts of more than just one person's written account may provide a clarity enabling a better type of full understanding. So, with all of that the person reading may come to fully comprehend the true meanings of the why, as well as what form of the matter that was written. And who knows, such people may even learn something. Also, people that do such may learn some personal things about the apostles, then too may even learn something about themselves.

Who were the apostles? Besides the ones that wrote the four gospels which are: John, Luke, Mark and Matthew there are those that wrote epistles or letters such as James the greater, Jude and Simon Peter. Also, there were the others that did no actual writing being Andrew,

James the less, Simon Zelotes and Matthias who replaced Judas. Surely, just because they didn't do any writing it didn't preclude them from gathering information for those that did. Such others were Philip, Bartholomew and Thomas. Considering the times along with their situation would they not have gotten help from their relatives such as their parents, aunts and uncles? Then what about their friends who also had friends?

If they had seen Jesus Christ, or knew the Baptist, would not some of them have been anxious to help? With even just some of those helping the ones doing the writing, would there not have been times when two or more may have given credit to what was reported? Especially if they had personally seen or heard what had happened, how would such information not have been able to be relied upon? Since being actual witnesses why would they not be credible?

Now with all of that information and reasoning, a question here is put below. Since both Zachary and Elizabeth were up in years, does it not make sense that such was their childhood and prime time in life that was way before the coming of Christ? So, with that information being known, would not most of their lives not have been a major part of the Old Testament? And is not in the written record of Mary, the mother of Jesus going to visit them not before the Christ was born? So, how could such matter be only in the New Testament and not in the Old?

When counting in tens from one to ten are not those same numbers included when stating a dozen. Are the ten eliminated when counting a dozen? Of course, they are not as they are part of the dozen. Since the starting cause of the New Testament hadn't even been born yet, how is it the older couple is not in the old? Were not the births, teen and late mid years of the couple not during the time period before Christ was born? Did the couple not live their middle years and grow old way before Christ was born? How then is it that they are deprived of not also being a part of the Old Testament? So, it is here, that the older couple was a part of the B.C. history years before the A.D. age. So why are they not depicted as such?

In history they don't eliminate animals from one age simply because they existed in two. So why do they not continue the same way in the bibles? Would not such a correction do them justice? Also, could it not help put things in a better perspective? Perhaps putting them in both the old and new would make for better continuity. And are not continuity matters of truth? But that may take a little effort. So as people like to do things that are convenient such will probably not happen. Of course, there is also tradition which here is nothing less than maintaining a wall. But then it again becomes all about the matter of the closed mind. It does however make sense not to apply the same logic doing the same thing with their son John. But surely with him, at least the Baptist should be mentioned.

John the Baptist was born months before Christ. So, if his birth scenario was put in the Old Testament would it not read correctly? Would not his parent's life as well as his birth extend the continuity of the Old Testament? Especially with the timing of his birth, how would such not allow easier coordinating understanding with the old prophets? Contrary to what people say about such things it would not hurt their religion not would it take away from their customary thinking. But in fact, it may even help both their thinking as well as their religion. Perhaps, a little common sense applied here may help. But then, there are those important matters that people in authority use. Such may be classified as excuses, as those used may be suggested that it's too complex or too inconvenient, or even assuming that no one would be interested.

And then there is the easy one of, that it hasn't been done before, or the old big excuse of being too busy. Gee, but aren't even couch potatoes busy?

Taken into consideration here, must be what is important. It's not that the matter is about changing names or time periods. In fact, the matter requires no changing of anything whatsoever. Since such matter could be handled easy why is such left in controversy making it seem confusing? Such could be done very simply, by taking the very matter of only the three that occurred in the immediate before Christ time of being born and merely duplicating it into the Old Testament.

Not to eliminate what is in the new, as leaving it there would maintain the same as well as helping in the matter of continuity. But such would take a little effort. And with everyone in such a hurry, who has time to worry about continuity? Yet it is that continuity is a substantially significant matter that involves everything.

PART IV.
MARITAL DISILLUSIONS
Chapter 7.
All Those Years Praying and Trying With His Wife for Children.

So, let us return back to where there was that simple man, Zachary trying to live his life as best as he could. Always praying for a son while trying to do what was right. Oh, how he must have been deeply frustrated, since not only, not having a son but also it was he being unable to produce any children whatsoever. Such feelings of that kind must have run deep in the man. Such stands to reason, as he knew he was not only past his prime but of age where he was past any possibility of aiding in causing of a child.

Would he not also have felt bad knowing he may have been the person preventing his wife from being a mother? Also, there must have been the realization that as every day went past his chances of becoming a father also went passed. Surely such thoughts ground deep into the mind as well as his heart. So as the years passed him by, while being eaten up by his inadequacy.

Zachary must have had bouts with some depression. Then to, would not such daily emotional feelings have caused him to lose hope? All those years of praying, while trying with his wife for children but realizing nothing. Would frustration not have turned to almost despair especially him being a priest? Of course, during all of those years there was also his wife. Most certainly she also had her lowly feelings. But maybe his feelings may have been a lit bit more hurting. Such feelings would have especially been magnified.

There he was with his years of combining his personal prayers for a child with making offerings during his priestly duties praying for a child. Then also his wife enduring the same emotional strain may have reminded him during his day of priestly duties to offer prayers on her behalf. And how would such not even deepen the hurt he was carrying? Why would he not have thought deep down inside, the feeling of why ask me as my office means nothing with God? Would not such moments, while still realizing nothing, add fuel to the fire of frustration?

So, it may have even been that Zach could have even reached the point where he might have given simply given up. Perhaps even having periods of despair such may have even turned to occasional anger with a hardening of his heart. Especially such could have really turned violent with his wife reminding him of being a priest having pull with their God. Then maybe there were even days when such words so affected him that he even complained.

Maybe he being full of hurt would have cursed responding of how he was no good, not having any pull with their God. Would not have such been possible for his thinking, considering how low he felt? Especially since his Lord God never answered his prayers? Also, it could have been in her desperation where his wife may have let her frustration show its ugly head. Perhaps she even pressured her husband from time to time suggesting that his God didn't find any favor with him. And then again maybe it was his thinking, where God felt that being a priest he shouldn't have any children. What else then could Zachary think, especially since it was that other priests were known to have had children?

How low some of the days for Elizabeth were? And then how low were many of the days of her husband? Just how low could the two have sunk not being in a state of depression? So, if a person had been walking in the shoes of Elizabeth or Zachary, how would such a person have felt? Would the person have gotten ulcers over the matter? Perhaps the person would have held it against the husband or the wife, thinking it to attach fault. Was there the blame game played out?

Maybe either person could have even turned bitter in total frustration. Perhaps giving the matter such serious thought, it went to the limit as even giving up as a marriage partner? How really depressed would such a person have become then thinking he or she really wasn't the high-flying person they thought they were? What about their personality? Could such negativity have been so much that it would have overtaken their personalities?

The Great Excitignly Holy John the Baptist

With such anger carried inside them, would it have been that one or the other had come to resent everybody? What then would either have been left with? Especially if the person had credentials such as Zachary who was a priest how would the office not be a further downer? Now if you had been walking in the shoes of Elizabeth how would you have felt? Would you have held it against your husband thinking it was all of his fault? Would not any normal person in such frustration reaching levels of anger, have turned bitter against Zachary? Or would such person have become so depressed that they would have felt that they were no longer the attractive sophisticated person they thought they were?

Then even carrying so much anger it turned into hate would you have given up even refusing to try? How much misery could the couple stand? Also, to be considered is how would his daily miserable mood not have affected his wife? Oh my, what miserable days there must have been in their little abode. Not to be overlooked is, with him hearing nonsense from those at the temple, it must have only fed his misery. And then, what would she have said to him when he did return home? Would she have given him a big smile while asking if he had a good day? Or would she have tried some offbeat humor as asking about some other person who was expecting?

Then even in the best of days would such not rub it in? Now it is that Elizabeth must have had her times of it. Some days it may have been where she simply couldn't stay in the house. She had to go somewhere or do something to get her out of her environment. Even today, don't people having similar problems do that? Don't they look for some place to go or something to do, for the purpose of getting their mind off their problem?

What has all of this got to do with John? Directly it has only a small amount of significance to do with him, but perhaps a lot to do with his parents. Maybe it was a way of strengthening them to be able to handle their son. What kind of ridicule would she have encountered from the neighbors? And then at the market place, would she not have been questioned? Statements made by people in social talk may have started out as fact but how much was twisted?

Rumors and assumptions like people do surely must have entwined turning the truth into who knows what. Distorted or false stories that may have been taken out of context must have grabbed hold. Such can only be imagined especially considering what gossip can do. And then for sure there must have been more excitement at the market places than had been in a long time. Would the woman not have been subjected to trying looks?Then from those jealous of having fallen into hard times, would she not have received undeserved words? And what about those words along with the mean looks?

Whether in jest or sincere jealousy would she not have been shown arrogant or even contemptible verbal abuse? Such would have certainly been received from those that were jealous of what earthly things the older couple may have enjoyed. During their mid years, maybe it was that Zach was especially helpless with her. After all, what could he ask when she returned home? Would he have simply asked if she had picked everything up? Perhaps in sarcasm, would he have asked if she had a good time? Or maybe he would have given a phony smile, while asking about one of the other women. Surely there would have been one remark that had even been expecting

Could he have been enjoying such a terrible day where he couldn't restrain his anxiety? Maybe he even pressed his wife, asking how some other woman that was expecting were doing? What other digs could he have made to further ruin their day? But there is no record of either acting with such meanness. So, it must be taken that in love, they respected each other. How could people of today consider judging them without not first considering the hardness of the times? But yet it is that they do so, without even giving any thought to the full circumstances.

Even a look at people today living in poverty, shows how with them it is they respect each other. But those living in luxury, who do they respect? No there is no difference as it is not about the times, rather it is all about the times the people lived in. It is not what they had but more over it is about what they didn't have or, what was not available during the time period.Oh sure, and how easy it is for people to give their opinion. Saying things people may suggest that they were used to it.

Sure, they accepted the way things were as having been raised in the same conditions. But used to it as the people being comfortable? Such leaves a lot to be desired. Then, when it is suggested that they try on for size, living in the same conditions the matter loses any being of funny. But to go and actually alive under the same conditions only heaven knows how one would react. Only eating what they catch with a homemade fishing line, spear, or bow and arrow does not get it done. Rather such would only end all discussion. So much it is for people that are in a rush.

So much in a hurry are some where they refuse to take the time to think or others that chose not to think. How could either comprehend what they are reading? Then there are such things as surprises. And who doesn't like a surprise? Whether little ones or big ones, as long as they're good ones, really, who doesn't enjoy an occasional surprise? However, the kind of surprise that Zachary was about to encounter, well, just maybe not every person would have been able to handle such. One could classify it as a stressful time while others might think of it as just being something different.

Not only was it such a time of which he was to partake in. But it either way it was of that particular moment of time when he was unaware of what was to occur. Also, he was never warned or advised by anyone that such an occurrence was going to happen. Nor was he informed of when. There was nothing special scheduled for his service that day. Also, there wasn't anyone scheduled to be with him to offer any sacrifice.

For all intended purposes, the only thing Zachary knew was that he was scheduled to solely perform the priestly duties. It was during one of the regular week days where it was to be of the regularly daily service. Also, it was to be at the regular time of day. Then also there was nothing special planned, nor was there any form of offering scheduled. So as far as Zach knew it was to be only the incense that would be offered. Also, it was that neither Elizabeth nor anyone else had told him of anything to be different that day. Just another peacefully easy day, with his self at the altar, may have been what he was anticipating. Also, when considering his age, maybe it was what he was hoping for.

Since nothing out of the ordinary happened in the early morning, what was there for him to think of? His life had floundered to the point of where he may have even been in a rut. So it was, at the time, there was nothing for Zachary to look forward to. For him the man as well as the priest it was to be, as the day dragged on, just like any other day. So, in considering his position along with his personal circumstances could such have not been Zachary's state of mind? Just another day of the usual service and then it would be back to his home life routine. But at least during his performing of his duties he could lose himself.

Even if for only the short time that it would take, for a while Zach may have that felt he could find some mental rest. But as it was, little did he know how big the small service room was about to get. Nor did he have any idea, how privileged he was about to be.

Surely, had his wife known what was to occur that day, she certainly would have started her day off differently. But as it was oo was in the blind as had no idea. So, as it was, the two must have started the day just like all the rest.

Simply going through the motions, it was each one doing their normal activities. But wow, were they to be surprised for it was that the day would certainly not end like all the rest.

PART V.

SURPRISE TURNS TO FEAR

Chapter 8. Suddenly, What appeared out of Nowhere!

Shocking it was, as it happened! Surprise time it was for Zachary! Suddenly, what appeared out of nowhere, unexpectedly is the figure of a person. Whoa, just imagine being in the shoes of Zachary the priest. All alone he was, when as he turns, only to find someone standing at the end of the altar. Yet according to the written record, isn't that what happened to the priest? Also wasn't it that the entity was not announced? Not only did Zachary arrive at the altar alone, but he was not expecting anyone either.

Oh my, but also there is the fact, that not only did Zachary not hear the person approach but never saw the person when he entered. His nerves must have exploded when he turned then seeing the unexpected presence of an entity standing about him. A person could almost feel the instant tenseness in the air as his eyes caught sight of the angel. Who or what was this being, Zachary's first thought must have been? Also, he must have asked himself, how did the being ever manage to get in there? Especially being a stranger, would he not have been stopped? Surely some of the scribes or guards would have seen to it that he was turned away.

There was only one entrance to the room. Then to, even if he was able to slip past the first set of guards, surely the other priests would have stopped him. So, with all the religious people around following traditional policies regarding entry, how did the person ever gain entrance? As sacred as the services were at the altar room entrance for sure other priests would have denied any person entrance. Such would have been even if force was found to be necessary.

More alarm there must have been as the priest's mind was struck hard. Stunned he was when not knowing Gabriel, suddenly the angel spoke

The Great Excitignly Holy John the Baptist

Zachary's name! Imagine a total stranger approaching a person that was in seclusion, then speaking the person's name. Would not any individual at that moment experiencing a similar situation, not have been at least alarmed? Easily Zach would have remembered how it was that he didn't know the person. So, he must have had immediate concern in wonderment of, how was it that the person knew Zachary's name?

Such concern there had to be, especially since the two had never met before. So, who was he, Zach must have thought? Any person that may have experienced similar would understand. Then too where some form of a near death was experienced beyond his or her saving self, may have a better understanding of Zachary's mind at the moment. Perhaps the moment wasn't fully realized as being life threatening. That was, until after the scenario was over. Then a moment later the person realizes something beyond the norm. Had his or her life been saved by someone who was not visibly there what would they be feeling?

Also, those who have ever been suddenly confronted in total surprise by a stranger would have some real comprehension of the emotions felt. Maybe anyone approached by an unexpected stranger would also know how alarmed one becomes. What a powerful moment to experience. Sure, for the younger person there may not be such a distressed feeling. But, being of the older generation wouldn't that have added to the insecure feeling of the priest? Then add to that the physical weakness of Zachary would have surely crossed his mind. So, with all of that going on in the mind, would it not be most reasonable for persons to understand how being in an apprehensive state of mind a person would get?

Now it was that Zachary was also a mortal human. And how would such unexpected presence not have caused him to be even in a shocked state of mind? Perhaps a reader may think that the author has put too much emphasis on the matters stated. But are not such things of importance to people? Then if not of any significance, why even today do people carry guns and knives for protection? Anyway, as it was neither did any of his peers or his family advise him of what he was about to encounter. Nor did any of them forewarn him of an appearance by any stranger.

Therefore, it can only be taken that the old man had to be totally unprepared for what was about to happen. Not even suspecting as not expecting anyone to enter, how could he not have been alarmed? Yet there he was, Zachary the priest all alone. Not alone, as almost instantly he was standing in the presence of someone having authority. But attempting to reason to himself he must have thought, what authority? Certainly, the priest would have known him or at least he would have been expected had the person been of any religious authority. Neither religiously, nor traditional or custom wise was Zachary even remotely knowledgeable of the person.

Truly the priest was not ready for what had occurred. Surely, he must have been so scared that in the least he was at least stuttering. Then when the angel spoke, wow! How would the voice not have been to the fragile old man, an earth-shattering moment? Why such a thought? Because, since Zachary did not attempt to move away or run, what other thought could there be? And why, was because he must have been too scared to move. What great news the angel had brought. Yet poor Zach was not ready for the person let alone any news. Who was this person, the brain of Zach must have kept repeating? Scared along with being old surely would have been enough for the priest to handle.

But it is that they must be combined with the fact that the angel had not been scheduled or announced. So, why would his brain not have kept on asking the same question, over and over? After all nobody interrupts a service being performed by a priest.Since what the priest was conducting was a holy service there would not have been any rude appearances.

Such respect there was that unless it was a matter of a life and death emergency situation, absolutely no one entered. It just doesn't happen no matter who wanted to enter. Especially, it was in those days of reverence and respect, that no one would even contemplate doing such a thing as to interrupt the service simply to convey some words of news. Now it is such news is shown in the written record of the apostle Luke 1: 13- 17. But here in this paragraph, it is only mentioned the part 1: 13- 14 because it is where it all started. It is from the written record, where the angel stated, "do not be afraid Zachary, for thy petition has been heard, and thy wife Elizabeth shall bear thee a son, and thou shalt call his name John".And the angel continued," and thou shalt have joy and gladness and many will rejoice at his birth". How would any man feel should a total stranger advise him that his wife would be pregnant?

The Great Excitignly Holy John the Baptist

Is there any room for thinking along the lines of being insulted? How about such insinuation that someone was fooling around with the man's wife? Would those type of words not move a man into hate, even violence?

Wow, then if that was not enough, not only was the sentence one of news but also of an order. Had the angel not presented Zach a directive of what his own son would be named? Hearing such words would any man not be insulted by someone attempting to tell him who would be the father? Then to assert what name he was to give his son; how much could the man take? But instead of expressing instant gratitude, what does the priest do? Did Zachary first give any real thought to whom he was listening to? Had he given any thoughts as to where from the person came that was addressing him? No, of course not, after all Zach was an elder. Plus, it was that he was also a priest.

Maybe he felt that due to his position he was certainly due some respect. And as a man with some ego, what else could he do but show his manliness? So, full of typical human pride along with his arrogance the priest displayed his hardened heart. First thing was that Zach was told that his prayers have been answered. But here it is again put of how was Zach to know how the person knew anything of what his prayers were about? Then considering that mode of thinking, especially it may have been that Zach felt that the person didn't even know to whom he was speaking.

This was way too much even for a young person or someone who already had communication with an angel, but at his old age how would it not all been a frightening experience? Eyesight of the old man wasn't what it used to be years before where maybe he couldn't see clearly those things which were close up. But the angel wasn't a thing, nor was he far away as the altar wasn't that big. Therefore, the angel would not have been more than three or four feet away. Would, if he were a foot closer, made a difference? Also, it may have been as men think, he must have felt, what business was it of the intruder anyway? So, with all that has just been said, does Zachary show appreciation or say thank you for what he was just told? No, of course not!

Then as being the normal person that he was, Zachary couldn't wait to express his doubt with authority. So, if a person were in the shoes of the priest, how would the person have reacted to the entity being there? Would the person if, of his age have attacked the angel? Would the person have run outside calling for help? And if so what would the person have done, when some of the other priests came to the rescue then only finding no one there? What story would a person have told when others not finding anyone else around?

Surely the angel would not have waited around for others to introduce themselves. Then to, no matter what story the person would have offered, would they have believed what was told? In all fairness the man's age must be considered, after all who would not have thought Zachary was dreaming or even seeing things? So then how would a person have reacted to the angel's first words? Would a person have given a response similar to that of Zachary who tried to show his intelligence? As taken from the record it is shown where the priest raises his question.

Not only asking, but also answering his own question, while simultaneously expressing doubt. "How can this be", Zachary questioned? Now it is that such is shown, as recorded in, Luke 1:18. Therein it is stated as written, "how shall I know this for I am an old man and my wife is advanced in years"? Of course, at the moment, the priest had merely stated facts of truth. But the problem was that the angel didn't ask for a response. Not only did he not ask for a reply but in fact did not ask him if he would be able to handle the situation. Isn't it wonderful that there are times when people, as the saying goes, put their foot in their mouth.

Usually such is done by speaking without any thinking. But really, this had to have been the ultimate. This was not only doubt being expressed, but a complete showing of his utting up of a blockage. Also, there was his pride showing as having the need to assert his knowing more than the angel. Maybe before asserting himself, Zachary could have asked the person where he came from or who his boss was. At least it would have set a more subtle tone. An interesting fact here is that the angel was bringing him not only a salutation but fantastic news. Such was not news of the day nor was it just any news.

Wow! It was the information that it was the absolute great news that Zach had been praying and waiting to hear for many, many years. For sure the day was not the same as it started out. There it was, the very type of good news, which after all those years, that he and his wife had both been endeavoring to hear. And then, it was that they were not only the very words he longed to hear but that, the words had been given directly to him. Wow, there it was all wrapped up in one phrase. To him it was the kind of news that blows the mind of which the man and his wife had been waiting for.

There is that moment in time when everyone is presented with the opportunity of a lifetime then bumbles it and, so it was with Zach where without him realizing it Zachary was treated as someone special. Evidently, Zachary hadn't given true thought to the angel's first words. Those words as recorded are again stated as found in Luke, which are, "do not be afraid for your petition has been heard". Did it go through his ears from one to the other without stopping? Or was it simply that his mind had been truly overtaken by fear? How could such words, not have alerted Zachary to the thought that the angel was someone of a holy entity?

Everyone from his neighbors to his friends, as well as his relatives was fully aware of the couple's problem. All people that he knew were all aware that the older couple was beyond their child bearing years. So, why didn't he think that it could have been a person sent from his Lord God? It wasn't as if the angel was talking about one of the other or even high priests or one of those Levites. Nor was he referencing anyone in the administration department.

Surely Zach wouldn't have been going around advertising to everyone that he was petitioning God for some favor. So, how would the angel have known about the petition, if he wasn't from heaven? Yet, even after the angel had stated how it was, Zachary put his negative question. How it was, was surely defined when the angel had spoken of no other than the Lord their Lord God. Understanding the situation as well as the man, just maybe the priest had other thoughts. Perhaps he felt it must have been more important for him to demonstrate just who was running the show there.

In his bossy negative haste to disclaim what was being told, Zach had erroneously hurriedly forced his doubting question on the angel. And even after such boldness he still didn't show any respect. Here it is, that the author believes perhaps Zach may have said something else. Perhaps, he may have spoken something else of which had been forgotten or wasn't relayed to Luke. It's not what wasn't spoken but what was recorded seem to have left something out.

Anyway, from the record it is in Luke 1: 19, where it is that the angel identifies himself along with why he is there. Not only did the angel in specifics provide the priest with news but also asserted just who he was along with who he represented. Such can be realized by giving full consideration to what the angel stated. It is as taken from the written matter, wherein the angel stated, "I am Gabriel who stand in the presence of God, and I have been sent to speak to thee, and to bring thee this good news". Even then, Zachary could have at least taken a moment to realize the power of God. How could he not have realized the power of the words that had been spoken, "am Gabriel who stand in the presence of God"?

How much more holiness could the angel convey? What a statement! "standing in the presence of God." Wow! What an assertion, and who could even think of stating such a thing? Such words would hardly have been spoken by someone playing a prank. What a huge significant couple of words they were to hit the man's mind! And then, there was Zachary who was a what? Why he was a practicing priest of much faith. But where was his faith then? And also where was his common sense?

Evidently, such power had to have been showing through the spoken holy words being put before him. Did their significance not register? Surely Zach had the moment where he could have acted. But perhaps Zach was terrified to the point where he couldn't even think straight. Maybe along with being scared, it was that he was also skeptical. Why not, aren't people cynical and negative about new things that people introduce or things that happen? But at least he could have shown more respect. Perhaps he could have even fallen down or prostrated himself. Then to, in the least he could have gone to a bended knee.

Could the man not have done something while also stating an apology? Then to, without much effort Zachary might have simply mentioned how he didn't understand who he was hearing from. But then, perhaps that would have meant that Zachary had time for the person. Now with time dragging on along with all of those matters the incense had probably all but burnt up. Yet did Zachary try to improve the situation? Did he attempt to do either? Oh no, not this holy man that was being so proud and contentious. It seems as though Zach felt it more important to demonstrate his authority.

Maybe there was also his gruff tone showing his arrogance. For sure it is apparent that the old priest was determined to show just who was boss. He would show the angel or person or whatever he was, that was standing there, just who Zachary was. After all, for Zach at the moment, it was him being an elder priest, only important for him was to stand his ground. So, perhaps there was no wine or water there to offer the angel, nor any food, but could not Zach first have shown some hospitality? Was he in a hurry or did the man have the time where he could have at least tried to be a little amiable? But instead, what does the priest do but insists in trying to force his thinking. Of course, such attitude only dug his self a hole. Without his realizing it, it was one of such size that he could not get himself out of.

As it was the priest had more than ample time to show at least some respect. But as determined from the record, it is apparently taken that instead what Zachary did was to demonstrate his authoritative boldness. Suddenly however, it was where Zach who was shown just who the boss was. Surprise it was as for the priest, it was definitely not him. Also, it was that Zach was to find himself treated to the angel's awesome power. So it was, as Zachary stood with his pride watching, he received the angel's summary. Certainly, what he heard was not what he expected nor wished to hear. What followed was an exercise of authority as what was given was a notice of power. Such was a resulting brunt of what his negatively proud doubting brought. Evidently by then, the angel may have been on a time schedule. And even if not, surely he was aware that he couldn't dilly dally.

Since the service that day was one of the short ones he knew time was short. Then to, he had taken enough verbal abuse where he was hearing no more. Wow! A person could almost feel the exploding tenseness in the atmosphere. As both looked at each other through hardened glazed eyes, the atmosphere heated. Most assuredly it was that the angel Gabriel wasn't about to return to his boss, not being successful. With his superior being the Lord God, he would not have returned without having done what was expected of him. For sure he wasn't thinking about attempting to explain how Zach wouldn't listen. So as ordered,

Angel Gabriel had his job to do, and it would be done. Evidently the scene reached its peak where one way or another, it was that Zachary would not only listen but pay attention. With nothing in the record to indicate otherwise, it is evident where no questions were asked by the angel. Apparently, no questions of interest were asked by the angel, as whether the priest was paying attention or how he felt about the matter. For sure though, the angel was not about to hold class for the priest to learn how to pay attention. But then, it was that the angel had already not only explained who he was, but in fact what authority he represented.

So, with that being said, the words of the angel should have been sufficient. At least no such information is noted anywhere where Zachary attempted to establish some common sense or show respect. Then it must have been, for sure where Gabriel wasn't interested in hearing any more of the human being's unnecessary verbiage.For sure it was that the angel was on a mission where he had to do as he was instructed. Such can be fully construed by what happened next of which, such is recorded in Luke 1: 20. There it is from the written record where the angel put forth the way it was to be. So, while Zach stood in awe, he could only listen as the angel put forth his edict. And what an overwhelming order it was.

Startling was not only the phrase itself that was expressed, but the tone of authority which delivered it. For sure Zach must have been humbled beyond anything he ever experienced. At no time could he have ever foreseen what was to be told to him. Then the bombshell of the phrase exploded. Containing the harsh penalty was the words conveyed. And Zach had earlier thought it to be probably just another one of those usual days where nothing exciting happens. Such means probably struck Zachary harder than any illness he had ever coped with. As taken from the written record it is stated the sureness of authority where Angel Gabriel stated, "behold, thou shalt be dumb and unable to speak until the day when these things come to pass, because thou hast not believed my words, which will be filled in their proper time."

Wow! What a shock it must have been. Especially at his age then also to struggle with the hardship of the time period. A short look at the first part should be done, wherein is stated, thou shalt be dumb and unable to speak. Not a simple request or only a moment of words being spoken, rather they were in fact the application of authority. Even more so they were an issuance or power. And if that was enough to cope, then there was the second part which signified that what the angel had first spoken about regarding Elizabeth having a son. How much more assurance could the angel have imparted to Zach? How much more of a burden could it have placed on the priest? Why a burden as this was all good news of which he had been praying. Suddenly the man had come to know that information of which his wife did not know.

Yet it was that since the priest was unable to speak, how would he be able to explain? What a predicament! Then he was told how long it was to be that he would not be able to speak. Such it was where the time was to be until the day when the things that the angel foretold had been accomplished. Such was not a stating of time by the hourglass, clock or the moon but by what was about to happen. Important it is to notice here the sequence of what was stated. Then also just as important is the detail that the angel used. But most essential it is to note, that the angel did not present any options or choices. Also, to be considered as important, even though, by most people are not, are the words that followed. Such as recorded in the written record is that the angel even went into giving the cause. Actually, he was not under any obligation, where the angel would have to give any explanation for his actions.

Highly significant it was that the angel had explained how Zachary had insulted the very word of God Himself. Such holiness can be interpreted from the phrase that was spoken yet, extremely important are those same words which people refuse to read or overlook. As taken from the written record, it is where the angel stated, "because thou hast not believed His words". Extreme attention should be paid to the two words as it clearly establishes that the angel was not speaking of his own but rather the Lord God who sent him. Had the angel been speaking of himself he would have maybe said something like, not believed my words. But in fact, he did not say any such thing to infer to himself.

Sure, Zachary had spoken only those thoughts of what he knew. However, it was that the angel had spoken words of the heart which was from his Lord God. So, it was in not believing the words of the angel in affect meant that Zachary didn't believe what the messenger from God was telling him. Where were the defining words that established such authority as well as who sent the message? First it was that at no time, did the angel even remotely mention that he was offering a suggestion. And second it was where he fully stated how he was relaying a message. Such was where the angel stated how he was sent to give the good news.

Extremely significant yet overlooked is that His forth coming was foretold by the ancient prophets, Isaias in 7:14 and Jeremias in 31: 22, 30:21; 31:33 and Lamentations 4:20; plus, Machias in 5:2 which relates to the same. At no time did the angel leave anything up to guessing. There were no questions in the message he was delivering. Nor did he leave any question as to who sent the message. And then the finality of it. It was where the angel specifically stated how long Zach would remain unable to speak. Then to ensure just who Zachary was hearing from the angel stated how he could come to rely on what the angel had told him. Of course, what that meant, was that once Zach had realized that his wife was pregnant, he would then know of the length of his punishment.

How much longer his condition was to last would then been able to be fully determined. Now it is, what may support some of the author's presented opinions is the phrase used by the angel. Such important matter is where the angel stated, "because thou hast not believed my words." This was the angel's statement directly informing the priest of the precise reason why he was being punished. Was the pride inside Zachary deteriorating as the words pierced his ears? Also, it is to be noted where Gabriel asserted the way it was to be in using the words, "my words which will be filled in proper time".

Such matter is credibly verified as recorded in, Luke 1: 36. With all of this information being so specific, everything is so explicit it doesn't require use of any imagination. Taking one phrase at a time it can be seen where the words were very direct. Not only how they were stated, but the specific words themselves disallowed any misunderstanding. Any possible ways of confusion were denied, as the angel did not use any words that could have been misunderstood or misinterpreted.

The fact is that the angel presented only such statements of words that did not present any opportunity for thinking otherwise. Furthermore, this can be determined because he did not use any words stated that could have required decision making. Important here is to remember that Zach was never asked such things as if he would like to consider such. Also, it is, that nowhere is it shown where Zachary was provided any options. He was not asked, nor given such things for consideration such as choosing or decision-making words such as, maybe or perhaps. Nor were there any such phrases spoken such as, as take your pick or it's up to you to choose. For sure the angel had covered all possible questions that could have possibly arisen. How interesting it is that humbleness is similar to courteousness in that neither one doesn't cost anything.

Yet, if not used such absence of one or the other can lead to many consequences. And surely it was that the angel was courteous. Then also it was that the angel did speak with such specifics as not leaving any doubt. He could not have been more precise or more direct about what he was conveying to the priest. Perhaps eating humble pie is what Zachary should have done at the beginning, but evidently he was not used to such confrontations. But it is for sure that he then had a whole plate of it before him. Sure, the time had turned out far from anything he had imagined that morning. At least he would never be able to complain about the day having been boring.

But then what he was experiencing as the meeting closed was only the beginning. For it was by then that any changing of attitude would have been too late.Such damage Zachary had caused was already done. Giving thought to such little matters, it is that people do not even think of. Of course, they also don't fully understand the emotions that were probably manifested.

Yet such emotions all with being high strung will surely change a person's attitude. Anyway, little did Zachary know how much humbler he would have had to get. After all, he still had to face his wife. What could be more exciting for a man than to have to explain to his wife the matters regarding the event he had just encountered? Wow! Then too, especially since she would have known absolutely nothing of the event where would he have started? Would the priest not have been walking around in a daze?

How did he be able to justify even to himself what had transpired, especially since only he had the experience? Was he pinching himself to see if he was still alive? Maybe during some moments, he may have seriously thought that he had a dream.

Also, it must be considered that his wife was totally in the dark, as never knew anyone that had seen an angel. Then also, she was totally in the blind, as did not know the content of the message which the angel had given her husband. But then neither was his wife aware that he had in fact seen an angel.

Wow! Was there some fun time in thee ole home that night? Well, at least it would not have been just another boring evening sitting around gazing at the stars. And for sure it was not the same type of evening as what either had thought the day would have been like at the start of the morning.

Chapter 9.

How Much Heartache Both Must Have Suffered!

How nice it must have been when the angel departed. All was quiet with Zachary then again he was all by himself. Then to, not even being able to talk to his self, it was surely quiet. With everyone outside waiting was there not at least some air of suspense? Because of the extended amount of time the priest had taken, it was way past the usual daily amount. How would such a long time not be out of the ordinary? How would such a condition not have left the people in wonderment of what took so long?

But for him it was simple, as all Zach had to do was leave. But then his departure must surely have been different than those exits he had made so many times before. A telephone would have been nice but there was none. How about a portable note pad and pencil or pen? Nope, none of those forms of writing things were available. Oh of course, there was his voice. But he didn't have one of those either. Yet it was that the priest had one when he went in, but there he was leaving. Not a sound from Zachary was able to be heard.

Wow! Such a moment in time it must have been for good ole Zach. What could he have been thinking? Surely the crowd had been thinking. Especially it was, there must have been some people who preferred him over the other priests, just waiting to greet him. There is no indication in any of the records that he was sprinkled with any kind of angel dust. Nor did any of the records show where he was glowing or had some sort of radiance about him.

What must be considered here is not one or the other, but in fact twofold. Not only what had happened inside must be considered but also the past living conditions of the priest as well as his wife. Tis a shame, that none of the apostles wrote about their personal life situations in depth. However, it only takes a little bit of considering the matter to formulate some understanding.

How much heartache both must have suffered as the years passed them bye.

The Great Excitignly Holy John the Baptist

What emotional strain they had been going through all those past years may not be able to be fully put into words. Not only had Elizabeth among her friends received occasional negative remarks, but also it would not be fair to discount those at the market place. Was she put in a class, by people where it was assumed she to be greedy? Did they falsely think that she prevented children as preferring the easy life of a priest having money?

Then too were there the assumptions of her wanting to have the nice things? Surely there were those that weren't doing so well or having their own financial problems. Also, there was Zachary who received similar unintended innuendos. Often there may have even been those hurtful insinuations. Some words there may have been from time to time that may have even struck at the heart. Important here is to comprehend how he had to cope with such not only from his friends but also as well as from his peers. But then to, maybe it wasn't always what they directly stated.

From time to time maybe it wasn't even what they said, more rather what they didn't say. But their looks, oh my how looks can say a lot. At the right time, in the right place perhaps words were not even necessary. Perhaps, some may have looked down their nose at him. After all, maybe they even harbored erroneous feelings against him similar to those that women had against Elizabeth. Would their wrongful words or actions not have been similar in meaning?

During certain times would it not have been extremely difficult for the couple? Such may have been when both had been put through the wringer on the same day. People without realizing it can cause some awful brutal times to fall on others. And then, during those days with both at home, would they both have not been caught in a much disturbingly distraught time of it? If one didn't' say something to the other about another person speaking a derogatory maybe the other had something to say.

Understanding how people love to spread rumors as well as speak about things they truly don't about there must have been some days when both had heard enough. Then there's those in places of authority who hear and talk to others yet void of knowing the full circumstances. But then here it was a different day in time. In a matter of only over an hour Zachary's life had been turned upside down. How would it ever again be the same?

Especially, it must be considered then, where during that year he was not the same young man that had been longing for a son. Not only that but it was that the priest was an old man, beyond his time for causing children. Then also the same, he was aware was the same with his wife.

So, there he was, that old man Zachary who probably thought he had seen it all then having to face his new never before added burden. What was he going to tell his wife? And then to, how would he be able to explain all of it to her? Thoughts about such things must have crossed his mind over and over as he walked. But as it was he couldn't talk. Therefore, there would be no simple attempt at trying to explain. And then him trying to explain that she was going to become pregnant.

Wow! What a hurdle to overcome! What a big mess he had got himself into. Was he thinking how his wife would probably think he was being cruel, attempting to play such a joke? Maybe as he walked the priest was still in a daze. But would Zach not have thought of such things? Perhaps explaining of not being able to speak may be even relatively easy. He could have always indicated that he fell down or lost it by choking. But, getting across to his wife of her conceiving of a child, well that was another matter.

And for sure such an important matter was not going to be so simple. He was not a fortune teller nor was he some sort of witchdoctor. Yet, there it was that Zachary would have to somehow inform his wife of her going to conceive a child. Wow! There it was, where she being the woman, and yet it was that her husband who was going to inform his wife about her conceiving a child. Even the simple phrase itself may have suggested some form of foolery. How, would such not have been a highly mountainous project even for the most sophisticated doctor? But as it was, her husband was not a doctor. Plus, it was fact that he as well as she was not only old in age, but was well past the age of having children.

Why would Zachary not have been actually afraid of going home? Considering his situation, as he walked in haste were people confronting him with innuendos while asking personal questions? How did he act? Did he smile as well as wave as if on camera? Or did he act as a politician going after votes? But then it was where he was unable to speak, so how could he have acted?

There really isn't anything in the record to indicate how he acted or that his wife was there. Nor is there anything mentioned regarding his neighbors and whether they were there. Certainly, any of them could have helped to lend a helping hand. But as it was, none of them were there. Such left the priest with just one big sized small mess. There he was where this man a priest of organization, of learning and holiness who always found himself in control. Yet this day, how would he not have been totally confused? Who to turn to?

Where could he go for help? But then what kind of help? Who could have provided the kind of help he was to need? Perhaps it was more like, where he realized that he was in a state of total chaos. What miserable feelings he must have had. Oh sure, there was the growing instant joy which only he could enjoy, after all there was the father to be, finally able to realize that he was going to have a son.So, in considering the situation, how long was that joy to have lasted? Slowly but slowly the doom and gloom must have taken over. Perhaps the situation with the angel brought him down to reality. Comprehending his situation would have been that of realizing that no one would believe him. Then along with being unable to speak what was he thinking about for the next day? But for Zachary it wasn't to be a simple mess that would be straightened out in a day or two. Rather for him perhaps there was to be much emotional pain and suffering endured.

Maybe as he walked he was able to have seen those things coming. Especially it would be where no matter how he may have tried to explain he would find it useless. Surely there were those still with the cynical and negative attitudes as well as those with closed minds. And for sure there are always those people that are always ready to offer those things.

Way of the world it would be where the ones that would cause hurt would be those close to him.Such it may have been where they said one thing but in their hearts they were feeling something different. Maybe they would smile mentioning how they understood. Then to perhaps others may have told him how he had been working too hard and to see a doctor. But then to, what about the fact that no one was there to see what happened to Zach?

The Great Excitignly Holy John the Baptist

And for sure, there were those persons that would have questioned the other priests. Such would have been curious to find out if they had seen anything. How would such gossip not force the other priests to act? Would they have not questioned his behavior? A big factor here was that he may have lost all credibility. Totally isolated Zachary's position was where he had no witnesses. Such could only have meant that he had no one to vouch for him. Then not being able to speak, such must have caused him to be further disabled since he was unable to describe any of the details. But then even if he could the man had no physical evidence to show which could have supported his story.

Where in the Koran does it state the time span of which Zachary would be dumb? Does it state matters of something as that he was struck dumb for three days? Where does it state the purpose of the three days? But without any name of who wrote the matter, how does it not raise the issue of credibility? Especially, since left out is what for was the sign? Why is it left out, the why of only three days, as why not five or ten?

Also where is a reason given as to what the three days stood for? Since there is no stated purpose of what the three days were to do, what value is the three days? Also, where does the Koran show what happened immediately after the three days? Then it is asked, which three days? There is no signature or name of the author, nor any names of any witnesses. So, without identity of such persons, how does the matter then not end as a game of guessing being the only thing remaining? Since there is only one person that did the writing without witnesses, when does the fantasy of using the imagination stop?

Also, how is the use of imagination then not the only way remaining? But what then does such leave but fiction? Then to, is not the book leaving out factual matter known from a past written document? How is such leaving out of information or omission of such matter not forms of deceit or trickery? However, in contrast here it is that Luke by his written matter can be taken that he had contacts with those that were present around the time of Elizabeth and Zachary or even maybe their son. Therefore, it is highly reasonable to deduce that Luke had the opportunity to gather his written information directly from one of them or other relatives. Also, it may have been where he received such information from others that were close to the couple.

The Great Excitignly Holy John the Baptist

Persons close to any situation, as in any close friendship would have provided as much information as they knew. Especially, such reports would have been easy to obtain once John was born.

Are not people curious? Would those people back then not also have been curious? Surely his wife wanted to know everything. And wouldn't she have been proud to tell what happened, if asked by others? So, who would be the better to know or find out of what had transpired regarding the event? Then also being able to find out what words were exchanged; how would such not be to Luke's credibility since he was actually there around the event's time period? So, it is asked, what if any would someone not around until centuries later know? Most important it is that persons who came centuries after the events did not even know Zachary or Elizabeth or even any of his immediate relatives.

However, it is, that such matters are found in detail as recorded in the written matters of the apostles. And it is that such matters speak for themselves, since it is those twelve apostles are found in the Bible. Why is it important to keep in mind the number of the twelve? Because it is that there were seven other original apostles which were very close to the four that did the writing of the gospels. Those seven of which are named herein must be considered as important to what was written by the four. Perhaps those seven may not have written anything. That is a big possibility because it was they being laborers of one kind or another were without the knowledge to read or write. But for sure there was no reason why from memory they would not have assisted the others.

Even today, every reporter has associates or scouts that relay information on what they heard or saw. Whether from first hand of others who heard or saw then in relaying what they found out or even have witnessed, it was probably done by memory. However, every little bit that each may have contributed must have helped. Also, it must be taken into consideration about those other seven. They having been around the time of Zachary surely must have helped Luke as their having spoken to the couple. And then, if not directly from one of the couple or John, perhaps such matter was received from others that had heard first hand themselves from the couple.

When there are things different or not considered the norm, are there not always those persons who wish to punch holes in new stated matters?

The Great Excitignly Holy John the Baptist

And would those or similar persons, also not rush to punch holes in the matters of the priest? Maybe they will use trickery by only making half statements. Or perhaps they will even offer some opinions, as if an authority. But if void of the specifics of why and for what purpose, what good will any opinion be?

Maybe others will issue statements that contain omissions of fact. Then to maybe even resorting to the disregarding of the matters depicted in previously found paragraphs. Also, maybe there would be not the showing of the prior or leaving out the full matter of what transpired after. But if such is done, how would such omissions not present confused situations or twisted matter? And how would such playing with words not only leave questions but require more guessing? So, in considering the aforementioned, the author has put a suggestion. He offers that such persons interested in using such tactics should refer to the above in chapter (6) six for all responses.

There are simply too many connections that are constantly overlooked. An example would be where the question could be raised did not the seven live somewhat close to the area of the older couple? It is easy to consider that they rendered assistance to the four by the written record of the information shown in the letters or epistles. Those written documents at least provide fact that there was communication between them. Maybe either of them going for food or other materials while shopping they may know Elizabeth or even one of her friends? Would not it have made sense for the seven to help the other four where they could have interviewed people? Then why not the older couple personally? Or perhaps could they not have spoken to the older couple's neighbors? Especially, have questioned those that were present during the celebration of John's birth? Why is it, that such probabilities are overlooked?

Even today junior reporters or persons writing for institutions bulletins have persons helping them. Such assistants though speak with people or witness events don't get their names in the columns or bulletins. Although they provide the writer with the information, it is only the writer's name is shown. And so, it could have been back then also.

Especially, since during that time period there was no such means of fast transportation. For the poor people all travel would have been by foot. At all times in all means of getting around the country side, even if by donkey would such not have had to have been a sure inconvenience if not difficult? Transportation, for sure, was not what the developed countries have today. With that taken into consideration would it not have made sense for the six apostles that did write to rely on others for assistance?

One thing that should really be considered is how one of the writers being a witness may have acted? Especially when one would have become aware that he forgot some of the speech or the actions. Would he not have asked the others for their input? Such may have happened had they been a witness as also having been there in person. Then too those may have also had friends or relatives that may have known the persons that heard or saw things.

Even today with people having note pad and pen they might get distracted or forget to jot down the exact words. Then when attempting to transcribe the matter it becomes that what was not noted becomes lost. Of course, if they recall every detail there is no problem. But, if they can't remember does not that little matter gets lost? Then what if they knew other people that had been present at an event or ceremony, would they not have inquired of them? These matters are most important to keep in mind as a lot of people don't think of such but think that the four had themselves seen or heard everything they wrote.

Reliability is what matters. Since such written matter is to be relied upon it is important to constantly remember the time period along with its primitive means of writing. Also important is that it may help to be aware of how the information was gathered as well as who the ones were that did the gathering. Having addressed the issues mentioned above let us now return to the event at the altar where once the angel departed how foolish Zachary must have felt.

Why me, he must have thought to himself? Would he not have been feeling at least belittled? And so it was, with the service over along with no one around to help him, the moment of penalty must have really struck him hard. For sure the entire occurrence had to have been an immediate shock. When he arrived earlier in the day to fulfill his duty Zachary was all healthy. He had no trouble speaking as well as no speech impediment. Therefore, everyone that he had been in contact with earlier was fully aware of how healthy the priest was at the time. But then it was after the service where he was a different person. Not only was he unable to talk, but there was no one around to speak on his behalf. Yet it was that the service was over which mean that he had to leave the altar area and go outside. What a big moment it must have been.

It wasn't so much that Zach had to leave the altar room, but was fully aware that once he did he would have had to face all those people. On his mind it must have been that he was fully aware that the service had taken way more time than usual. Would he have been concerned thinking about what everybody would say? But most important was what would he be able to say of why the service took so long? First it would be where he would have to face the other priests. And then not only what would they say, but would they stop asking questions?

So then, what could he do, or rather how could he do since he couldn't speak? For sure with their curiosity would they not have pestered him? Would those that had participated in the praying

not have wanted to know what happened in there? How would he explain? And then also there were the people who were anxious or mad simply because of the service taking so long! How did he possibly cope? How long could he have endured the onslaught of the crowd's questioning? What a moment it must have been for the man! What a time it was for Zachary who was a priest! What a messed-up situation on a day that just seemed to move along so easy, then too what an experience! However, no matter what had transpired up until that time, from then on nothing would ever be the same again for him.

So, there it was where the old quiet priest, Zachary was about to embark on a new way of life. Without any training or education relative to the situation that was given him, he had no idea how to proceed or what to do. For sure it was for him the educated person that he was, to be a new way which he had never ever envisioned. With all of his worrying about those matters mentioned, would he at the time have given thought to just how troublesome his life in the upcoming months would be?

Questions galore for sure there would be, as who would have begun to understand what went on inside during the service? As with most people inside organizations there are those friends that form a click.

Also, there are those certain people that find a need to attach to each other. Such it may be where persons become intimately close with each other. So, close it is with some people that some can get to the point where even the most personal problems are discussed in trusting total confidence.

Would Zach not have had such persons around? Was it one or two persons he could have conveyed the entire matter to looking for any support? And then could they have not told such matters much later to one of the apostles they may have known? Of course, years later, he would have told his son all about the event. Then too, he could have also given the information to whomever it was that inquired. Immediate assumptions must have been flying high among the people in the temple plaza. Especially those that had been praying while also waiting for him to conclude the service. Surely there were people who knew exactly how long the service would have taken. No doubt about it, that the regular attendees must have all been aware that the service had taken a much longer time than the usual schedule that was planned. And would they have not been asking each other whether there may have been some sort of added offering?

Were there others that were concerned thinking something was wrong? So, with all of that, would not curiosity have abounded where people everywhere from one end of the temple to the other not have been talking? Gee, for the people it was a time of something different. There may have been feelings of excitement since something out of the ordinary was going on. And it would have only taken one person to initiate a quick rumor. When he finally showed himself had gossip not already started? People close to Zach that had been waiting for him to come out must have at least suspected something. But suspect what? How could they not think something out of the ordinary must have happened? After all such was not normal for Zachary to take such a long time.

Having performed the service so many times, the priest had to have been very proficient. Then to as it was since there were no persons presenting an offering it was well known to everyone that the service would be a short one. And hadn't those people after knowing how long he usually takes, being used to his time of service, not have assumed thoughts as to what happened? But what could they have thought?

The Great Excitignly Holy John the Baptist

Who can know other than imagine especially having not been there, but initially seeing his actions when Zach the priest finally showed himself how the crowd, priests and guards reacted? Was there anger at his taking so long or was there concern for his health?

Considering the time that the service took, would those people not have thought that something really special had to have happened? Yet they were aware that the priest wasn't carried out on a stretcher. So, it was the question of the day being what happened with the priest, what for and why?

PART VI.

AFTERWARD IT'S THE TEMPLE!

Chapter 10. A Person Could Almost Visualize the Crowd Going Wild!

Finally, the priest came into view. Upon Zach seeing the crowd maybe he made some ridiculous signs trying to answer their question. But for him being unable to talk, what could they have thought? How impatient people are. A person could almost visualize the crowd going wild almost as if at some sporting event. Where calls probably yelled such as, hey Zach what happened in there? Perhaps others would have been yelling, what took you so long?

Also, maybe there could have even been others yelling words of mean intentions. Because some people from being delayed so long while being in hurry may have taken it personally. Some people in meanness may have even yelled, hey Zach, you getting too old to be a priest? Was not he trying to respond making other signs pointing to his mouth? Then also would Zach not have made movements attempting to indicate some form of explanation? But who would have understood. Yet with all his efforts Zach was probably struggling with himself so much that he actually lost control. Perhaps some people may have thought he fell down and broke his jaw.

It was a touchy situation of which he had no prior experience at. Every question or innuendo became a huge confrontation which presented a problem. Maybe some could have even thought that someone had hit him with a club. Of course, there may have even been those that were suggesting that he was putting on some kind of an act. Whatever Zachary had tried doing, a big fact is that the signs the crowd was receiving had to them to be ridiculous. Such experience had to be new to them as they had never seen him do such nonsense before.

Up until that time he was just another priest doing as the others did, which always took about the same amount of time. Important it is to note, that during that time period there was no such thing as an already designed method of sign language. Sign language may have been something in the future, but for sure it was not around during those times. Significant is that there is no record of him having any relatives or friends that were dumb. Also, worthwhile noting is that there is no record of Zachary or his wife having any relatives or friends that were dumb. Such persons could have been a big help to him as at least he would have had exposure to others in the same predicament. At least had he known such, Zachary would have had some experience that would have allowed him to communicate with others. Oh, how such, even if only once in a while, would have been most helpful. Perhaps there may have been some people that felt that he may have had a vision. Or else, what could have transpired in there, they may have asked each other? After all it was a most solemn service. Not being a party there would not have been any clowning around.

Such matter was recorded by Luke where in his written matter he described the attitude of the crowd. As taken from the written record it is in Luke 1:21- 22 stated, "and they wondered at his tarrying so long in the temple. But when he did come out he could not speak to them". Would they have thought that he had seen a vision in the altar room? Perhaps, but that would have been very unlikely. It was unknown at the time of anyone having had a vision before. Therefore, what signs would the people have known to look for? There isn't anything in the written records of his attire or body depicting anything unusual.

So, it was most probable that while he wanted to get home, and get home in a hurry Zach kept waving while walking yet also making some hand signs to them. Where does the Koran mention those matters? Is it in the Koran that when Zachary came out of the temple he gestured to everyone what had happened? Really? He gestured to everyone? What kind of a gesture? Gestured indicates one. What type of gesture could he have possibly used that would have told them of his experience?

Is there anything shown that indicates the type or manner used? Then to, what number was to be everyone? Are there any figures or words in the Koran, given to suggest any clue, as to what the number of the people were? Is there any indication specified of who were those that made up the so called everyone? Are there any titles or names mentioned? Now it is that since the people were inside the temple walls how could he have motioned to so many? Especially if he was outside all the while with none knowing any type of sign language! Then to without sign language or such things as blackboards what type of a gesture could he possibly have made, especially to some many?

A meeting place for socializing as well as prayer, it was also that trading inside the temple was done. Important to remember is that the temple was huge. It was no where even similar to the local churches or synagogues of the modern era. And its main business was one of being for religious services. Now since those matters also entered into its availability while being a center of gathering the man would not have wanted to stand in their midst being made a joke of. With all of those things going on, for sure there would have been a good number of people, perhaps even into the hundreds.

How would Zach not have been under some pressure? But wasn't he already in a tense state of mind? Maybe it was even been possible by that time of day where the man had lost a little control. Perhaps he may have been a little hysterical? For sure the situation was not a simple matter as trying to tell people in traffic to stop or go. Imagine how such an older person having gone through what he immediately felt. Then trying to describe the whole matter of what took place inside, to a crowd. Wow, then at the same time, all without being able to speak. Such an attempt would have had to been a monumental task if not impossible. How would such at his age have not put a deadly enormous stress, where he was almost falling down?

What person, even today would have wanted to hang around? How would he have begun to gesture the full explanation of what transpired? Especially, since such an event would have required details. After all, the phrase does not state any limit of what he could have gestured about. As it is the phrase only states what went on. And it is that by itself indicates everything done along with what was said inside. Also, the service was not one of Hollywood or stage comedy, but a religious matter. Such it was where there were other priests and Levites in attendance but outside the altar room guarding the entrance. Now it was that back during that period of time the temple was the place. Since gentiles were not permitted even close, there would have been sufficient means taken to ensure the traditional policy.

The Great Excitignly Holy John the Baptist

Now it was that Zachary had been in the service of carrying out the custom prayer and religious tradition. Yet also, it was that those others were omitted. Would not attendance inside the temple walls have been made by a large crowd of people? Back during that period of time, the temple was the place. It wasn't like today where churches and stores are within walking distance down the block or driving that car. So, to keep out those not wanted to enter there would have been guards. Then to, since performed with great reverence the service was also combined with regularity of day and time. Such was the religious act of custom and tradition that it was well known throughout a very wide area. Surely such a holy service would have drawn more than just a few for tea as ten or thirty people. And even if there were only fifty, who would Zachary have gestured to?

How many at a time would he have even felt up to giving any gesture? Then to the point that they may have understood what his message was? Of course, then also there would be the thinking that he was able to convince three or four at a time. But how long would it have taken to explain about the angel? And then what about what was said between the two? How is it that such is also omitted? One should try doing the same with some friend or family members. Of course, the trick would be to keep a record of being able to determine how long it would take. Then would he have not had to do the same among fifty?

So, after trying to explain to the other priests and scribes, how would there not have been disagreeing and cynical Ness abounding? Yet in considering what he had just gone through what person in their right mind would have been concerned about the crowd? So, with that considered there must be a question asked. Was the priest after such a brow beating along with his age been in a stable mind, actually wanting to address the crowd? An important thing to consider is that people would have wanted to know the details of how. They would have pressed the how looking for exactly how he came to be in his physical condition.

Then trying to explain the how in his condition would have had to have been extremely difficult if not impossible. Explaining how anything that happens is not always that easy, especially if out of the ordinary. Then to have to explain the condition along with why, such would have been to overbearing. Something to compare might be telling someone of having a cold. How easy that probably would be. But, then attempting to explain why, along with how it was caught would not be so easy. But it is that everyone knows about colds, where his problem was more than a cold.

So, with that being said, if there was seventy-five people there, how long would it have taken him? But it must be taken into consideration that the situation was not the first thing of the day. Rather it was that Zachary had to have been under tremendous stress. Is it that the Koran of unknown authors and not a person, specifically states, everyone. Surely other words could have been used such as, a few, or several or even very many, but were not. Does not the book assert everyone which means without doubt, everybody? But then also does the book mention how its information was put in and what were the sources?

What do more omissions of information do anything other than present misleading matter? How does leaving more to guessing, void of fact, help in comprehending truth? Furthermore, being void of stating any type of the gesture he may have used leaves only more guessing. Just too much void of factual matter. And it is that such void is emptiness simply leaving everything up in the air to assumption, being without facts. Furthermore, it would have been almost impossible for Zachary to gesture the entire matter, especially to a crowd that was tired of waiting. What gestures could he have possibly shown that would have made sense? How would Zachary have possibly explained the what, or who the entity was? Now, there is the reality of, who would have believed him? Surely there were those that would have thought that he had lost his mind.

While others may have suggested that he was drunk. Also, others might have felt that he fell down and banged his head. Would other people have felt that he was beaten? Did the crowd get rowdy? Was there any reason for them not to get overly pressing for him to speak? Would there not have been the people getting out of hand with pushing and shoving? A matter to be considered is what were such people like that may have had gotten worked up? Then to, where some may have been angry when seeing his actions, how did they react? Even in today's world such can be seen happening in other countries on the news. Then perhaps a few may have even had some thinking of his describing of an angel. But then since none had ever seen an angel how would they have related his motions to having had a vision? Or, what would they have related his motions to? Would their thoughts have gone to an extreme? Even have gone to the point of him being a witch conjuring up evil spirits?

A most important item is how would he have explained what the angel said? Wasn't it really the words spoken by the angel that Zach acted upon to be irrational? Also, was it not the angel that caused his loss of voice? So how would anyone explain such many necessary things to so many? Also how did he perform such when not having learned any sign language? Oh, how easy it is for people of today in hindsight to offer their opinions. Everything is so easy to them to be explained, even to the point of what they would have done. Of course, they're already prepared to say how busy they are or offer other excuses. But Zach, well, he had no hindsight or experience to relate to. Also, since he didn't have any education in such matters how would he know what kind of signs to use? Did he get up on a ladder or do a dance or use pantomime? Plus, and most important is that he was the only person inside, all by himself. Therefore, who would have had any idea from the beginning as to what he was trying to tell them? Regardless of the questions the people may have asked or who asked them, he had no means of answering.

Perhaps with him remaining dumb maybe he had given simple hand waving signals. What else could he have done? Unfortunately, Luke did not include anything regarding how long it took for the people to come to conclusions. Nor did the apostle mention anything about the attitude of the people. Such would have given a clear picture of what Zach would have gone through. Surely there would have been those people that may have been in a hurry. And would they not have shown an attitude?

Here put are a few of the author's thoughts for consideration. Back then there were no such things as note pads, paper and pencils, weren't any such things as computers or blackboards. Now it was that most of the people during the time period were illiterate. So, even if he could write they, wouldn't have been able to read what he wrote anyway. Then, along with not having any form of developed sign language communication at that particular moment was at least a huge burdensome problem.

However, the biggest obstacle may have been that no other person had been inside assisting him. Therefore with no one else for the people to ask what had happened, how would the crowd not have been unable to fully comprehend what had happened or why?

Considering those things, all that the people knew was that the person passing by in front of them was unable to talk. With all of the obstacles he was coping with they were all added to by what the people didn't know. Then most important is to consider the number of people that were there. Some consideration must be given the fact that in the plaza there may have been groups of people. Such could have been a large group that had been there for the socializing as well as prayer time.

Then also there were those that were there for buying and selling things where the numbers could have been at least eighty if not a hundred and eighty or even twice that many. What is not known is whether there was any cause for celebration going on in the plaza. If there was such a happy event taking place it could have brought the plaza area to being filled. Maybe with those other things going on perhaps the number of people would have exceeded four hundred or even more. Then with the weather co-operating it may have been filled beyond the norm. However regardless of the numbers, with most people being illiterate the situation had to be one of discord. So, what remained was that there may have been some good guessing.

Also not written in the records is what Zachary did to avoid the public's curiosity. Did he put a covering over his face to hide his identity? Also, it may have been where he exchanged clothing with someone. Perhaps he was able to sneak out while accompanied by one of the other priests. Such could have been if he was able to convince one of them that he had a bad tooth ache. But more than likely it was not so much of him being unable to speak, as much as those thinking the worst. Would not some even have thought that he had been taken over by the devil? But even that would not have been instantaneous. Yet for sure the crowd would have to wait.

The people wouldn't have gotten the message of how it happened right away. Would not those persons attempting to comprehend what had happened take much time? For the priest being unknowledgeable in sign language, thus unable to convey any message regarding what had happened would such situation not have required a lot of time to explain? Had he been able to answer one question, surely whatever the answer may have been would it not have led to another question? And it is those details would have been absolutely necessary. Such had to have been paramount considering the confusion that was about the area. Also taking into account are all the various types of comments people could have made. With all of those things possible, how did he ever cope? Whether guessing or using the imagination one must appreciate how people often think the worst where surely there were those negative innuendos that would have been put by the people. Perhaps some may have yelled out that his age had caught up with him, hollering for him to retire. Then maybe others may have yelled out that he had a stroke. While others may have uttered he had been stabbed or beaten.

So, with neither him nor the crowd having any means of practiced sign language how would there not have been mayhem? Also, how would there not have been skeptical discord among the people themselves arguing with each other? Can a person imagine being there in the midst of the crowd with all of their pushing, shoving and yelling? Would there not have been people having one thought trying to force their way on others who may have had other ideas? Then others would have asserted that he was intoxicated. Don't people utter such thoughts when unknowing?

It shouldn't be too difficult to imagine how the man, a priest, all healthy up until only hours before was feeling. All speaking faculties were working when Zachary entered the altar area, then upon leaving he was unable to utter a word. Would he have been so upset that he hesitated in leaving, as trying to get his mind together? Then to, being in the midst of the crowd was he not also scared? Would such madness have caused him to fear for his life? Perhaps he may have felt that he was in danger as the crowd may have turned into a semi-violent mob. No doubt it was that he had to get away. Yet after coping with all that fiasco of confrontations it was that he still had to look forward to returning home.

Of course, the big thing was that Zach was still unable to speak. Any frustration about not having children or being angry about the matter had to have vanished. As it was for the moment there remained only the lowly feeling of knowing the burden he was about to place on his wife. But what could he do? How would he act with his wife not knowing what to expect? What a day he had gone through and it wasn't even over. Wow, perhaps maybe it was just beginning! Possibly thinking as hard as he could did he imagine all of the upcoming to be troubles? As he approached his dwelling what thoughts must have gone through his mind? Was he so ashamed that he wouldn't even be able to open the door? But it was that Zach had to go through it. After all it was his home. Then what would he do once inside? How would he act since he couldn't speak? What kind of an act could he have thought of putting on? How would he be able to explain his condition without his voice? Then also maybe he was likely afraid to provide the details for getting laughed at. At that moment, the last thing Zachary would have wanted to hear was his wife laughing at him. But what could he do?

How could he get her to understand his situation? Surely, he must have given thought to the idea that one statement about the angel would surely lead to another. And then, where would it end?Big problems developed, for as it was that there had not been anyone else present that had seen anything. That single fact alone meant that he was without any witnesses. Then added to that was that neither him or his wife or anyone they knew ever before had seen an angel. So, with all of that being known it must have kept him in a defensive state of mind. Though he wanted to tell the whole story, how could he? So unsure about everything perhaps he even doubted himself. Such a situation was just the right stuff for those of preconceived ideas or assumptions.

Wherefore it is, that nowhere is anything found of any description of his face being altered. Nor is there any written matter depicting any brilliance radiating from him. Then also there is nothing found in the record regarding his subsequent months of home life where some people may have come to visit him. And then it is presumed that none of the people there in the temple that day had ever known anyone else who had before seen an angel. Therefore, with that in mind, more than likely there were only a few that would have thought that Zach did.

Sure, there were some but more than likely it is others in wrong assumptions may have thought other things. But whatever they may have thought it really had no bearing on what had happened. Nothing thought or spoken could have changed the outlook in the confused mind of Zachary. Then came the real pressure as he approached his house. A person could almost imagine the tenseness in his stomach growing as he got closer and closer. There would be no band playing nor would there be any mob of people clapping while shouting compliments. No, it was to be the same type of approaching his place as was always before. There would have been no people waving flags or rolling out the red carpet. Maybe he was so overwhelmed by the entire event that his head was still spinning.

Whew! After all that the man had made it safely around the crowd as well as away from other Priests, Levites, Pharisees and Scribes. Such a state of mind he may have been in that even to the point of being dizzy. As it was though, eventually he would have to go inside. Then what? Other people he was able to walk away from but here it was where he couldn't very well walk away from his wife.

And so, after all that the man went through his biggest challenge waited for him on other side of the door. He knew things would not be easily handled.

Sure, it would be that she would not readily understand. But all the thinking of what and how to present his situation just made no sense. But he was aware that he had to get it over with as there was nobody else to speak for him. What a time in the man's life.

PART VII

HOME AND COMMUNITY, A BOILING POT!

Chapter 11.

Was His Wife Hollering Hello Sweetie as he Entered?

Suddenly, there he was across the threshold! Whew! All safe it was when he finally arrived inside his own dwelling. Was his wife hollering hello sweetie as he entered? Normally providing him a greeting when he returned would not Elizabeth have done the same? Especially, with her not knowing of his new physical condition, would she not have given a happy verbal greeting? Sure, it could have been that she may have had one of those lonely, miserable days. But wouldn't she have wanted such miserable feelings not to continue?

What would her emotions have been like when she saw his sad face? Then when she didn't receive any of her husband's usual responses, how did she react? Wow! Quickly came the moment when he stood face to face with his spouse. Since neither of the family sides had any training in sign language how did the man explain his newly developed situation? What a time for the both of them, it must have been. Confusion would have certainly been at the forefront of all possible intended discussion.

So, there was the husband of only hours earlier fully aware of his wife having no idea whatsoever as to what had occurred. Of course, if she did it would have certainly made his position easier. But as it was she was confronted with not only an unusual but totally unexpected type of situation. Not being prepared for his antics what would have been her first assumptions? As sure like any other woman, wouldn't she have had many? But really, what could have taken place, his wife must have thought?

The Great Excitignly Holy John the Baptist

Fully aware she was that her husband was a learned man as well as was healthy when he left. So, with that in mind, maybe there was the normal laughter of Elizabeth.

Did she assume that her husband was ok, but just trying to have some fun as joking around? Perhaps she may have even thought that her husband was doing something to pep her up. After all she was aware that Zachary knew about her having bad days. Then to she may have thought that maybe he was developing some form of a comedy. So, there was the husband of only hours earlier fully aware of his wife having no idea whatsoever as to what had occurred. In the least she would have realized that something was not right.

Something bad must have happened, she thought, but what? And what a mess it was as he couldn't lie to her. Meanwhile, what was he able to do since he knew he could not provide any detail? It would have been an effort for Elizabeth as she attempted to figure not only what had happened but what it was all about. So, in her thinking would she not have had assumptions trying to provide answers even before giving a question? Then to, maybe she was trying to guess why, while he was attempting to signal to her the what. Then probably the way people jump quickly to conclusions about everything, maybe she was thinking in the negative.

Of course, Elizabeth wanted to know everything. And why not, after all, it was that she was his wife. However, there was a very big stumbling block for Zach. What could he have told her? Perhaps he wrote a few words on their tablet. But with the matter being so complex there would never have been enough room. It certainly would not have been simple as having a headache. Comprehending the thinking of the man's immediate experience, how much could he have told her before putting a stop? If he started trying to explain to his wife exactly what occurred how much detail would he be able to write before she got mad?

Whatever he would have noted would it not have been taken by her the wrong way? Would she consider the first intentions as an insult? Zachary was well aware of his wife's depression on not having any children. If he was aware of anything it was that he knew he had to be careful in what he told her. But where would he start? Maybe he caused a few hesitations which were followed by delays. For sure it was that the man found himself on the spot. Probably a few excuses he may have used as having to do something else.

Describe the angel to his wife who knew that he was only a normal husband and not some single holy person. Perhaps for others it may have been easy but for him, how would he even start? But eventually, it was that he was running out of time. Terrific, the man was feeling as his heart was pounding knowing that all he had to do was to tell the woman that she was to become pregnant. Wow, what a challenge and how would Zachary say such of which she would not think he was dreaming? Of course, he had to start somewhere with telling her something. But really, how much would his wife take by watching, then trying to understand before she would get all frustrated in unbelief?

Did she have any idea how worn out her husband must have been. From his time spent coping with the angel was enough to drain his strength, then also there were the guards, priests as well as the people that he faced? As the day went the man probably felt as if he were in some court answering to some charge of lies. Would he have been able to fully explain such matters to her in his condition? Their immediate moments spent together must have really been a real test of their love and respect for each other. Surely for him it turned out to be nothing less than a monumental chore for both.

Always over time the older married couple was able to find it easy to communicate about everything. As always being up front, neither of the two ever held anything back from the other. But then what was this new madness that had the two of them as almost strangers to each other. This mess of such was of substance they had never before encountered. Wow! What was going on in his mind, she must have thought. Maybe while being in tears Elizabeth desperately tried so hard to understand. Yet all the while being frustrated she could see how her husband was struggling with his trying attempts to explain.

What a terribly upsetting time it must have been. Yet it must have been where all the while he was in total frustration. With all good intentions the man would have been trying to do his best. Certainly, the husband didn't want to cause his wife any hard feelings as was trying not to allow her to think he was making fun of her. Attempting to make some sense of what he was trying to get across to his wife had to be a draining event.

There he was a priest who had counseled other people regarding all types of problems. Yet he as it was he was truly lost for words. Would he have been repeating his motions over and over, just to get one point across? The rest of the day had to have been not only tiresome but also troublesome for both. All the while there was his wife spending her time trying so hard to understand her husband. For sure such trials could not be considered in any measure as a boring time.

While being like any other normal woman, did she have to force herself to overcome her preconceived ideas? And then, with the situation being one of entirely something new, maybe she was so upset that she was unable to even think. She couldn't even recall any situations the couple may have encountered where she at least could have made a comparison. So, along with both never having been confronted with anything similar, it must have taken all of her strength to keep from breaking down. But then to, maybe there were even some easy moments. At least for her it was where she could ask questions since she was able to speak while relying on the fact that he could hear. But for him things were different, as there was no instant or easy way of his providing reasonable quick answers.

In presenting these matters it is to consider the time in history that it took place not just the event. People are able to see on the news about the people in Syria and the surrounding countries what they put up with even these days. Consider back then, there were no such things as electricity to heat or cook with. Nor were there such things as dish and clothes washing machines. Also, there weren't any cars, buses or paved highways. No lights, no vacuum cleaners, no fans or air conditioners and no such thing as running hot water or baseboard heating. Now it is in all fairness that one must add those things on to the living conditions. Then with all of that it is necessary to consider the couple's unfortunate lives of not having children. But, would not the couple have thought, that with time passing their lives had settled into a quiet of what they were starting to enjoy? Surely each was aware that their bodies were slowing down. Were their minds not finding contentment in just each other?

The Great Excitignly Holy John the Baptist

Wow! And just when things were getting into a comfortable zone! Then comes the episode of Zachary with his visitor from his Lord God. One thing for sure stands out, which is that the living situation in the Zachary and Elizabeth household from that day forward would never have been the same as before. For them it may have been like starting their marriage all over. But at their age it wouldn't have been anything like when they were in their early years. Rather, what they were going to go thru would be anything but what they experienced when first married. Wow! And at their age in life to be handed such a challenge.

It wasn't as if they would have a good time even going on a honeymoon. Perhaps, it may have been that from time-to-time Zach tried to drop some subtle hints to his wife. It must have been horrible for him to the point that he was almost felt tortured not being able to discuss what was to happen with her. Rather, the question for him may have been whether they would even survive?

Now it is to return to the immediate matter where it must have been that Zachary with all that had happened had to have been totally overwrought. Not just was it the situation itself but the fact was that here was this simple man of simple means all by himself. But little did he know just how much turmoil his physical situation was to cause him and his wife. Then the really big moment finally came. It stared him right in the face probably causing him to remain motionless. Inside for a moment, there he was so happy to have arrived home, then all of a sudden he found himself truly alone as standing while facing his wife. At first Elizabeth must have thought her husband was pulling some form of a gag. Surely greetings to her husband must have been made but was her kindness responded to with what, his hand signals? Was it that he was waving goodbye? Or maybe he had a tooth ache or other pain in the jaw, she may have wondered.

How business-like Zach was as he was not doing any smiling. Perhaps she may have thought, now what is this idiot of my husband doing? If at first, she was not confused Elizabeth must have at least started to get mad. Why doesn't he stop fooling around, she may have wondered? Why doesn't he just tell me what the problem was? What could she have pondered? But as the time of day went by maybe she was finally able to conclude that his actions were no joking matters.

The Great Excitignly Holy John the Baptist

Would not her being curious about him, being unable to speak, have driven them both bonkers? At their old age along with all the other problems she is greeted with this burden. Then not being prepared before hand, what was she to think? After all, the man wasn't carried back to his abode. Nor was it that he had stumbled inside. There were no indications that he had been robbed or beaten. Nor were there any bruises that showed where he may have fallen down any steps. Then to, she was fully aware that when he had left her earlier in the day he was fine.

What trying times the two must have had! But her heart was there as she felt sorrow for him, especially seeing how overly distraught he was. So taken in she was, when finally realizing his effort in trying so hard to make her understand. Her compassion was pouring out all over while trying to comprehend so hard of what had happened. Now it was that with all of her husband's motions and facial expressions overtaking her, maybe such a time was all too much at once. So, if the husband was confused along with maybe doubting himself how much more confused would his wife not have been?

Perhaps with everything going on it may have even clouded her mind causing a blockage of immediate understanding. Why not? After all, this was not something that they planned or was expecting. For Elisabeth the entire unexpected situation had to have strained her nerves beyond anything she ever felt. So, there the two were all at once suddenly thrust into a truly new kind of situation. Oh my, how much fun they must have had. For sure it was that the older couple had found themselves in a different environment, as unable to communicate with each other the way they used to.

Oh, sure it was probably relatively easy for him to convince her that he had lost his voice. After all, by his motions along with the use of the note pad she was able to understand that much. But it wasn't enough as his wife wanted to know how. What motions did he use? How many different types of movements was he forced to use in order to explain? Or did he try to minimize the matter? For sure it was that what they were going through was a first for the both of them. Yet it was that things were never to be the same again. Was her immediate thought for his life? Surely Elizabeth like other people must have had preconceived ideas. What thought was she to believe?

Also, what would her neighbors along with the other people in the social groups believe? What could she have told them? There were no such things as drive thru clinics down the street. Neither were there any speech therapists or medical doctors during the time period. Actually, there weren't any specialists around either that could have rendered some assistance.

When the evening became strained by the pressures, perhaps he realized that she was not able to quickly understand. Maybe he even felt the strain of her pushing so hard to understand that it only caused more confusion. Then soon he may have realized that his actions were not helping her anxiety. Also, even if she did understand what he was trying to tell her, maybe his biggest concern was whether she would really believe him. Reaching a point of frustration, realizing the helter-skelter matter was going to be slow for her to comprehend, perhaps they agreed to continue the fiasco the next day. What a lousy position Zach found himself in. Then to what a miserable situation it was for the two of them!

What most likely made it ever worse were their ages. After all they weren't in their mid years when they had so much confidence. Then too, the couple was far from their young years when they had lots of pep and energy. Did the older couple work out a means of some form of communication? Surely there can be no doubt that such would have been necessary to overcome their challenging obstacles. So, with an ongoing plan they must have been at least able to devise some kind of understanding of when he was trying to communicate to her.

Surely there must have been times when her husband needed to speak to her. Of course, it was still easy for her to speak to him as all she had to do was call him. Some method, though crude, must have been figured out for alerting each other. Perhaps there was him ringing of a bell or banging on a pan. Whatever method they arranged may have been sufficient to at least allow the causing of some attention by her so that she could respond. Once things settled down to a chaotic orderly disorder, where his wife was at his side maybe he was able to slowly get his message across to her. But how long would it have taken? Then to, what message of what happened was he able to get across to her? Also, how much detail was he able to provide? And then if she found things too hard to believe what then?

The Great Excitignly Holy John the Baptist

While he was attempting to describe each moment, yet feeling her mood of indecision, then what? Such could hardly be taken as what people would consider as normal types of communication. But then during those close moments even a doctor would not have been able to help. Times back then were tough enough where for sure the old couple didn't need the added burden. Only a little imagination would be necessary to consider what an awkward time it may have been when she would have asked a question. Such trials the man must have gone thru. All the while with her coping with her husband's new way about himself.

Was it his stumbling to give a message or her stumbling to understand? Either or, for sure there must have been moments of absolute confusion. Perhaps from time to time, in their maturity perhaps they may have even found time for a pause to laugh. Important to continually remember is that since neither had previously experienced such between them, every day had to be a trial of struggle. Yet maybe in their maturity, after a while, they were able to find some humor in some of their struggling moments.

Sure, it was that the normal everyday living things that were done during those times would have been easy to go through. But then suddenly things had changed where every day had become not the same. Surely there must have been at least one time during the day where there was at least a moment without confusion. Then there were the weekend religious services. More strain may have been felt as may have been found for him to be different than those in the past.

Since he was without voice Zach would have been limited regarding services he could perform sols. Where chanting or hymns would have been part of a service, one of the other priests would have had to have assisted or even have taken his place. When such was necessary how did he handle it? Would he have felt a sense of embarrassment? Were his feelings of pride turned to hurt? Were there times when Elizabeth would have had to go with him to communicate with the high priest on his behalf? One can almost sense the low feelings he may have had. Especially it would have been during those times when he needed someone to speak for him. How would it not have lowered his self esteem? Yet for her those assisting parts may have been a blessing.

The Great Excitignly Holy John the Baptist

Maybe it gave her moments of uplifting as allowing a chance of realizing some satisfaction. Since Zachary was unable to tell his wife of the details so it was with everyone. Such can be understood by recalling what Elizabeth said when she first came to realize her being pregnant. For her to get out of the house to help her husband had to have given her some peace of mind. But also, there were those services during the weekdays, where once again he would have been alone. Perhaps those days didn't come fast enough as they may have restored at least some peace to his mind.

This a shame that so much information was not recorded in the bible regarding the couple's actions during those times. And then, how did they cope when a visitor showed up? After all, wouldn't there have been the curious, nosey neighbors? Also, what about those people she may have often gone shopping with? Wouldn't they have been newsy like most people? Perhaps over a few days the couple worked a lot of things out. At least for the older couple they had slowly managed to find some peace.

If nothing else they had to gain some sort of normalcy. Pulling together, their love for each other must have been tested from time to time. But being a woman of character, she knew what had to be done. And for sure after all those years any question of her giving up was not the answer. However, they managed, it was that the older couple was able to draw on their strong love and faith. Even being strained to the hilt they must have stuck together. Perhaps they decided not to allow their love for each other to be trodden down. So much were they relying on each other to keep their love that it was to them something sacred. Such may have been even to the point where they were able to perform those physical love making sequences of husband and wife.

Perhaps their being so focused on maintaining their love for each other that their being together overcame the burden of his lacking of speech. Of course, it is not known whether he previously had the gift of gab. Like some women, some men just never know when to shut up. Maybe he had been a real talker. One that liked to talk, maybe even where it would have gotten, from time to time, on her nerves. Perhaps he was the kind of nice guy that just liked to be sociable. When around people, perhaps he always felt compelled to enjoin in conversation talking about everything.

The Great Excitignly Holy John the Baptist

Whatever the subject matter pertained to, maybe, he was happy to discuss anything. Did he have a likeable personality? Was he gifted with the ability of striking up conversations? If someone else initiated some talk on a matter would he not have carried such into his abode? Of course, he would have dragged his wife into it. Perhaps it just may have even been that to her his problem was almost a blessing in disguise. Whatever or however it was that they did, somehow it was for sure that they succeeded in realizing their true companionship. Slowly but surely as the days went into weeks Zachary probably was daily getting more and more restless.

When was it going to happen, he must have been wondering? When is she going to become pregnant? When, when, when, was the question he must have pondered on. Then to, how much time will pass before it happens. Perhaps there were those nights when the question drove him to the point where sleep was not possible. Yet, the one thing he could not afford to do, was to have any more doubts as to who the angel was. Nor could he think any negative thoughts as to whether he was telling the truth. How much longer was he going to have to remain in his unwanted condition? Then to, did Elizabeth ever fully trust what her husband had been communicating to her?

Since neither of them was a fortuneteller he could only hope it would be soon. And she, what could she do but only believe what her husband had communicated. Yet it was that both had to wait. But, wait for what, she must have thought? Oh, how time can be so destructive. Did they ever fight? Was he humbled by her trust and affection? Or was he constantly tested by her doubting negativity? How far was their trust in each other stretched? Maybe in their wisdom from age they realized that their situation was beyond the norm. Perhaps they were even able to find some humor in it all. If ever endurance needed a defining there could not have been a better situation. Especially since both understood full well that neither one could do anything to change the cause of their situation. Then on whose side was time?

Every day that passed, such thinking must have caused him to sink lower and lower. With him not knowing what the length of the time was to be, would he then dwell on it when not busy? How much of the stress could he take? Would he have a breakdown as her time drew near?How much of the stress interfered with his home's stability? Perhaps his wife played a larger part in his stability, yet due to the lack of written matter is not known. Why not, as he was the one carrying around the information. It was he who had the problem. And it was he who had brought the mess into his living place.

Now it was that Zachary was no prophet, plus he was not a person of civil authority. So being just being the average man he had no notoriety. Yet, his faith and clean living must have meant something. His clean living was the material side of which he knew his Lord God would not be involved in. However, his faith was a different matter of which he knew was being tested. It was something he had to keep strong. Why? Because if he quit or gave up what would he have left? It was his faith that was the cause of the angel.

Oh sure, some would say it was his prayers while others would argue that it was his services that he offered. Then others might mention him simply being a good person. But in reality all combines into one thing, his faith in his God. Wherefore, here it is mentioned that all of that was about the time before Christ. So, there is a question that is asked. Why is the old couple not found in the Old Testament? But then, even today there are people who think there was only one big bang that the world came from. But when asking the same people which rock, plant, fish or animal they can speak to that has intelligence to speak, they drop the subject matter.

And so it is, when asked about the old couple of their not being part of the Old Testament it too becomes a mess. Such a question evolves into a debate that stretches like a rubber band. Meanwhile the days of Elizabeth being enlightened were drawing near. Because of her husband's physical condition constantly bearing down on him, in doing so it negatively affected his personality. Of course, all of that would have had a direct impact on Elizabeth.

Maybe with such a burden placed on her she began to crawl inside herself. Then without even realizing it, maybe they both started erecting walls around each other. And would such not have caused more anxiety? Oh, how time can drag, especially when being hoped for something quick to happen. Some days must have been really terrible as the two had to get their lives going.

But what could they do? They were both stuck in their own ruts, yet going in the same direction. Evidently the older married couple respected the marriage vowels as well as each other as they lived their marriage life. But then what choice did they have? So, what was the answer but time itself? It is easy to comprehend how the world must have closed in on them. Since he couldn't speak, he could hardly perform ceremonies involving naming of children or marriages.

Then what form of socializing could the couple enjoy since the husband couldn't speak?

Also, to consider is that since there was no technology back then what a small world they must have been confined to! Today confined may he an easy situation to handle but back then without any of the modern electrical and electronic conveniences it would have been mind testing.

CHAPTER 12

What a Position Elizabeth Had Found
Herself In.

Unexpectedly without warning something later on happened. It was one of those days where in a woman's life the unexpected happens. How could it happen? But it did, as suddenly one morning Elizabeth awoke realizing the stark fact that she was pregnant! Such situation is depicted in the written record of Luke. In his chapter 1:23-24, it states from the written matter, "and it came to pass, when the days of his service were completed that he returned to his own house

.Now, after these days Elizabeth his wife conceived". Was she able to intelligently, in a detailed fashion communicate with her husband Zachary. Oh, sure there were the signs along with the hand signals he made but still it remained that there were no vocal expressions. Patience being fully strained with Zachary to the limit, it must have been complemented by his wife. Sure, the woman was able to grasp the holy matters that took place during the time of her husband's service. Surely Elizabeth was knowledgeable about her husband's offering duties.

But what had suddenly come upon Elizabeth was something she was unprepared for. There it was with the woman having her situation of which she had not expected. Did she have any understanding whatsoever of that which had transpired during his service? What did she know? How much did she understand? Perhaps by her reaction it may be taken that her husband was unable to communicate to her about his being visited by an angel. Initially he probably attempted to inform her of what had transpired. But then him realizing her being not receptive, what sense would there have been in trying to explain even more?

Total frustration must have eaten at Zach realizing his speech failure as unable to communicate. As a result of their having a lack of any true discussion maybe he stopped with the details. After all, if she wasn't readily accepting the part of the angel, would he not have decided not to tell her about the forth coming child? So it is that she was lacking of any knowledge of his already knowing of what was oncoming. As such Elizabeth could not have even begun to think about what an angel visiting her husband may have said to him. Then also why would she down deep have believed him, even if really did try to tell her? No warning of any spiritual kind was ever given to her. Plus, there had never been before any previous occurrences relating to such matters in their family's history. All of that lack of knowing, as well as unable to find out could have only left her wondering.

An idea of what form of mind set Elizabeth may have fallen into is shown by Luke in 1: 24. Now it is where he only presents just a few words, but what power of feelings they give off. In that one simple phrase as taken from the written record it states, "and she secluded herself for five months." Had Elizabeth become somewhat strained? One thing that really presented an obstacle was that at no time were they both, being together at the same time ever been advised that such an event would have taken place.Such would have made things so much easier, but it wasn't meant to be. Even after reading of such matters found in the scriptures what then? How would they ever have been able to relate that the writings were actually telling of them?

Meanwhile, as the months had passed her cousin Mary had become aware that she was pregnant. No, it wasn't' by way of the telegraph but because she had also been visited by an angel. And in the written matter it depicts where the angel advised her of her cousin's pregnancy. What a position Elizabeth had found herself in. Had she been thankful for their years of prayers being answered such as like other women? Or was she into herself where all she could do was think the worst? Was she just like any other person worrying about other people? Would Elizabeth have been over concerned about what other people were going to think? Did she find herself wondering around in the home constantly looking for things to do?

At times would Elizabeth have found herself talking to herself? Especially with her husband unable to speak while being without other relatives in the home, would not the silence have driven her batty at times? Then without any such things as a radio or tv what did she do to keep herself occupied? How did she finally explain her condition to her husband? Considering her anxiety over his situation along with her new position, did she tell him right away? Would she have waited for that right day? Was she scared of what he may have thought or was she all excited? Would she have told him the day she came to realize of her soon to be a mother? Then whenever she did tell him, what had she thought seeing his reaction? And then to, what would have been his reaction? Would he have been thinking like other people ready to say, see I told you so? Or would he have just given a smile, understanding how his wife had been in the dark as to the child's holiness?

What a day of calamity that one must have been for the both of them. As the days passed surely the shock had slowly but surely worn off. Once she did tell her husband were they both getting concerned about what the neighbors would have thought. Would they have given thought as to what other people such as those at the market place would have been thinking? And then, what about her cousin, did she ever hear? Such is answered in the record of Luke. At 1:26-28, wherein it is stated what Luke wrote about just how her cousin found out. As it was Mary had already been advised of her new situation.

As taken from the written record in 1:26 it states, "now in\the sixth month the angel Gabriel was sent from God to a town of Galilee called Nazareth, to a virgin betrothed to a man named Joseph, of the house of David and the virgin's name was Mary. And when the angel had come to her, he said, Hail full of grace, the Lord is with thee. Blessed art thou among women." Then it was where the angel advised her of how she was to have a child along with her Son's holiness and greatness.

Important to comprehend is, as shown in the record there was her explaining of her not being able to understand. But the angel responded advising how it was to be through the Holy Spirit as well as asserted how he was to be the Son of God. Then before he departed angel Gabriel also advised Mary of her cousin's situation. As the record shows in Luke 1: 36- 37, the angel stated, and behold, Elizabeth thy kinswoman also has conceived a son in her old age, and she who was called barren is now in her sixth month".

Then the angel really cleared the air. Fully displayed his authority he asserted just who and how everything was able to be. As shown in the written record he stated, "for nothing shall be impossible with God." Noted it should be that the angel didn't say anything about whether God would have thought about the matter or left up to humans to decide. Also, it is that those matters are found in the record elsewhere. Perhaps not in the same words, but they do provide similar meaning. That is shown by the written matter of Matthew.

Here it is taken from his written matter in chapter 1: 18 were it states, "now the origin of Christ was in this wise, When Mary his mother had been betrothed to Joseph, before they came together, she was found to be with child by the Holy Spirit". Essentially it can be realized that the one apostle is saying the same as the other but only in different words. Though the words are different there is same intended meaning. Then in 1: 20 Matthew further states, "but while he thought on these things, behold, an angel of the Lord appeared to him in a dream saying, do not be afraid, Joseph, son of David to take thee, Mary thy wife". Clearly asserting the who along with the how the angel further stated, "for that which is begotten in her is of the Holy Spirit".

And so it was that Mary found out matters about herself that were to be. Most significant is how she found out just how it was to occur. Also, she was given another surprise when she was informed of her unexpected cousin Elizabeth's condition. How important that piece of information was which a lot of people overlook. Not only was it matter that others did not know about but most important was that it should have bolstered her belief in God.

Meanwhile, how did Elizabeth cope with those little groups of people that made up their own way of thinking? Especially those who erroneously assumed what she must have done? Those who knew that her husband was simply too old, what did they think? Then also, those that were aware of him being way beyond his time, would they have been the first to assume such things? Did such people or the false assumptions have any effect on the lives of the two? Also, there were the unfounded rotten rumors that miserable people surely had started. Such miserable attitudes could have been shown by the various people. Could such not have only added an extra burden that neither would have wanted?

Who would have believed him, that he being old as he was could be the father? After all, by that time it had to have been well known that he had lost his voice. Along with that would people not have wondered what else in his old age the man had lost? Then, if such burden were not enough, the man had a position of notoriety. Being a priest/rabbi in the temple his position must have been precarious to say the least. How did he handle the cynical Ness that must have been abounding? Also how was he able to justify him and his wife's situation, especially among his seniors? Was there talk going around about them? Was there any malicious gossip going around about her?

Everyone knew Elizabeth for years had been trying for a child. Talk there was and most probably there was the malicious kind. Or in the least there must have been those spoken erroneous assumptions that always end up in the talking arena. It would have only taken one person to mention what was only assumed. A person could have suggested how she may have been seen with so and so. Also, it could have been where someone could have added so and so a number of times. And before anyone would have realized what happened, there was the word going around that she was also seen with another so and so.

Oh, how easy it is for wrong gossip to spread. And the problem here is that people almost feed on such as needed to be spread around. Then when in a small community area wise how fast, as almost like news? Then being of many people would it not have been as quick as the tongue? People know the condition, where it's everybody knows everyone. Such would have been especially easy back then where it was the time when there were no telephones or vehicles. With the market place and temple being the center places for gossip surely it spread like butter on hot bread. Why, was because everyone had to use the same market place since there was only one.

Oh sure, maybe they were only small stores and outside tents. But it was that they were all at the one and same location. Such was day in and day out. So anyway, as time passed how did the two not react to each other, with more confusion? Also important is, how did he ever cope about his situation with his wife among his religious peers and counterparts? How easy it is for people in today's world of having modern conveniences to assume things. Then too, how easy it is for wrong gossip to spread. With people always ready to assume things is the very reason why the time period back then should be fully considered. Also, maybe it was that the hardship they endured better prepared the older couple for the future tribulations. Some problems with the religious authority the couple would certainly realize from their own son's actions while he was growing. These matters might require any reader to at least make an attempt to understand the times. Can a person imagine situations just from reading?

Life's hardships of the time period should be really considered, especially in conjunction with the people's strong religious beliefs and practices. Are those matters not of most importance? Such serious consideration not taken could lead to assumptions that the bible is merely a made-up story. Even erroneous thoughts of hocus pocus for the bible could be thought, even though it is factually based.

There are those days as well as were back then of many different as well as variations of opinions of verbal and written matters by religious persons as well as others. Yet only guessing with assumptions along with their omissions really leaves people confused. Then doing so for the purpose of twisting of what is fact into that which is false or not true puts matters beyond true comprehension. Such falsity leaves people at the point where they are misled. Why? Mostly, because they do not follow up or compare with other. Is it not so that people usually only see or review what is immediately in front of them? But, how is omitting matter not a form of lying? Yet by people not reading along with not connecting with other matter they end up confused. Or even worse is that they not only are denied the full truth, they take the easy way of putting it all away for another time.

What benefit is there not to know the full truth? Or, then what difference does it make to the person that doesn't care whether they are reading false matters or lies? Yet such people will gladly express their opinions in a discussion. Should matter not contain all supporting information? While omitting a fact or several facts, is such matter then either not true or presented in deceitful controversy? So, what is gained by twisting of what is fact into that which is false or not true other than disallowing true comprehension? Then too, how is omitting such known matter not a form of deceit or lying?

If such only leads to misunderstanding or if not caring how does a total loss of any form of comprehension not result? But then, isn't it so that at first such is never suspected or expected. It is the human element where hate in people just naturally gets started. Even if not paying visits or being visited, didn't Elizabeth still have to go to the market for food? Not having any daughters or sons posed a serious problem. Who would be there to help them as Elizabeth and Zachary were all alone? Only persons who may have experienced such loneliness at one time or another could fully appreciate their situation.

Certainly, it would have been a comedy riot for everyone if her husband, who couldn't even speak, went to do the shopping. There standing was the vendor asking what do you want or can I help you. And how would he have reacted? All Zach would have been able to do would have been to hand the person the whatever. But what about the specially prepared foods that needed to be ordered? Also, there would have been food or stuff needing to be attended to in a certain fashion. Then how would he explain the desired result? What about those around being in a hurry, would they not have been pressing?

Everyone around could speak, so naturally asking him questions they would naturally expect answers. Was he able to overhear the whispering as someone was able to make reference about him? Did he hear someone say, he's the priest of the pregnant wife or something similar? So, what would those people have thought? Talking while expecting him to speak out was the naturally way of things. But then only hearing nothing in reply from him, what would they have thought? What would they have thought of him, especially when Zachary simply ignored them?

Yet, what else would he have been able to do? Which of them offered any help or assistance? Or better which of them did not turn their backs on her? And what did they think? Nowhere in any records is it found any indication of anyone coming to the aid of either one. Now is asked, would they have come had Zachary not been a priest? Oh, how nice people are among their own kind. Yet all one has to do is watch the news to fully realize how people all over the world are still the same. And all the same, all full of cynical Ness, selfishness, greed and negativity. Just as it is in other countries so it is in the other states, counties and neighborhoods.

How sad it is that after all these centuries gone past that the world hasn't grown up yet. Was there fear of reprisals, from Elizabeth committing bad acts? It is according to scriptures where such a woman's situation occurred there was strain. And such strain there must have been. Would it not have been beyond what was shown in the records? Such it was known that the woman was barren, yet how did she explain her new condition to her friends? What could she have possibly told them? For sure, would not the nosey ones have pressed for an answer? How sad and bitter she may have become.

Surely there must also have been those that probably even put on their faking act of believing her, no matter how she tried to explain. Then those same people, what did they say when in company or conversation with others? Since Elizabeth was the known wife of a priest, perhaps would that not have generated some gossip? How could she do such things must have been the thoughts of some. And did they start any false rumors because they didn't know? Did they stand up for the older couple? Or finding it easier being in front of others to just knock them, because they couldn't defend themselves?

So, were there at least some people that were even somewhat understanding? If there were any that were compassionate why is there nothing in any records to indicate such? Amazing it is, how there is no record of anyone offering their help or physical assistance. Also, it is again questioned, how did she at first manage to explain her matter with her husband? Was she telling the truth? Sure, her husband was aware how but such it was that she didn't know. Over time she must have gone from going out regularly to sometimes. Then finally her anxiety and depression must have caught up with her as she secluded herself more and more. How afraid she must have been to confront others. What about those persons giving their best sarcastic or snobbish grins?

What a depressed state of mind the woman must have had to the extent of isolating herself. Actually, recorded is what Elizabeth had said to herself. Such words depict just how down on herself were her thoughts. In Luke 1:25, as taken from the written matter, he mentions what she said, "thus has the Lord dealt with me in the days when he deigned to take away my reproach among men". Wow, how her endurance must have been tested! Evidently, she carried such thoughts until she was visited by her cousin Mary. No warning or advance notice did she ever receive. However, it was that her cousin was on the way. And then, it happened? Suddenly and unexpected Mary also full of doubt arrived at the home of her cousin. All bitterness Elizabeth must have had, that added to the burden of her husband Zachary, quickly disappeared. And it is where such can be comprehended if only event the smallest of some thoughts are given consideration.

Such event is depicted as found in the record as reported by Luke in 1:25. Now it was around the time during her sixth month that the angel Gabriel visited Mary the betrothed of Joseph the carpenter. It is recorded by Luke that the angel advised her of certain things. But it seems that she being so young and innocent that she didn't fully comprehend the complexity of what was told her. As taken from the written in 1:30-32, the angel said to Mary, "do not be afraid Mary, for thou hast found grace with God. Behold, thou shalt conceive in thy womb and bring forth a son". Then the angel let her know just how special she was when he continued asserting, "and thou shalt call his name Jesus. He shall be great and shall be called the Son of the Highest".

Now it was that Mary probably was at least somewhat confused if not doubting where she asked how such could happen. Then, as stated in Luke 1:35 the angel replied by advising her how such would happen. The written matter in Luke's record clearly mentions what that the angel asserted. It is evident by the strength of the words used that the angel had not given an opinion or presented a request. Rather it was again that the angel was delivering a message. Further taken from the written record the angel continued in stating, "the Holy Spirit shall come upon thee and the power of the Highest shall overshadow thee; and therefore, the Holy One to be born shall be called the Son of God".

At no time can any question be raised as to the authority of who the angel represented. And for sure it was that there was nothing left to any guessing as there was no need for imagination. Those statements not only replicated but confirmed what the ancient prophets had foretold. However, it should be considered of Mary's young innocent age. Totally not planned as well as the event not expected, she must have been scared to the point of being quite shaken. Then of all things if that was not enough, even though not asked, the angel advised her of her close cousin Elizabeth's being pregnant. As taken from the written matter, it states as recorded in Luke 1:36-37, "and behold, Elizabeth thy kinswoman also has conceived a son in her old age, and she who was called barren is now in her sixth month, for nothing shall be impossible with God". If that wouldn't have shaken the bones of a person not even into their teens, nothing would.

Innocent though she was, in Mary's heart she believed, however being a down to earth person, there must have been some human doubt. Such would have been natural when thinking about how young she was. Of course, as Elizabeth was with Zachary, her parents weren't going to listen to such foolishness. And Joseph, how would he understand? In those days there was no such thing as mail service or telephones. Therefore, Mary would have had no way of communicating with her kinsfolk. But in desperation needing to find truth she personally went to see Elizabeth. Who else could she have turned to? She was determined to find out for herself. Yet, it is that God showed his loving understanding.

Being aware of her troubles He had His angel tell Mary about Elisabeth's condition. And it was where the angel Gabriel advised Mary of the woman's pregnancy. See, Luke 1:26 along with 1:37. So it was that after all of the contention with her parents as well as Joseph Mary set out to find just what was going on. With all of the cynical Ness about her, she must have felt compelled to find out for herself. Then, there was nothing left but the big moment! Oh wow! What a moment when Mary arrived at the home of Elizabeth! Yes, it must have been an extraordinary time of excitement where jubilance abounded. Not only unplanned but unexpected was her arrival. It must have been a full surprise that the older couple had. Such impact did the meeting of the two cousins make that each had something to share.

After Elizabeth gave her welcome, Mary in full astonishment realized what the angel had told her was coming to pass. Mary broke out in her humble prayer of acknowledging her situation. As found in the record of Luke 1:40-55, wherein as taken from the written matter it is where she said, "my soul magnifies the Lord, and my spirit rejoices in God my Savior". Of course, when Elizabeth and Mary first saw each other it didn't take many words for each to realize how they were beneficiaries of their Lord God. For Elizabeth it must have been breath taking as for sure it must have immediately dawned on her all the matters regarding her husband.

Meanwhile it was found recorded about Joseph being visited by angel. As taken from the written matter it states, "an angel appeared to him

(Joseph, her betrothed) in a dream saying, do not be afraid, Joseph, son of David, to take to thee Mary for thy wife, for that which is begotten in her is of the Holy Spirit. And she shall bring forth a son, and thou shalt call his name Jesus". His forth coming was foretold by the ancient prophets, Isaias in 7:14 and Jeremias in 31:22, plus Machias in 5:2 which relates to the same.

Now it is that Jesus was born of Mary as recorded in Matthew 1:20-21 Also the manner of the birth of Jesus is recorded in Luke 2: 4- 7. But the fact is as shown in the written record that his birth was months after John the Baptist. So, can anyone truly relate to Zachary, the man? Certainly, he had to have been in the most controversial situation of his life. His character had to have been challenged along with his wits which must have been tested to the limit. Believing what the angel had told him Zachary was only able to watch how those persons reacted to his wife as well as himself.

Whether from a distance or in close proximity all he could do was listen while he waited. For those that didn't know what had occurred that certain day in the temple but hearing them, he must have had some ear opening moments. Especially such would have been while listening to their unwarranted arrogance or skepticism. Perhaps there was even an occasional laugh by such persons but they would have been only fakes. People may have even smirked as they followed their thoughts of making fun of Elizabeth's apparent condition. And were any of them his so-called friends?Now, when such confronting moments occurred it may have even caused Zachary to recall his doubting time with the angel. More deep-down suffering must have struck his heart as his emotions quivered. But also, maybe he had thoughts of any day he would find relief.

When faced with the realization that he couldn't publicly support his wife whenever she was verbally attacked why would he not have felt disgust? Yet, how could her husband act or do anything to respond when she herself could not explain the controversial matters. What made things even more difficult was that she could not, nor would not lie as making up a fictitious story. During those hard times of rigorous daily life would not his spirit have been torn at? Such was he in a stressed-out mind, especially when having been encumbered with his wife's developed situation. He was not only unfamiliar but fully inexperienced as well as had never been taught about his type of situation.

What was so critical was that her as well as his situation entailed religious matters. While not having anyone else to speak with that had a similar experience it surely must left him feeling all alone. Who could he have talked to? What person was around that could have given him any good advice? Truly a strain on the marriage there must have been. Such it may have been especially when his wife's new situation was contrary to the normal behavior of much older women. Also, it was that the couple had been raised in strict Jewish religious customs and traditions. His training along with his beliefs had to have taxed his mind. Hot and cold emotions must have run wild at times especially when he was aware that he was being looked down upon as well as talked about.

Doesn't such gossip find it's way around? Also receiving similar negative looks from his friends that were surely around, how did such not take its toll? Then to how much more hurt would he have encountered? Most especially may have been when being advised by his wife of her receiving the same? People can be so cold and heartless at such lonely times, without even realizing it. Then there are those people that do so with intent.

Yet, they do so while not knowing, yet without even making any attempt at trying to comprehend the person's miserable state. Oh, how such occurrences must have really dug into his heart. Then when such was received by his wife from his friends, how much more could he have taken. Not only does one have to read that which is written in the gospels but also compare. As then not to do so could hamper true or full comprehension. Highly significant is what is hidden in between the lines, because that also is most important. Unfortunately, people read a bunch of words in a line or one paragraph, then assume it as the final definition.

But what was said before as well as what the sentence states could have a bearing relative to the meaning it intended. Then also it is what is stated afterward along with what matter it relates to could bring on a new slant. It is that all matter of all sources must be taken in context to arrive at a true picture. Also, it is what happened afterward along with what the sentence describes provides a lot of meaning. Therefore, it is that without the before, along with the after the result could be completely erroneous. Such before and individual matters combined helps to prevent the depicting of the then present to be taken out of context in a misleading fashion. Especially is true regarding what may have been fully intended but misinterpreted. Such means would be unfair as well as putting erroneous assumptions into any type of various situations described.

Attempting to justify someone's actions or discover something about people or an event requires more than just reading one or two lines. If all information of written matters is not reviewed then compared, how can the matter or situation be fully and truly comprehended? Then also to justify someone's actions or discover something about people or an event to be fairly accurate for allowing truth, it requires more. Such requires more than just reading one or two lines. Then where people don't do so, then start talking about the situation or matter without knowing all of the details what would such talk lead to? And if writing the same is done for sure it doesn't take much imagination to comprehend the damage it could do to the parties written about.

Meanwhile it was that Zach while knowing recalled what the angel had told him. No doubt he was fully aware of his wife's anxiety, that was, until Mary showed up. Negative towards their Lord God, Elizabeth had been for allowing her condition to happen. Such attitude is found depicted by Luke. Herein it is shown aforementioned where Luke showed such in 1: 25. Surely her bad feelings must have had some bearing on her husband's thinking. Would she be alright after the delivery, such concern had to have ballooned inside him with heavy feelings. But then the husband couldn't do anything about that either. How much more of coping with all of that could he have endured? Surely, Zach must have felt completely helpless.

After the initial months went past of struggling with her condition maybe Elizabeth was given cause for hope. Following the time of her being visited by her cousin Mary, would Elizabeth not have even been climbing the walls with anticipation? Perhaps she being visited by Mary was a true surprise as it was truly unexpected. But it was the type of heart-warming emotion that put it on a higher level. So much feeling there must have been between the two that one could almost feel it a mile away. Such heartfelt feelings there were that all the money in the world would not have been able to generate such genuine feelings. Yet, did she let her young cousin know of her concern because of her age? Would she have caused Mary to be concerned?

Doing so much worrying as any mother would have done. All the while at the same time she must have been looking forward to having her first baby. How could her mind not have been frizzled? Then too from time to time she must have had some fun as she drove her husband crazy. Surely her husband was feeling the same, except maybe he was overly concerned about how well she would fare. Would there be some, a few, or many unexpected complications?

Would her old age hold her back? Maybe the age factor would deprive her of much needed strength, then what? So many negatives must have gone through her husband's mind. Maybe Zach recalled that the angel never mentioned anything about any of the health matters. And then, how would he be able to care for his wife? If there were serious or critical complications, what would he do? Oh, how Zach must have worried. Surely it had to have been where he was unable to put such a serious matter out of his mind. Then too, maybe his worrying may have even reached a crucial point. Sometimes it may have even been where he had gotten sick over it.

Upon recalling that day of the certain time in the temple, he couldn't help but remember that the angel didn't mention anything about how his wife's health would fare afterward. A complete lack of knowing how she would fare must have eaten at his gut. How sad it is that all the worry in the world solves nothing. But it surely can bring on other health things to worry about. Worry yes, but for sure during those months it was different. However, the two older people may have prayed before, during those last months the couple must have set new praying records.

Especially that last month their actions must have really been something. Was their mood all happy in expectation, or all depressed thinking of the things that could go wrong? Wow, what a time of struggle in an old couple's life. But as it was, with all of each one's concern along with all of the worrying neither could do anything to prevent what may go wrong. And then if there were some problems to occur, then what? But for sure there was no way that either could prevent any mishap.

As each day went passed it was they must have understood that there was nothing they could do, as what was meant to be was to happen. As with most people that endure a long-term problem he may have fallen into a mental rut of false assumption. Listening to other people perhaps he may have even believed that all that happened was just some freak of nature. Yet it was with Zach where he had started to realize all the things of which the angel had told him. Then as it caught up with him he came to understand how he erroneously gave such little credit. But as it was that the days were coming about of all that had been foretold.

And it is where there was in an even earlier ancient time when such was foretold. Yet without any mentioning of John's name, it requires use of the thought process along with knowledge of the time periods. Wherefore it is that when taking into consideration the full extent of what was written the words fit no one else but the Baptist. Such fascinating information is found in Jeremias, pronounced Jeremiah, in chapter 1:4 to 10. Some would suggest how it could refer to other persons. However, when required to put the matter, before along with the following of the other persons conduct, such suggestions failed.

Life is full of so much, that it requires much more than simply reading words. If one doesn't do something with that which is read, what happens to that which was read? Such may be applied to Zachary's mental state in relating to his situation. If he had lost clarity in listening to other people where would his mind have been?

As it was the months and long days had passed. Finally, it was where the day of reckoning quickly approached. Was the older couple going around on pins and needles as they passed each other throughout the day, every day and each week?

Were the two really ready for who was coming, or rather what was coming? A person can only imagine the thoughts the two must have had. Was either thinking of the worst? Were they worrying about losing the baby or even the mother? Maybe she was able to say things but her husband still all mum unable to speak.

What a most difficult time period they went through. Was he praying for her or she praying for him? Maybe they even prayed together, after all their faith must have really been strong, but one can only ponder. And then there was the time element to be considered.

PART VIII.

MESSENGER ARRIVES AMID SELF INTERESTS.

Chapter 13. Did the Parents React as Others, Once the Child Was Born?

Finally, after all of those months came along their son. Their prayers had been answered. What the two had been praying and hoping for years. No doubt those months in waiting must have taken the father's nervousness to new levels. Such a strong character he had would also be shown in his son. But perhaps the real burden was concern for his wife during delivery. At her age, how would her body hold up may have been his concern. Maybe he had even dreaded the time knowing that it was to be his wife's first baby. Yet with all of the worrying that the couple did, the boy was born just fine. With the boy and Elizabeth being healthy she had to be in a state of bliss.

Did the parents react as others, once the child was born? Did Zachary remember what he had been told by the angel? At such an exciting time in a parent life who remembers or even cares what was said or happened months before? Especially, was Zachary able to remember being told how holy great his son that was born of his times was to be? What a time of joy for Zachary. But especially even more so for Elizabeth who may have doubted what her husband had been telling her. What a time in the couples lives it must have been. So excited they were, the couple was probably tripping over each other with praises of their love for each other. Such event was recorded in the written record of Luke. In his chapter 1:57- 58 it is depicted as taken from the written matter which states, "now Elizabeth time was fulfilled that she should be delivered, and she brought forth a son, And her neighbors and kinsfolk heard that the Lord had magnified his mercy towards her, and they rejoiced with her."

The Great Excitignly Holy John the Baptist

How exuberant Zach must have been, aware that both his wife and baby were in good health. But it was where he was still voiceless. Fascinating it is how it is mentioned that the neighbors and kinsfolk rejoiced with her. But where were they before hand?

Were any of them around to render assistance to the older expecting couple? Yet it was that Zachary unable to speak was still unable to talk. Sad the father must have been coping with being excluded from the others that were all of a sudden having a good time rejoicing. Did they keep him in a corner isolated? Were they still giving him the shunt? How were they of such self-righteous minds full of assumptions feeling? Was the mood that he was being punished? Had they taken it for granted that Zachary had done something evil?

Were false rumors about him still abounding? Or, were they covering over her, thinking that she was the one that did wrong? All the while taking it out on him to protect her? Maybe, not as many of the original erroneous assumption remained. But for sure as the way of the world, it should be remembered that such cynical and negativity still remained as none of the people knew about Zach's instance with the angel. Could old wrong thinking have ignited new erroneous assumptions? How easy it is the way people jump to conclusions. Especially, when void of the fully true information they simply jump to erroneous conclusions. Either way, for sure there was probably still a good mix of gossip being around. A very strong clue is here shown where in today such important matter seems to be overlooked. Yet here it is taken, that there are no written indications that he was able to enjoin with those that were celebrating.

Furthermore, as a matter of fact, it is specifically mentioned of his wife, and only his wife's name mentioned of having enjoyed with others in the rejoicing. How low he must have felt. Here it was after all of that waiting that his son had finally been born. And Zachary, well maybe for an instant he had believed that all had come to pass. Maybe as any man in a similar state of mind may have been he could have been fully looking forward to his voice returning. But such was not the case as he remained dumb, unable to speak. Oh, the mental torture Zachary must have experienced as the following days went by. Yet, it was not meant for him to be totally left out.

The Great Excitignly Holy John the Baptist

Rather Zachary would surely have his moment in time which he probably forgot all about. There was still the one big issue remaining of which such substance was even mentioned by the angel. Time had passed where the man's son still had to be circumcised. Oh yes that all important period when also his son would be given a name. But the new father probably forgot all about it. Why not, as for sure it must have been that he had more important things on his mind. His wife was physically ok plus it was where he had his son who was also healthy. But for sure it was that Zachary was to have his day complete. After all, regardless of who was present or what their status or authority was, Zach was the father.

So, it was where as the days passed, a name had to be decided upon for the new boy. Wow! What an exciting time it must have been! Controversy and discord must have abounded everywhere. For sure all the kinfolk and friends of authority being excited must have put in their opinions of what name they wanted the child to be called. Those kinds of busy bodies which are always around letting their curiosity show. About everybody else's business, for sure they must have come out of the woodwork. Not bothering or being concerned about Zachary or his wife before when the couple could have used at least some mental support. When the woman was carrying everyone was probably too busy with themselves being about their selves. But then, at the time it was a different period.

For everyone it was a time of celebration. People were all about having a good time probable even showing their willingness to be a part. Even those that the couple hadn't seen in months probably showed up. Over the course of the days there must have been some communication of the matter between the new parents. Although Elizabeth respected what her husband wanted, her being the nice person that she was, Elizabeth respected the other persons' opinions. Now the way it may have been the way people are, things must have gotten out of hand.

Such reached the level where they were attempting to force their way of what they wanted. It can only be taken where they were only interested in wanting to have the baby named the way they wanted him to be named. Reading in between the lines must be taken where, it can be realized how they were strictly adamant.

Even with the woman being the wife of a priest seemed to have made little difference as it all about them. And so much so was their aggressiveness with all desiring to show their influence. Such it was where they were actually demanding of having him named after his father. But, what about Elizabeth, didn't she have an interest? Wasn't she the mother? So, should not her wishes have come first? However, even with all of that aggravation to put up with, the woman still tried nicely to be amiable as she pleasantly kept on trying to advise them otherwise. Yet, the words in the recorded text clearly indicates, emotions of pressure. Evidently there was more than the simple making of suggestions.

As the record indicates others were demanding to have their way regardless of what the parent wanted. But then with the father unable to speak it could have only   meant that his voice was missing. Therefore, with that in mind, it must be taken with her being by her lonesome against the mob. Evidently there were also those that had influence in the community. However boldly it was where the woman seemed to have held her ground refusing to budge. Maybe it was over and over where she stated her opposition of him being called their name of which she didn't have in mind. Everything had to have been about Elizabeth since her husband was still unable to speak. All of those matters are found in the written record of Luke. As taken from his written matter in 1: 59- 60 it states, "and it came to pass on the eighth day, that they came to circumcise the child, and they were going to call him by his father's name, Zachary".

Who were those people inferred as they? Who were they, to decide what the child's name was to be? Gee, here it was the mother of the child, after years of grieving she was finally able to have had a son. Yet she was actually forced to argue with those that couldn't have been previously bothered about the couple. Not to forget was that Elizabeth in her old age had carried the child for the normal term. Just who were those people? Rather it might be asked, what kind of people were they? Had they no respect for what the new mother had just gone through over the past years? Also, what about what they may have put her through during those years. Hadn't some of those same people tortured her enough during the period before the woman's time had come?

The Great Excitignly Holy John the Baptist

Just when does it become enough for a woman then of her old age? Especially since the woman had gone through months of receiving undeserved turned up noses and unwarranted innuendos. Plus, there were probably those unfounded insinuations. And then after having put up with all that, then having just given birth? Surely it was that as Elizabeth spoke, Zach understanding the zealous crowd along with their overbearing mood, must have at least pointed to her in support of his wife many times to show his support for her. But those people swimming in their own self righteousness showed no respect for Zachary. Their own little preconceived erroneous assumptions had ruled the days.

Now it is that such matters may be reasonably determined by considering the tone that can be taken from the written words. Thought must be given to the extended time along with the situation at hand to fully grab the atmosphere. Such substance is shown clearly in the written record of Luke. As shown in his written matter the apostle's writing not only depicts of their arrogance, but also her temper. Such in 1: 60 states "and his mother answered and said, not so, but he shall be called John." There is the further proof of how they acted by the tone, which most surely can be taken from the same words. Clearly such is depicted where they refused to accept the words of Elizabeth.

Wow! There it was, she the mother actually having to cope with those people that utterly mentally ran all over her. One can almost feel the attitude of her being treated as if she was merely some sort of a maid or some other attendant. Who were those people that attempted to forcibly require Zachary to provide the baby's name? How selfish she must have thought they were. But really, it may have been how ignorant they were to have asserted themselves in such a fashion. It is important to remember that they were fully aware that Zachary could not speak. Yet having ignored him all the while, then it was they forced his involvement.

What did they expect the father to do? Did they really think he would have gone against his wife's wishes? In today's world such could almost be expected. Perhaps they thought that he would have simply waved his hands, in disgust motioning that he agreed? Such would have given them all the power they were attempting to muster up. Maybe they even anticipated him throwing up his arms as if saying he didn't care.

Or, perhaps some may have even thought he would have walked out as if refusing to participate. When is enough, going to be enough of the bickering, the disgusted mother must have felt. What will it take to have the arguing stop, Elizabeth may have wondered?

What kind of unplanned and undeserved miserable celebration had erupted? Had those kin with the wine flowing along with the so-called boisterous friends turned the joyous situation into a rowdy mob party? By all of the harassment they had put her through, could it not be that some still had reservations as to who the father was? Also, perhaps there were those harboring the thoughts that she had an affair with someone else? Maybe there was ever thinking that she was forcing the child's name as a punishment? Perhaps such matters can be construed from the matter shown in the record of Luke. In his writing, noted full well is their demonstrating of their persistence.

So much was their intent that the crowd was prepared to force their way on the parents. They had their proof of why which was all they needed. Now it is that such is shown in the record as at 1: 61- 62 as taken from the written matter it states, "and they said to her, there is none of thy kindred that is called by this name. And they kept inquiring by signs of his father, what he would have him called". Obviously by the summary of the words the crowd refused to let up. Instead, only the more did they try to force their way. After all of those years of monotony there it was in one day the couple had more excitement than they had in all prior years combined.

Amazing it was but the crowd knew all about her families past names plus was also aware of the father being unable to speak. Oh, how some must have reveled knowing Zach was unable to speak. For sure there was no concern on their part as to the husband putting up any argument. Surely they must have felt how they had the upper hand where that they had the mother cornered over a barrel. It was to be either their way or no way. Yet, it was to be that eventually where the crowd would actually regret their arrogance. However, for sure during the moment they must have felt really good, as having cornered Elizabeth. Had the mob succeeded in demonstrating their authority? By then they most assuredly must have ruined the day with their over whelming obnoxious behavior.

The Great Excitignly Holy John the Baptist

By pitting her against her husband, had they made it almost impossible for her? Then too, did they not also put her husband on the spot? Oh boy, how the emotions must have been flowing. Had everyone felt so superior where they thought how they must have had her feeling alone? Especially being fully aware of her unable to speak husband being useless? Perhaps the group may have even felt by the number of them they had power which would have shown her just who would have the last say. And meanwhile there was Zach unable to say anything. Unable to talk he couldn't even speak up for his wife, yet all the while he was forced to see her being brow beaten. Sure, it was that he was unable to talk, but how amused the crowd must have been while watching Elizabeth hand the tablet to her husband.

Simultaneously while in wonderment, the quiet mumblings of sarcastic remarks must have been ongoing all about the place. Then quietly with everyone watching the father simply inscribed the baby's name. What a moment it must have been as he handed it back to his wife where she held it up for all to see. No doubt that the community eventually heard the details of the so-called celebration. And then if that wasn't enough he had to realize that such was from some of his so-called friends. Wow, and to think it wasn't even any child of theirs. What a day it must have grown into for the older couple.

Suddenly there it was, as if a curtain had been raised, it was Zach's turn, as he came to the rescue. Perhaps all the while he had been forced to simply sit in a corner watching the hounds have their moment. But then what happened next must have really brought the curtain down. All instigators must have dropped their jaw in awe seeing what happened. And then, how taken back the crowd must have been upon seeing Zachary's reaction. No, there wasn't any violence, nor was there any arm waving. Rather there it was where the husband simply showed his support of his wife. No yelling, no loud verbal abuse language did the father use but surely, he lowered the boom.

Such a simple yet fascinating few moments and it is all found in the record of Luke. As taken from the written matter in 1: 63 it states, "and asking for a writing tablet he wrote the words, John is his name, and they all marveled". All the while immediately it must have been how elated and uplifted was Elizabeth! Was there instant quiet as the crowd bit their tongue? What would have been the reaction of the group? Of course, while those same kinsfolk and neighbors quickly found out just how wrong they were the father must have been in a state of absolute bliss. Such feelings must have been overflowing especially between the older couple as their love for each other overflowed. Then also perhaps some were to realize how badly they had treated the couple.

Suddenly they must have all felt that a bomb had exploded as the atmosphere ignited with something. But was it joy? Or was it fear? How startled the small crowd must have been at what happened next. Now it is that some people argue how Zach couldn't have written his name as there were no such things as paper tablets and pencils in those times. Perhaps there weren't those exact things for writing, as the word writing may be assumed to refer. However, during those times there were in fact other things. True they weren't made for long sentence writing or for big letters but for very short notes they sufficed.

Although papyrus was around during those times it was of such material that was used for the long types of writing. Then there was leather, but that was probably too expensive plus it was needed more for apparel wearing. Also, there was the soft wood which would have allowed characters to be scratched. With the use of a sharp knife or other sharp instrument such indents would have been sufficient. But most likely at the time what Zach most probably used was a flat piece of soft clay. Such would allow the carving of several characters which after use could be reused. Only a little water applied over a few minutes would have kept it ready for use.

Now it was that during that time period, most people then were illiterate. Not only did they not have any learning of writing but most important was that they were unable to read. But those of high positions such as priests and the well to do class of the military as well as politicians and authorities would have had reading knowledge. So, it was with Zach being a priest having learned to read and write so to his wife would have learned. Therefore, using either a wooden or clay tablet it must have been most easy for Zach to have carved John's name that could have been read. But read by whom? Surely there must have been some that were rejoicing who had reading ability.

Maybe it was a land owner, or ruler of some type or even one of the other religious friends. But whoever it was, it would have only taken one or two persons in the crowd to advise the others of what the tablet stated. One of the most powerful moments in time of history where the person's name was ever written on clay or wood that had such an impact. Since the tablet only stated one word it would have only taken one person with just the basic reading skills to decipher what Zachary had written. But what a moment in time it was containing only a word.

At that specific moment it had impact being much of a powerful meaning. So much was it where it must have had such an impact that it bothered those looking where they were affected even until they left. For sure it must have quieted down those that were boisterous about what the child's name was to be. After all it was their idea to force it on Zach to make the decision, and did he ever put them in their place. Sure, it was that he was unable to talk, but how amused the crowd must have been while watching Elizabeth hand the tablet to her husband.

Simultaneously the quiet mumblings of sarcastic remarks must have been ongoing all about the place. Then quietly with everyone watching the father simply inscribed the name of John. What a moment it must have been as he handed it back to his wife where she held it up for all to see. Jaws were probably dropping by the seconds as the crowd came to realize that their arrogance and oppressive means was all for naught. But little did the guests know that they were in for even a bigger treat.

Unaware it was, that they were about to experience a moment that would shake their faith down to their sandals. Yes, it was that there was to come, bigger things that would even more baffle them. Yet what could have happened that would have caused such calamity among the group? It would have had to have been something truly out of the normal. Such it would have had to have been that would have caused people to shudder with all sorts of thoughts. Suddenly without any warning the crowd was stunned. In one quick moment it happened. No, there was no band playing, no cymbals or drums giving an encore .

Just a quick immediate quiet. Suddenly, Zach stood up while being able to speak! Alarmed it must have been that the people were. Especially those people standing close to him, able to hear him speak and wow, did he ever speak. It must be recalled that over the past nine months they were all used to him being dumb. All that time he was unable to talk. Imagine the name calling that had gone around during the time.

The Great Excitignly Holy John the Baptist

What title would they have applied to make fun of him? Perhaps some may have labeled him as the dumb priest. Then to maybe others had even titled him as the father of someone else's child.

Surely as people like to kick those that are down there were probably even others that were wrongly applied. Yet at that one moment, all things were made right. No, the priest didn't start rebutting those other people but rather applied his speech to the one who he knew John was all about. Oh, how the people must have listened in their state of shock. But as it is those matters can also be found in the record of Luke. In 1: 64- 65 as taken from his written matter it states, "and immediately his mouth was opened and his tongue loosed and he began to speak, blessing God".

At that moment when he did speak, how would it not have been earth shattering to the entire group? And wow, did he ever speak! It must have been that the man was filled with the wisdom of the Holy Spirit. Further along as taken from the written matter it depicts where he continued on what Zachary spoke. In 1:65 it states, "and fear came on all their neighbors; and all these things were spoken abroad in all the hill country of Judea". As most new fathers become so it was that Zachary must have also become all excited. Not only did he put forth a simple prayer, but offered praise of thanksgiving. Then also at the same time he prophesied not only what for, but also for whom his son would be doing. With others watching his actions along with being all ears the atmosphere must have been electrified.

Suddenly it was when to the others came the big surprise. As taken from the written matter of Luke in 1: 67- 72 it states, "and Zachary his father was filled with the Holy Spirit and prophesied, saying, "Blessed be the Lord, the God of Israel, because he has visited and wrought redemption for His people, and has raised up a horn of salvation for us, in the house of David His servant, as He promised through the mouth of His holy ones, the prophets from of old, salvation from our enemies".

Continued did Zack speak," and from the hand of all who hate us, to show mercy to our forefathers and to be mindful of His holy covenant". Then it is continued at 1:73- 78 which states, "of the oath that He swore to Abraham our father, that he would grant us, that, delivered from the hand of our enemies, we should serve him without fear, in holiness and justice before Him all our days, and thou child shall be called the prophet of the Most High, for thou shalt go before the face of the Lord to prepare His ways, to give His people knowledge of salvation through forgiveness of their sins, because of the loving-kindness of our God, wherewith the Orient from on high has visited us".

Speaking as one with authority the father had really lowered the boom as he foretold about whom, what and for what his son was to do. Now if that wasn't enough to shake the minds of those listening, lastly it is shown where Zachary finished. In Luke 1: 79 as taken from the written matter it is stated, "to shine on those who sit in darkness and in the shadow of death to guide our feet into the way of peace." It is noted here the phrase, thou shalt go before the face of the Lord. So why are those words so significant? Because it clearly portrays, his son, John's position, as walking closely before the Lord, during the Lord's same time period. Those words made it impossible to be interpreted as just a someone,

John as being of someone in the far distant future also, it denied any confusing of what John's duty was to be. It wasn't that he would simply be going around talking about something to happen centuries in the future. Rather it clearly indicated how John would be the messenger of the day, which would be advertising of the Christ that was immediately behind him. Plus, it is to be noted that John the apostle also provides some credit along the same thinking way. Yet it is that John does not duplicate what Zachary spoke, but in so many words said the same thing. A big fact here is that the matter can be realized by comparing the two. In John 1: 6- 8 it is recorded what the apostle stated, "there was a man, one sent from God, whose name was John, this man came as a witness to bear witness concerning the light, that all might believe through him. He was not the light, but was to bear witness to the light."

Meanwhile back to the celebration, where it is asked, why would those people at the celebration have had any fear? After all, wasn't it supposed to be a time of a happy celebration? And doesn't a time of rejoicing normally indicate some celebration in happiness? That is unless some of those people were guilty of false assumptions or spreading rumors of untruth. Also, it may have been very difficult for those that had given undeserved mistreatment to the couple. Perhaps another reading of chapter three may help connect the matters.

The Great Excitignly Holy John the Baptist

Well, any way for the new parents it was certainly a great time of great joy. With much rekindling of hearts, the days would be looked forward to. Another big change for the older couple but a at least it was to be a happy change. After all that of which the two had been through, finally it must have ended in a period with days of continuing celebration. Certainly, Zachary the father must have always had thoughts of plans for a son as most fathers do. That was until he got visited by the angel. And how would his son eventually fill his father's shoes?

Regarding that period of time that had passed there is no information that could be found on the parents. Where about they may have stayed or moved to, or what they did, nothing could be found. Although there is a lot of speculation it is that nothing was found in the written record. But it is this author offers one reason, which may be that some of the apostles' writings may have been lost to a fire or when put upon by their enemies. Then also, perhaps there was so much going on about John the Baptist and the Christ that maybe the old couple was simply forgotten.

In all the commotion, then taking into consideration how people can twist things, who knows what may have taken place over the years? It is the author's view that the parents having been very old when John was born after several years they may have simply died sometime thereafter. Then not being of any importance to the rulers or the people the burial of the old couple was just not recorded. Also, it was that since they were not of royalty as other people that passed away, it was only religiously that they had to be buried. Perhaps once buried, then over a short time they were simply forgotten as just other older persons. But even that doesn't make sense.

After all the commotion the two had caused there is just too much time lost for some coverage not to have been made. Such lack of information just doesn't make sense. Such especially rings loud with there having been known even well outside the community. Recalled should be of Luke stating how the people reacted. And for sure it is that such reaction being written about indicates a matter of heavy emotion. As it is from what Luke wrote it can be taken that much heavy emotion had existed. As taken from the written record such is shown in 1: 65 where it states, "and fear came on all their neighbors; and all these things were spoken abroad in all the hill country of Judea". Noted here is that Luke didn't constrain the matter to the neighbors or the relatives but to those abroad. Now if such was the event that it caused widespread news, how could such people being known then suddenly be forgotten?

Consider the number of people involved along with the incident. It just does not make sense that nothing could be found on the how and what John did while he was growing up under his parents. Surely what Zachary had spoken of his son should be combined with what the prophets wrote about his son.

With all of that taken together how could the lives of three people not have some record written somewhere? That is unless the parents passed away and John was raised by a friend or someone else. Then what about all the people that were at the celebration? Would they not have been curious from time to time as to how the family of three were doing? For John to have grown into manhood it would have taken at least a few years. Not just a couple, but from birth to being a man would have taken in the minimum of twelve years. Would some of the neighbors not have had some knowledge since having been curious? Could they not have supplied some information that they knew or heard? Yet nothing is written anywhere.

It is suspect that after all that transpired at the event that there was no one with information. Surely there must have been persons that would have inquired from time to time as to the parents. Would not some people have wanted to know how the couple was doing? Then others may have been curious how Zachary was doing while others may have been concerned for the child. Whatever happened to each of the three individually? Where there being no information found on at least Zachary, how is such not beyond the norm? There is just too much information over such a long period of time missing about such important people. The many circumstances along with the numerous amounts of people that were involved presents cause for written recording to have been made.

Such has led the author to believe that actually at some time there must have been written matter of the old couple's later years. If not much, surely there would have been at least some written record of something happening over the years. Especially when considering the number of people along with their interest, such absence of information is not normal. Who stood for John? Sure, there were his parents but what about where was their best man? Was there no aunts or uncles even if not by blood? Would some friends have not wanted to participate? What about God parents? With all of those persons so concerned were there none? How unlikely it would have been that no one was interested. Surely out of all those people concerned with what the child's name was to be, there would have been at least a few that would have wanted to be somewhat involved.

From the words that were written, it can only be taken that perhaps, Luke lacked information. But what about Mark who wrote only a little bit about John. Why didn't he write anything about John's early years? Then there was the other two apostles Matthew and John who both wrote a considerable amount of information about John in his matured years. But why didn't they write anything about his growing up years? Why did all of the four not write at least something about John's parents' later years? With all of those questions unanswered the author believes that at least one of them did, but what happened to the writings? Maybe the old couple just lived without any exciting days. Really!

Over a period of twelve years would there not at least have been something that would have been worth writing about? Were there no birthday parties? When John reached the age of manhood was there no celebration? Perhaps they lived simply like other older couples where there just was no news. Something is just not right. Evidently Luke could not get any type of information from those people that knew John's parents. Nor could he find anything special regarding John's growing up at home. But such doesn't even make sense. Perhaps it could have been because of John's holiness where the parents couldn't keep up with him. After all John's purpose was already ingrained in him. But would that not have been cause to write about? Such must be taken into consideration, especially with what Zachary had not only known but foretold about his son's holiness.

Was such missing material due to all the commotion that John along with Christ was causing? But taking into consideration the twelve apostles along with all the people they knew such would have been very unlikely. Perhaps the death and burial of the elderly couple being a local thing, may have become simply insignificant.So, it is put, what was done or what occurrence happened that somehow caused all the record of at least twelve years of the three as well as others that were involved to be lost? How sad it is, and most unfortunate that after having so much written record of all of what the old couple of Zachary and Elizabeth went through before their son's birth there is absolutely nothing to be found on their subsequent years.

Here it is once again asked why is John the Baptist parent's lives not mentioned in the Old Testament? Sure, the older couple eventually became a short part of the New Testament. But it is most certain that their beginning as well as their early married years was well before the time of Christ. Then along with the years of getting old being the greater and largest part of their lives was in fact all in the Old Testament. Why because they were about before the birth of Jesus Christ who was in fact the start of the New Testament.

So really, why is the beginning of the older couple not in the Old Testament? With all of the mystery about the parent's demise along with John starting his ministry in the desert the author suggests what must be considered as fact which cannot be disputed. It is that John during his childhood days could not have had a better teacher of the scriptures than his father. Since Zachary was not only a priest it must also be considered that he was educated. Not only did he know how to write along with being able to read but, after all of those years must have been well versed in the scriptures. And what a teacher he would have made. Then with all of that knowledge, there can be not doubt as to what a pupil John would have been.

And now it is to moving forward into the life of their great excitingly holy son, thee only, and true messenger of the Lord God, who had to be not only special but, holy beyond that which was only human. It is that the Baptist was not to be spreading the word about some other high priest or public official but rather of the Son of the Highest God.

The Baptist could not have been just another human as people consider humans of flesh and blood only as the highly significant substantial essence of his task prohibited the Baptist from being just another ordinary human. What he knew from the old scriptures he learned from his priestly father Zachary.

However, his knowledge of the kingdom of God and the Messiah being in the midst of the people had to have been ingrained in John the Baptist from other than earthly sources.

Since no other holy person knew the Christ but him all thinking regarding the Baptist being only a preacher is left without any credibility.

So as the facts depicted support this let us move forward into the time of the great excitingly holy John the Baptist. And now it is to move forward into the life of their great excitingly holy son.

CHAPTER 14.

Should People Believe in the Prophets of the Old Testament?

Finally, after all of those months came along their son. Their prayers had been answered. What the two had been praying and hoping for years. No doubt those months in waiting must have taken the father's nervousness to new levels. Such a strong character he had would also be shown in his son. But perhaps the real burden was concern for his wife during delivery. At her age, how would her body hold up may have been his concern. Maybe he had even dreaded the time knowing that it was to be his wife's first baby. Yet with all of the worrying that the couple did, the boy was born just fine.

With the boy and Elizabeth being healthy she had to be in a state of bliss. Did the parents react as others, once the child was born? Did Zachary remember what he had been told by the angel? At such an exciting time in a parent life who remembers or even cares what was said or happened months before? Especially, was Zachary able to remember being told how holy great his son that was born of his times was to be? What a time of joy for Zachary. But especially even more so for Elizabeth who may have doubted what her husband had been telling her. What a time in the couples lives it must have been. So excited they were, the couple was probably tripping over each other with praises of their love for each other.

Such event was recorded in the written record of Luke. In his chapter 1:57- 58 it is depicted as taken from the written matter which states, "now Elizabeth time was fulfilled that she should be delivered, and she brought forth a son, And her neighbors and kinsfolk heard that the Lord had magnified his mercy towards her, and they rejoiced with her."How exuberant Zach must have been, aware that both his wife and baby were in good health. But it was where he was still voiceless. Fascinating it is how it is mentioned that the neighbors and kinsfolk rejoiced with her. But where were they before hand?

Were any of them around to render assistance to the older expecting couple? Yet it was that Zachary unable to speak was still unable to talk.

Sad the father must have been coping with being excluded from the others that were all of a sudden having a good time rejoicing. Did they keep him in a corner isolated? Were they still giving him the shunt? How were they of such self-righteous minds full of assumptions feeling? Was the mood that he was being punished? Had they taken it for granted that Zachary had done something evil? Were false rumors about him still abounding? Or, were they covering over her, thinking that she was the one that did wrong? All the while taking it out on him to protect her? Maybe, not as many of the original erroneous assumption remained. But for sure as the way of the world, it should be remembered that such cynical and negativity still remained as none of the people knew about Zach's instance with the angel. Could old wrong thinking have ignited new erroneous assumptions?

How easy it is the way people jump to conclusions. Especially, when void of the fully true information they simply jump to erroneous conclusions. Either way, for sure there was probably still a good mix of gossip being around. A very strong clue is here shown where in today such important matter seems to be overlooked. Yet here it is taken, that there are no written indications that he was able to enjoin with those that were celebrating. Furthermore, as a matter of fact, it is specifically mentioned of his wife, and only his wife's name mentioned of having enjoyed with others in the rejoicing. How low he must have felt. Here it was after all of that waiting that his son had finally been born.

And Zachary, well maybe for an instant he had believed that all had come to pass. Maybe as any man in a similar state of mind may have been he could have been fully looking forward to his voice returning. But such was not the case as he remained dumb, unable to speak. Oh, the mental torture Zachary must have experienced as the following days went by. Yet, it was not meant for him to be totally left out. Rather Zachary would surely have his moment in time which he probably forgot all about. There was still the one big issue remaining of which such substance was even mentioned by the angel. Time had passed where the man's son still had to be circumcised. Oh yes that all important period when also his son would be given a name.But the new father probably forgot all about it. Why not, as for sure it must have been that he had more important things on his mind.

His wife was physically ok plus it was where he had his son who was also healthy. But for sure it was that Zachary was to have his day complete. After all, regardless of who was present or what their status or authority was, Zach was the father. So, it was whereas the days passed, a name had to be decided upon for the new boy. Wow! What an exciting time it must have been!

Controversy and discord must have abounded everywhere. For sure all the kinfolk and friends of authority being excited must have put in their opinions of what name they wanted the child to be called. Those kinds of busy bodies which are always around letting their curiosity show. About everybody else's business, for sure they must have come out of the woodwork. Not bothering or being concerned about Zachary or his wife before when the couple could have used at least some mental support.

When the woman was carrying everyone was probably too busy with themselves being about their selves. But then, at the time it was a different period. For everyone it was a time of celebration. People were all about having a good time probable even showing their willingness to be a part. Even those that the couple hadn't seen in months probably showed up. Over the course of the days there must have been some communication of the matter between the new parents. Although Elizabeth respected what her husband wanted, her being the nice person that she was, Elizabeth respected the other persons' opinions.

Now the way it may have been the way people are, things must have gotten out of hand. Such reached the level where they were attempting to force their way of what they wanted. It can only be taken where they were only interested in wanting to have the baby named the way they wanted him to be named. Reading in between the lines must be taken where, it can be realized how they were strictly adamant.

Even with the woman being the wife of a priest seemed to have made little difference as it all about them. And so much so was their aggressiveness with all desiring to show their influence. Such it was where they were actually demanding of having him named after his father. But, what about Elizabeth, didn't she have an interest? Wasn't she the mother?

So, should not her wishes have come first? However, even with all of that aggravation to put up with, the woman still tried nicely to be amiable. She pleasantly kept on trying to advise them otherwise. Yet, the words in the recorded text clearly indicates, emotions of pressure.

Evidently there was more than the simple making of suggestions. As the record indicates others were demanding to have their way regardless of what the parent wanted. But then with the father unable to speak it could have only   meant that his voice was missing. Therefore, with that in mind, it must be taken with her being by her lonesome against the mob. Evidently there were also those that had influence in the community. However boldly it was where the woman seemed to have held her ground refusing to budge. Maybe it was over and over where she stated her opposition of him being called their name of which she didn't have in mind. Everything had to have been about Elizabeth since her husband was still unable to speak.

All of those matters are found in the written record of Luke. As taken from his written matter in 1: 59- 60 it states, "and it came to pass on the eighth day, that they came to circumcise the child, and they were going to call him by his father's name, Zachary".

Who were those people inferred as they? Who were they, to decide what the child's name was to be? Gee, here it was the mother of the child, after years of grieving she was finally able to have had a son. Yet she was actually forced to argue with those that couldn't have been previously bothered about the couple. Not to forget was that Elizabeth in her old age had carried the child for the normal term.

Just who were those people? Rather it might be asked, what kind of people were they? Had they no respect for what the new mother had just gone through over the past years? Also, what about what they may have put her through during those years. Hadn't some of those same people tortured her enough during the period before the woman's time had come?   Just when does it become enough for a woman then of her old age? Especially since the woman had gone through months of receiving undeserved turned up noses and unwarranted innuendos. Plus, there were probably those unfounded insinuations. And then after having put up with all that, then having just given birth?

The Great Excitignly Holy John the Baptist

Surely as Elizabeth spoke, Zach understanding the zealous crowd along with their overbearing mood, must have at least pointed to her in support of his wife many times Would not he have done so. to show his support for her? But those people swimming in their own self righteousness showed no respect for Zachary. Their own little preconceived erroneous assumptions had ruled the days. Now it is that such matters may be reasonably determined by considering the tone that can be taken from the written words.

Thought must be given to the extended time along with the situation at hand to fully grab the atmosphere. Such substance is shown clearly in the written record of Luke. As shown in his written matter the apostle's writing not only depicts of their arrogance, but also her temper. Such in 1: 60 states "and his mother answered and said, not so, but he shall be called John." There is the further proof of how they acted by the tone, which most surely can be taken from the same words. Clearly such is depicted where they refused to accept the words of Elizabeth. Wow! There it was, she the mother actually having to cope with those people that utterly mentally ran all over her. One can almost feel the attitude of her being treated as if she was merely some sort of a maid or some other attendant.

Who were those people that attempted to forcibly require Zachary to provide the baby's name? How selfish she must have thought they were. But really, it may have been how ignorant they were to have asserted themselves in such a fashion. It is important to remember that they were fully aware that Zachary could not speak. Yet having ignored him all the while, then it was they forced his involvement. What did they expect the father to do? Did they really think he would have gone against his wife's wishes? In today's world such could almost be expected.

Perhaps they thought that he would have simply waved his hands, in disgust motioning that he agreed? Such would have given them all the power they were attempting to muster up. Maybe they even anticipated him throwing up his arms as if saying he didn't care. Or, perhaps some may have even thought he would have walked out as if refusing to participate. When is enough, going to be enough of the bickering, the disgusted mother must have felt. What will it take to have the arguing stop, Elizabeth may have wondered? What kind of unplanned and undeserved miserable celebration had erupted? Had those kin with the wine flowing along with the so-called boisterous friends turned the joyous situation into a rowdy mob party?

By all of the harassment they had put her through, could it not be that some still had reservations as to who the father was? Also, perhaps there were those harboring the thoughts that she had an affair with someone else? Maybe there was ever thinking that she was forcing the child's name as a punishment? Perhaps such matters can be construed from the matter shown in the record of Luke. In his writing, noted full well is their demonstrating of their persistence. So much was their intent that the crowd was prepared to force their way on the parents. They had their proof of why which was all they needed. Now it is that such is shown in the record as at 1: 61- 62 as taken from the written matter it states, "and they said to her, there is none of thy kindred that is called by this name. And they kept inquiring by signs of his father, what he would have him called". Obviously by the summary of the words the crowd refused to let up. Instead, only the more did they try to force their way.

After all of those years of monotony there it was in one day the couple had more excitement than they had in all prior years combined. Amazing it was but the crowd knew all about her families past names plus was also aware of the father being unable to speak. Oh, how some must have reveled knowing Zach was unable to speak. For sure there was no concern on their part as to the husband putting up any argument. Surely, they must have felt how they had the upper hand where that they had the mother cornered over a barrel.

It was to be either their way or no way. Yet, it was to be that eventually where the crowd would actually regret their arrogance. However, for sure during the moment they must have felt really good, as having cornered Elizabeth. Had the mob succeeded in demonstrating their authority? By then they most assuredly must have ruined the day with their over whelming obnoxious behavior. By pitting her against her husband, had they made it almost impossible for her? Then too, did they not also put her husband on the spot? Oh boy, how the emotions must have been flowing.

The Great Excitignly Holy John the Baptist

Had everyone felt so superior where they thought how they must have had her feeling alone? Especially being fully aware of her unable to speak husband being useless? Perhaps the group may have even felt by the number of them that they had power which would have shown her just who would have the last say. And meanwhile there was Zach unable to say anything. Unable to talk he couldn't even speak up for his wife, yet all the while he was forced to see her being brow beaten. Sure, it was that he was unable to talk, but how amused the crowd must have been while watching Elizabeth hand the tablet to her husband. Simultaneously while in wonderment, the quiet mumblings of sarcastic remarks must have been ongoing all about the place.

Then quietly with everyone watching the father simply inscribed the baby's name. What a moment it must have been as he handed it back to his wife where she held it up for all to see. No doubt that the community eventually heard the details of the so-called celebration. And then if that wasn't enough he had to realize that such was from some of his so-called friends. Wow, and to think it wasn't even any child of theirs. What a day it must have grown into for the older couple. Suddenly there it was, as if a curtain had been raised, it was Zach's turn, as he came to the rescue. Perhaps all the while he had been forced to simply sit in a corner watching the hounds have their moment.

But then what happened next must have really brought the curtain down. All instigators must have dropped their jaw in awe seeing what happened. And then, how taken back the crowd must have been upon seeing Zachary's reaction. No, there wasn't any violence, nor was there any arm waving. Rather there it was where the husband simply showed his support of his wife. No yelling, no loud verbal abuse language did the father use but surely, he lowered the boom. Such a simple yet fascinating few moments and it is all found in the record of Luke. As taken from the written matter in 1: 63 it states, "and asking for a writing tablet he wrote the words, John is his name, and they all marveled."

All the while immediately it must have been how elated and uplifted was Elizabeth! Was there instant quiet as the crowd bit their tongue? What would have been the reaction of the group? Of course, while those same kinsfolk and neighbors quickly found out just how wrong they were the father must have been in a state of absolute bliss. Such feelings must have been overflowing, especially between the older couple. Their love for each other overflowed. Then also perhaps some were to realize how badly they had treated the couple. Suddenly they must have all felt that a bomb had exploded as the atmosphere ignited with something. But was it joy? Or was it fear? How startled the small crowd must have been at what happened next.

Now it is that some people argue how Zach couldn't have written his name as there were no such things as paper tablets and pencils in those times. Perhaps there weren't those exact things for writing, as the word writing may be assumed to refer. However, during those times there were in fact other things. True they weren't made for long sentence writing or for big letters but for very short notes they sufficed. Although papyrus was around during those times it was of such material that was used for the long types of writing.

Then there was leather, but that was probably too expensive plus it was needed more for apparel wearing. Also, there was the soft wood which would have allowed characters to be scratched. With the use of a sharp knife or other sharp instrument such indents would have been sufficient. But most likely at the time what Zach most probably used was a flat piece of soft clay. Such would allow the carving of several characters which after use could be reused. Only a little water applied over a few minutes would have kept it ready for use.

Now it was that during that time period, most people then were illiterate. Not only did they not have any learning of writing but most important was that they were unable to read. But those of high positions such as priests and the well to do military as well as politicians and authorities would have had reading knowledge.So, it was with Zach being a priest having learned to read and write so to his wife would have learned. Therefore, using either a wooden or clay tablet it must have been most easy for Zach to have carved John's name that could have been read. But read by whom? Surely there must have been some that were rejoicing who had reading ability.

Maybe it was a land owner, or ruler of some type or even one of the other religious friends. But whoever it was, it would have only taken one or two persons in the crowd to advise the others of what the tablet stated.One of the most powerful moments in time of history where the person's name was ever written on clay or wood that had such an impact. Since the tablet only stated one word it would have only taken one person with just the basic reading skills to decipher what Zachary had written. But what a moment in time it was containing only a word.

At that specific moment it had impact being much of a powerful meaning. So much was it where it must have had such an impact that it bothered those looking where they were affected even until they left. For sure it must have quieted down those that were boisterous about what the child's name was to be. After all it was their idea to force it on Zach to make the decision, and did he ever put them in their place. Sure, it was that he was unable to talk, but how amused the crowd must have been while watching Elizabeth hand the tablet to her husband. Simultaneously the quiet mumblings of sarcastic remarks must have been ongoing all about the place.

Then quietly with everyone watching the father simply inscribed the name of John. What a moment it must have been as he handed it back to his wife where she held it up for all to see. Jaws were probably dropping by the seconds as the crowd came to realize that their arrogance and oppressive means was all for naught. But little did the guests know that they were in for even a bigger treat. Unaware it was, that they were about to experience a moment that would shake their faith down to their sandals. Yes, it was that there was to come, bigger things that would even more baffle them. Yet what could have happened that would have caused such calamity among the group? It would have had to have been something truly out of the normal.

Such it would have had to have been that would have caused people to shudder with all sorts of thoughts. Suddenly without any warning the crowd was stunned. In one quick moment it happened. No, there was no band playing, no cymbals or drums giving an encore just a quick immediate quiet. Suddenly, Zach stood up while being able to speak! Alarmed it must have been that the people were, especially those standing close to him able to hear him speak. And wow, did he ever speak. It must be recalled that over the past nine months they were all used to him being dumb. All that time he was unable to talk.

Imagine the name calling that had gone around during the time. What title would they have applied to make fun of him? Perhaps some may have labeled him as the dumb priest. Then to maybe others had even titled him as the father of someone else's child. Surely as people like to kick those that are down there were probably even others that were wrongly applied. Yet at that one moment, all things were made right. No, the priest didn't start rebutting those other people but rather applied his speech to the one who he knew John was all about. Oh, how the people must have listened in their state of shock. But as it is those matters can also be found in the record of Luke. In 1: 64- 65 as taken from his written matter it states, "and immediately his mouth was opened and his tongue loosed and he began to speak, blessing God". At that moment when he did speak, how would it not have been earth shattering to the entire group? And wow, did he ever speak!

It must have been that the man was filled with the wisdom of the Holy Spirit. Further along as taken from the written matter it depicts where he continued on what Zachary spoke.In 1:65 it states, "and fear came on all their neighbors; and all these things were spoken abroad in all the hill country of Judea".

As most new fathers become so it was that Zachary must have also become all excited. Not only did he put forth a simple prayer, but offered praise of thanksgiving. Then also at the same time he prophesied not only what for, but also for whom his son would be doing. With others watching his actions along with being all ears the atmosphere must have been electrified.

Suddenly it was when to the others came the big surprise. As taken from the written matter of Luke in 1: 67- 72 it states, "and Zachary his father was filled with the Holy Spirit and prophesied, saying, Blessed be the Lord, the God of Israel, because he has visited and wrought redemption for His people, and has raised up a horn of salvation for us, in the house of David His servant, as He promised through the mouth of His holy ones, the prophets from of old, salvation from our enemies, and from the hand of all who hate us, to show mercy to our forefathers and to be mindful of His holy covenant. Then it is continued at 1:73- 78.

There it states, "of the oath that He swore to Abraham our father, that he would grant us, that, delivered from the hand of our enemies, we should serve him without fear, in holiness and justice before Him all our days, and thou child shall be called the prophet of the Most High, for thou shalt go before the face of the Lord to prepare His ways, to give His people knowledge of salvation through forgiveness of their sins, because of the loving-kindness of our God, wherewith the Orient from on high has visited us".Speaking as one with authority the father had really lowered the boom as he foretold about whom, what and for what his son was to do.

Now if that wasn't enough to shake the minds of those listening, lastly it is shown where Zachary finished. In Luke 1: 79 as taken from the written matter it is stated, "to shine on those who sit in darkness and in the shadow of death to guide our feet into the way of peace."It is noted here the phrase, thou shalt go before the face of the Lord. So why are those words so significant? Because it clearly portrays, his son, John's position, as walking closely before the Lord, during the Lord's same time period. Those words made it impossible to be interpreted as someone, John being of someone in the far distant future. Also, it denied any confusing of what John's duty was to be.

It wasn't that he would simply be going around talking about something to happen centuries in the future. Rather it clearly indicated how John would be the messenger of the day, which would be advertising of the Christ that was immediately behind him. Plus, it is to be noted that John the apostle also provides some credit along the same thinking way. Yet it is that John does not duplicate what Zachary spoke, but in so many words said the same thing.A big fact here is that the matter can be realized by comparing the two. In John 1: 6- 8 it is recorded what the apostle stated, "there was a man, one sent from God, whose name was John, this man came as a witness to bear witness concerning the light, that all might believe through him. He was not the light, but was to bear witness to the light."

Meanwhile back to the celebration, where it is asked, why would those people at the celebration have had any fear? After all, wasn't it supposed to be a time of a happy celebration? And doesn't a time of rejoicing normally indicate some celebration in happiness? That is unless some of those people were guilty of false assumptions or spreading rumors of untruth. Also, it may have been very difficult for those that had given undeserved mistreatment to the couple. Perhaps another reading of chapter three may help connect the matters. Well, any way for the new parents it was certainly a great time of great joy.

With much rekindling of hearts, the days would be looked forward to.

The Great Excitignly Holy John the Baptist

Another big change for the older couple but a at least it was to be a happy change. After all that of which the two had been through, finally it must have ended in a period with days of continuing celebration. Certainly, Zachary the father must have always had thoughts of plans for a son as most fathers do. That was until he got visited by the angel. And how would his son eventually fill his father's shoes? Regarding that period of time that had passed there is no information that could be found on the parents. Where about they may have stayed or moved to, or what they did, nothing could be found. Although there is a lot of speculation it is that nothing was found in the written record.

But it is this author offers one reason, which may be that some of the apostles' writings may have been lost to a fire or when put upon by their enemies. Then also, perhaps there was so much going on about John the Baptist and the Christ that maybe the old couple was simply forgotten. In all the commotion, then taking into consideration how people can twist things, who knows what may have taken place over the years?

It is the author's view that the parents having been very old when John was born after several years they may have simply died sometime thereafter. Then not being of any importance to the rulers or the people the burial of the old couple was just not recorded. Also, it was that since they were not of royalty as other people that passed away, it was only religiously that they had to be buried. Perhaps once buried, then over a short time they were simply forgotten as just other older persons. But even that doesn't make sense. After all the commotion the two had caused there is just too much time lost for some coverage not to have been made.

Such lack of information just doesn't make sense. Such especially rings loud with there having been known even well outside the community. Recalled should be of Luke stating how the people reacted. And for sure it is that such reaction being written about indicates a matter of heavy emotion. As it is from what Luke wrote it can be taken that much heavy emotion had existed. As taken from the written record such is shown in 1: 65 where it states, "and fear came on all their neighbors; and all these things were spoken abroad in all the hill country of Judea". Noted here is that Luke didn't constrain the matter to the neighbors or the relatives but to those abroad.

Now if such was the event that it caused widespread news, how could such people being known then suddenly be forgotten? Consider the number of people involved along with the incident. It just does not make sense that nothing could be found on the how and what John did while he was growing up under his parents. Surely what Zachary had spoken of his son should be combined with what the prophets wrote about his son.

With all of that taken together how could the lives of three people not have some record written somewhere? That is unless the parents passed away and John was raised by a friend or someone else. Then what about all the people that were at the celebration? Would they not have been curious from time to time as to how the family of three were doing? For John to have grown into manhood it would have taken at least a few years. Not just a couple, but from birth to being a man would have taken in the minimum of twelve years. Would some of the neighbors not have had some knowledge since having been curious? Could they not have supplied some information that they knew or heard? Yet nothing is written anywhere.

It is suspect that after all that transpired at the event that there was no one with information. Surely there must have been persons that would have inquired from time to time as to the parents. Would not some people have wanted to know how the couple was doing? Then others may have been curious how Zachary was doing while others may have been concerned for the child. Whatever happened to each of the three individually? Where there being no information found on at least Zachary, how is such not beyond the norm? There is just too much information over such a long period of time missing about such important people. The many circumstances along with the numerous amounts of people that were involved presents cause for written recording to have been made. Such has led the author to believe that actually at some time there must have been written matter of the old couple's later years.

Did the Hebrew religious factions in conflict with the teachings of

John not push them to take measures that may have eradicated the parent's lives? If not much, surely there would have been at least some written record of something happening over the years. Especially when considering the number of people along with their interest, such absence of information is not normal.

Who stood for John? Sure, there were his parents but what about where was their best man? Was there no aunts or uncles even if not by blood? Would some friends have not wanted to participate? What about God parents? With all of those persons so concerned were there none? How unlikely it would have been that no one was interested.

Surely out of all those people concerned with what the child's name was to be, there would have been at least a few that would have wanted to be somewhat involved. From the words that were written, it can only be taken that perhaps, Luke lacked information. But what about Mark who wrote only a little bit about John. Why didn't he write anything about John's early years? Then there was the other two apostles Matthew and John who both wrote a considerable amount of information about John in his matured years. But why didn't they write anything about his growing up years? Why did all of the four not write at least something about John's parents' later years?

With all of those questions unanswered the author believes that at least one of them did, but what happened to the writings? Maybe the old couple just lived without any exciting days. Really! Over a period of twelve years would there not at least have been something that would have been worth writing about? Were there no birthday parties? When John reached the age of manhood was there no celebration? Perhaps they lived simply like other older couples where there just was no news. Something is just not right.

Evidently Luke could not get any type of information from those people that knew John's parents. Were there Jewish radical factions using life threatening means to cause total absence of the couple? Nor could anything be found regarding John's growing up at home. But such doesn't even make sense. Perhaps it could have been because of John's holiness. Was it that the parents couldn't keep up with him and his teachings. After all John's purpose was already ingrained in him. But would that not have been cause to write about? Such must be taken into consideration, especially with what Zachary had not only known but foretold about his son's holiness.

Was such missing material due to all the commotion that John along with Christ was causing? But taking into consideration the twelve apostles along with all the people they knew such would have been very unlikely. Perhaps the death and burial of the elderly couple being a local thing, may have become simply insignificant. So, it is put, what was done or what occurrence happened that somehow caused all the record of at least twelve years of the three as well as others that were involved to be lost? How sad it is, and most unfortunate that after having so much written record of all of what the old couple of Zachary and Elizabeth went through before their son's birth there is absolutely nothing to be found on their subsequent years.

Here it is once again asked why is John the Baptist parent's lives not mentioned in the Old Testament? Sure, the older couple eventually became a short part of the New Testament. But it is most certain that their beginning as well as their early married years was well before the time of Christ. Then along with the years of getting old being the greater and largest part of their lives was in fact all in the Old Testament. Why because they were about before the birth of Jesus Christ who was in fact the start of the New Testament. So really, why is the beginning of the older couple not in the Old Testament?

With all of the mystery about the parent's demise along with John starting his ministry in the desert the author suggests what must be considered as fact which cannot be disputed. It is that John during his childhood days could not have had a better teacher of the scriptures than his father. Since Zachary was not only a priest it must also be considered that he was educated. Not only did he know how to write along with being able to read but, after all of those years must have been well versed in the scriptures. And what a teacher he would have made. Then with all of that knowledge, there can be no doubt as to what a pupil John would have been.

And now it is to moving forward into the life of their great excitingly holy son, thee only, and true messenger of the Lord God, who had to be not only special but, holy beyond that which was only human. It is that the Baptist was not to be spreading the word about some other

The Great Excitignly Holy John the Baptist

high priest or public official but rather of the Son of the Highest God. The Baptist could not have been just another human as people consider humans of flesh and blood only as the highly significant substantial essence of his task prohibited the Baptist from being just another ordinary human.

What he knew from the old scriptures he learned from his priestly father Zachary. However, his knowledge of the kingdom of God and the Messiah being in the midst of the people had to have been ingrained in John the Baptist from other than earthly sources. And since no other holy person knew the Christ but him all thinking regarding the Baptist being only a preacher is left without any credibility.

So as the facts depicted support this let us move forward into the time of the great excitingly holy John the Baptist. And now it is to move forward into the life of their great excitingly holy son.

PART IX.

UTTERED SOUNDS FROM THE NEW VOICE.

Chapter 15. Had the People Actually Found Someone That Could Lead?

And so it was that the holy John the Baptist made his appearance. Such event may be understood as is found in the records. According to the recorded matter of Luke he advises who was ruling as well as the time period. As taken from the written matter in his chapter 3: 1, it states, "now in the Fifteenth year of the reign of Tiberius Caesar when Pontius Pilate was procurator of Judea". Those words not only give the time period but also provide information as to who was ruling during the period. Then he provides additional information linking the Baptist. As taken from the written record of Luke it states, "during the high priesthood of Annas and Caiaphas the word of God came to John, the son of Zachary, in the desert".

This matter of the Baptist being in the desert is also confirmed in the record of Matthew the apostle. As taken from the written record in his chapter 3:1, it states, "now in those days John the Baptist came preaching in the desert of Judea." So, it is as according to the record where he went right to work preaching while also spreading the word in the area around the Jordan. Fully depicted in the written records it was that John's preaching was always the same. His message was that the people were to repent for the kingdom of heaven is at hand. People should not take this phrase lightly as it is of hard factual matter.

As stated in Matthew 3:2 it is that similar but different words, yet of the same meaning are shown in the record of Mark. Such matters are shown in Mark's chapter 1:4. Taken from his written matter it states, "there came John in the desert, baptizing and preaching a baptism of repentance for the forgiveness of sins". Also, there is similar wording of Mark found in Luke 3:3 and supported by John in 1: 6- 8 who used slightly different words to say relatively the same thing. Evidently John didn't find any resistance among the people. In fact, according to the written record, over a very short time he must have been overtaken by them with their showing of their belief. Amazing it is how similar his words are to the words that Isaias used as he foretold of John's coming. It is shown in the record where Isaias had preached those same words that would be used. Such matter is also shown in Luke 3:3-6 as well as found in Matthew 3: 1- 3.

Nowhere are any words found, that were used by the apostles, to cause guessing or allow for having any contrary thinking. Plus, there is shown that simply too much information exists by at least a couple or three that substantiates what the others had written. It wasn't a few people on a single day saying the same thing. Then also, nor was it where a lot of people over several days had stated different matters. But rather it is as shown in the records that all of the people from Judea, as well as the region about the Jordan went to see the Baptist.

Noted is that the record states how all those from Jerusalem also went to go to see the Baptist. Those words as written are not able to be picked apart as some simple maniac throwing a picnic or going around as some mad man. Since the people were all going out to see him it can only be taken that there must have been a wide spread acceptance of what he was preaching, as well was as doing. Now it is asked, where is there shown in any record of any skepticism what so ever about what he was preaching along with his baptizing? Nowhere can such doubt be found. If there was, surely, would there not have been a shortage of people showing up?

A person while reading then also while trying to understand can almost feel the happiness as well as the joy when the crowds were around John. Perhaps the men were just following along, but for the women perhaps they were the ones doing the leading. Surely there was a lot of singing and joyous clapping along with shouts of praise. But whether he was preaching or baptizing it must have been where the people also joined in prayer.

Was John not finding his time spent not only amusing, but satisfying? Had the people actually found someone that could lead? Was the Baptist showing them how to believe in themselves? During those times of oppression there must have been a lot of hymns sung. Then also along with the baptizing there must have been much clapping as crowd after crowd showed up. Not just the same people but new first-time persons were showing up. And the big thing was that they stayed, not just to listen but to actually take part.

Surely, as the people prayed along with their joyous actions, it showed their being interested. But it is fact that the people got baptized which showed that they were not just sitting on the side watching. Rather it was a sure means of saying that they were in full participation. But even more important is that it was a genuine showing of complete acceptance and belief. Not only did the people believe in John his self but also trusted in what he was teaching. Most important is that the people believed in what he was preaching. Oh, how there was peace in the valley.

As contrary to the rulers, he was not ordering the people around requiring them to give and do or not do. Then too it wasn't just the civil ruling persons but also the religious ones that aligned themselves with the civil authorities. John was not merely explaining the what, of the commandments but also the why. But highly significant was his message that the kingdom of heaven is at hand. The significance is that he was preaching of the then present time which in fact is contrary to what some people assert. Some think he was talking about the future but it is as taken from the various records he was always talking and preaching in and about the present tense.

As the Baptist stated it was that the Messiah was in their midst. How powerful the word is. Taken in the context of time his dynamic words denied any misconstruing. As the Baptist stated the kingdom is at hand such phrase explicitly as used meant nothing less than the then present time. Nowhere is it depicted in any from where his words were not about the future as prophets did. Rather it was at all times as the records show, he was spreading the news that the kingdom was already there.

Now it is that opinions and theories are of no substance regarding the matter because they do not change the substance that is presented in the written records. Since the written matter is presented by more than one person it prevents theories. Another fact is, that nowhere is it shown that John ever spoke about himself being of any prophet or holy greatness. Nor did he ever attempt to demonstrate that he was some sort of chief of some kind. Also, nowhere is it found anywhere that he ever charged any money for his services. Then to, it is not shown in any records where he may have used his preaching as a means for making financial or political gain.

As such the records are then clear of any indication where he may have provided his service for establishing a position of power. Here it is that the important question must be put forth. Since the Baptist was so full of knowledge that people followed him by the droves, believing in what he taught, while him not seeking monetary or power gain, then for what was his purpose of preaching and baptism? Something else to be considered is the way people talk about gatherings. Maybe they might say, well there were a lot of people there, or maybe they would say, some of the people showed up. Meanwhile others might say something like, well you know, it was a pretty good crowd.

Also, what may be heard is often as suggested where it seemed as if most of the town was there. Then others might even go so far as to offer about how people were drifting in and out. Yet it is a fact of which was not what the apostles reported or even what they intended. Truly it is clearly explicit as well as definite of what they were saying. Use of the word, all, was used more than once, but most important is not only stated by one but also by another. Only can such expression be taken of which was intended to mean that all the people went out to seek him. It was not just a few or some, but as the word was stated, it means everyone went to see him.

Wow! Not only interesting it is but also actually it may be considered comical where one group or person suggests where John was one of thousands of ascetic radicals running around at that time. Thousands of ascetic radicals, really, but where is the number as to how many thousands? This is so funny it borders on hysterical. And then running around? How closed is such a mind is it to make such a wild statement? Gee, thousands is a large quantity yet where is it shown they supposed to have been running around?

Significant here is that none of the entities fail to name even ten that John could be compared to. Nor do the entities explain about what the dress of the radicals was. Also, it is that none of them provide any explanation what so ever about what their theory of running around was supposed to mean. Also, they fail to even address any of the multitudes that followed him. Were those people within the crowds all radicals too? What about the civil authority that followed him, were they also radicals? But it is the entities really depict their closed minds of self. They show their false or lack of authority in failing to substantiate their statements with credible facts.

Then there are those entities that claim he wasn't a prophet or merely a prophet foretelling of way in the future matter. However, it is that without even realizing it they were somewhat correct in that John was not really a prophet by what meaning people usually think of one. Fact of the matter is that the Baptist was the only holy person being the messenger to walk before the Lord God announcing His presence. John was the only person that walked while announcing about as well as during the time of Christ who exactly meets that identifying matter foretold by the prophets.

Where such is doubted then such doubting persons should show what person can be identified as filling the description of John who meets the prophets' descriptions. Such is simply too much matter to even remotely consider as coincidence. Refusing to consider such it is where others really by choice don't want to learn any more than what they already don't know. Would those entities be disclaiming the prophet Malachiah? And then would they also be refusing to accept Zacharias? But weren't they sometime around the time period of Nehemiah?

Such presents matter that requires a question. Were not those two of the same God as of Nehemiah? Is there such a thing as a mind block? Yet, how convenient it is for entities to make suggestions to simply erase prophets that were prophesying from the same God? Could it be simply because those entities don't want people to turn the pages and learn? Closed minds are similar to people who refuse to consider all but their own preconceived ideas.

So, with all considered how does such not evidence that Mohammad was not a prophet? Especially since such supports that he having come some hundreds of years after Christ Jesus! And it is those matters not twisted were already existing as being from the past. Which raising the issue of, was he a self-appointed holy person or causing himself to be addressed as a prophet? Was it his taking information from other religious entities' sources then twisting it suit his own means? Such is raised as shown by his very statements. Then add to that the omission of facts as well as people and then what remains? Surely it presents false if not vague obscuring pictures.

If doubt as to what here is put, then where is the proof? And where are witnesses? Then perhaps to be considered is all it took was for people of ambition seeking power or wealth to play on those that are weak or have no faith. Soon the imaginations of weak people along with those having no strong religion were preyed upon. So what credibility is there in other books, as well as the Koran which is of such omissions and unreliability? Then to, if use of force is the only means of certain religions to maintain, then what does such reveal about the substance?

Since God is all love and loving all, how can use of force to enforce the religion be morally correct? Force whether physically or through use of intimidation or blackmail used as a means to force any religion cannot be just nor be justified. Since such method or means directly opposes the will of God how is it not then contrary to the Lord? And since it opposes the will of the Lord God how is it then not evil? In today's time of knowledge and technology all one has to do is watch the news from around the world. How is use of their religion by men to use as an excuse for their actions in the present time is nothing more than what was repeatedly performed in the past? Perhaps such force even being the ruling power of the government provides the base for easy swaying of many minds.

Then there is the conformance by some following along as from seeing others doing such then also going along. Yet it is those unknowing already in conformance were doing so as being under forced pressure. Persons being subjected to force surely makes conformance easy. So it is that such use of force is a means of preventing of any other readings or gaining knowledge of any other religion. Further, such means and methods strengthen the so called uncorrupted or original new society. Of course, such means over time denies the individual from thinking.

Will there be entities that may attack this matter? Will they do so with vicious words, referring to their matter as being the only true matter? Yet with all use of words will they be able to clearly prove with support how their matter could be taken as true? Such matter is questioned must be questioned when void of fact by any person's personal knowledge. When steadily deprived of freedom of thought and options what would people be left with? Of course, such oppressive force then is not matters of choice but brain washing. Then after time those same people do it to themselves voluntarily. Why? Because by then, for them they know of no other way other than what was taught.

Of course, while on the subject, an interesting question is that, where is there any old written record of any persons seeing Mohammad dying? Surely for such a celebrity there would most certainly have been many about him. Also where are there any records of him performing any witnessed miracles? Then too, where is there any record of witness writing of what truly happened to him. Oh, sure there are a lot of unsupported theories. But then too there are many assumptions accepted from the assertions of opinions made by self appointed authorities.

Such is while taken in the aforementioned it can be readily seen where various writings from various entities associate Jesus Christ with others as a prophet. Or by sleight of hand, they include him in matter pertaining to prophets. Yet it is they do not produce any matter that can compare any of their prophets with Jesus. Fact is, that clearly shown in the written records it is where witnessed by more than two persons Jesus Christ have raised dead people to life. Such was not one person but several. And where is there written of any other person, prophet or other that had done such along with having witnesses that wrote of him, especially of raising other persons as well as himself up from the dead?

Yes, it is named people are written as witnesses of having seen and eaten with him afterward. Fascinating is how people will refuse to read of the witnesses yet only assert their opinions. But legal or law neither always mean morally ethical or truth. However, assumptions like theories and assertions that are not supported are just that, which is nothing more that unsupported statements. Also, opinions are not fact, even though such may have created rumors to the extent of being believed.

But it still remains, that if there is no factual written record to support such statements of opinions, what value are the statements? How are they then nothing more than opinions full of useless words? Also, if there are no witnesses of written record supporting the contents such can only be taken as novelty. So, with that in mind, will people which came from families who were forced into an oppressed mind religion refuse to read the gospels? Will they merely skim through or go through the motions of reading but in fact not reading the details? In such actions are they not mentally of the mind block being asserted? If the material would not be read in detail how would it not deny any full means of comprehension?

Wherefore it is that though appearing that they are reading, in reality they merely skip through what is the real truth. Gee, but then reading a second time they may come to comprehend that there is more to it, than simply glancing through while listening to a contrary prompter. Perhaps it is also, that the matter of unknowing that fascinates the imagination. Such allows people to dream and for those that may have little or live in poverty, dreaming may be all they have. Given time such may cause the accepting of what anybody says. Such accepting may be done even if only reading nothing more than opinions.

But opinions stated void of factual matter, still remain just that, which are words of unsupported opinions. Those kinds of missing things are easy to sway peoples' minds.Since there is no answer, the imagination allows people to assume whatever they wish. Then where force is used behind the omission or twisting of matter the person become engrossed in the false matter. Gee, but wasn't it till about the fifteenth century where people even in the high places believed that the world was flat? But wishing and theories do not replace factual supported matter. Of course, it may be like the saying about, how it is being hard to teach old dogs new tricks.

Also, it's just like the big bang theory, where so many people think it is fact, when the only fact is that it is only theory being unproven statements. Once it is discovered how many volumes of bangs that established many galaxies with untold number of planets, what then will they say? Also, it is scientific fact that rock whether a result of a volcano or mass explosion does not and cannot by itself cause to exist any living matter. Such living matter must be either planted or caused by the wind dropping particles. Yet people void of factual knowledge believe what it is that is put in front of them. How easy it is to have no belief in any creator which leaves what? That man made himself?

Oh, sure then there is the one where it is claimed that man was derived from animals or fish? Then if that being considered it should also be considered that all beings were developed from amebas. Once factual matter is left out, omitted or considered as unnecessary what remains? What can such matters when fully considered leave? Those unproven assumptions or theories, of which neither is supported by fact, still leaves remaining anything, but surely, they are not fact. Also comes along the unproven opinions, gossip, rumors and phony laws. Then when repeatedly applied with force to ensure adherence it becomes like glue.

So, by omitting Malachiah which came some years after Nehemiah it shows the entity's limited knowledge of the Old Testament. Of course, it must also be noted that the entity omitted Zacharias whose prophesies are awesome. Now it is that an entity put that there will be no more prophets till the messiah. Such a statement requires that a question must be asked. Whereas, it is that were the prophets foretelling of the Messiah not identified and fulfilled by Jesus Christ?

So, is asked, why does not such entities address those prophets also? And then there is the big fact of the Christ's person along with His working of miracles of which were witnessed. Not only were His miracles witnessed, but so were seen by at least two or more persons, as well as often by several persons. Then also, not one miracle was there, but there were many with some being in front of civil authorities. Plus being significantly important is that as found in the written record of the books of the bible there were different types of miracles. Then too they were done with different types of people which had different types of needs.

However, it is of the utmost significant importance knowing that people refuse to address those things. Now with that in mind a fact to reckon with is that of all the miracles performed by the Christ that were written about there is no record anywhere, by anyone that disputed any of them. Not one person is found in the written records attacking such matters as being not true. Wherefore it is highly essential to note here about those persons that were not credible. Wherefore it is in the Christian bibles there is recorded the matter of the high priests attempting to discredit him, but even they could not find anyone to do so. So then is presented a question.

The Great Excitignly Holy John the Baptist

Since the other prophets are believed then if there is no other person that meets the identity provided by the prophets then what is to be truth that can be believed? Most important here is the question that if there is to be another Messiah, will he arrive in the same fashion as foretold by the prophets? If not then what will it do to the prophets' credibility? Will then, he be born in the same place as was the Christ, or on in a tank or a rocket ship? Also, will he work as many, as well as the different and type of miracles that the Christ worked? Of course, people full of assumptions fail to give proper understanding appreciation of those that were there at the time of Christ.

Yet it was those very people having seen wrote what they saw as witnesses or wrote what they received from actual witnesses. But then why believe them? After all, was there not more than one? And just how many were there? Then also, did writers of the time not have associates that may have helped them by reporting what they saw or heard? Would not the writers have taken information from whatever second party sources were available as to what they may have seen or heard about? Then too, were they not some of them living there about during the time period? Then also present at the time of one or more miracles?

And unlike Hollywood, all of the miracles performed were instantaneous, as without any practice session. Not only were they not magic but also not practiced feats. Of all them that were performed there was never any admission charge or donations required. Just as back then, why believe in such things as miracles? Or why believe in anything? But if a person, like so many choose not to, then what does that leave for the mind? Is science to be relied upon to do the thinking? But science still has no true factual idea where mankind came from but only guessing type theories. How does such thinking not kind of put such persons above everything?

After all, is not what then remains is only self? Yet who can show where and how they created their self? It may be, especially when realized that they cannot even create water. But one should not mix one thing with another. As making water from other chemicals is not the same as creating it from nothing. However, it is the written statements of at least six of the witnesses still remains for those interested in truth. But then with people so full of self, money and ambition who has room for truth?

The Great Excitignly Holy John the Baptist

So now it is asked, what has all of the preceding to do with John the Baptist? Such minds sets and actions of the shown entities has everything to do with the Baptist. It is that he had a mission established by God Himself of one sole purpose which was to walk before the Messiah which had already arrived. Fulfilling his purpose of preparing the way of the Messiah is depicted by John spreading the word of Jesus Christ. Such is fully depicted in the record as shown by the apostle Mark. There it is as taken from the written matter the Baptist his self defines the matter leaving no doubt.

It is in his chapter 1: 7 by a witness where John stated, "one mightier than I is coming after me whose sandals I am not worthy to stoop down and loose". Most important here is to consider that John never spoke about the next year or other later years. Nor had he talked about someone coming in the future regarding the matter of when Christ was coming. Rather it was he said, after me. That combined with John talking about being unable to lose the strap of his sandals clearly signifies the, at the time being the present.

However, most highly significant is the single world used by John that clearly establishes his talking of the then present time. That word is, am. And it is that his stating, "am not" clearly denies any thinking of future matters. Almost in his tone of voice it may have conveyed a sound as if Jesus was so close that John was being chased. Yet it is that even that matter was expounded upon, which was his mission. And it is those matters are specifically stated in the various paragraphs of the apostles. For sure the methods, actions and words of the Baptist directly or indirectly all helped to support his delivering the message along with his bridging mission.

Not one prophesying as a prophet being one who only foretells or predicts things regarding future times. Nor was John one as having words with or about God. Rather he was the heralding messenger who conveyed his message of and about the then present tense. And it was that the message was that of announcing the peoples prayed for Messiah having already arrived. Not just arrived somewhere, but in fact then being in their presence. What the Baptist was telling them was that He was already in their midst. Such being in their midst was that the Messiah was right behind him. Now it is that such closeness of both being among the people is clearly proven by the written records.

The Great Excitignly Holy John the Baptist

It is stated in the written record where the two did meet at the Jordan. Yet people seem to discount the meetings significance. If nothing else it proves beyond any doubt that they were both around during the same time.

There were two religious' factions of the Jewish people at the time but John did not align with either. For his main purpose was preparing the way of the New Testament which was the Lord God. His sole purpose being that of bringing both factions to understand that the Messiah who was in fact the New Testament was already there in their midst. Here presented is the question, does the Koran state that the role of John was to call people away from the legalism that had corrupted the faith of the Jewish people?

Which matters of legalism, as was it that of the civil ruling party or the Pharisees. Maybe it was the Sadducees or the Levites? Does it state or omit his primary mission being of preparing the way of the Lord God? Does the book allude that the faith of the Jewish people was corrupted? Why does it not define of give examples of the corruption? Does it state how or mention any defining as to which faction of the people? Was it those of the orthodox Jews or those following the scribes? Perhaps the reason there is so much twisted matters and omissions of substantial matter in other books along with the Koran may be because the writers were not there during the time period. Where they too confused from taking material from other religious sources? Perhaps they even failed to understand the corruption in their own religion that prevented them from comprehending what was truly going on.

If the faith of all the people was corrupted, how would John have had any following? Also is there omitted what it defined as corrupted? Since their faith was in the one true Lord God and no other, how could it have been corrupted? Does the book define which group more corrupted than the other, whether the elders, Levites or priests? While thinking about the Pharisees, what about the Sadducees and common people? Were they supposedly all having been corrupted? Perhaps there was corruption, but is the book attempting to assume that the entire faith of the nation of all the people was corrupt? How does a book of misleading phrases and omissions suggest corruption when it is of itself contrary and of controversy? But then is it not the way of the world, that when something good comes along there are always the negative factors of twisting or omitting that follow?

And sure, enough those with the negatives eventually made their presence known. Why? Because the Lord who was right behind His messenger John time wise, was performing miracles. And it was that those miracles could not be explained by any of the rulers. Also, it is that no other religious person or ruler at the time was able to work any miracles. And since the rulers could not work any miracles nor provide any sensible explanation of why Christ could do such powerful things, there remained for them only one option.

A resorting to the way of force was the option that remained. Oh my, what a challenging time for John, having to cope with all those closed minds. But then, they without knowing it were actually fulfilling the written scriptures of the prophets. Of course, since the rulers could not dispute nor explain his actions except with opinions, all they could do was to use force. After all, what the Christ was doing was not only what no one else had ever done, but could do. Yes, it was that those miracles Christ performed were beyond what humans could do.

Considering only their power of authority and money was their interest. As such their stance was not to look at the good he did. Rather they found their ways easier to turn His marvelous performance into their human jealous and greedy evil ways. Why because the Christ's along with John's following was depriving them of their contributors. After all, what would they live on? Especially should all the people have stayed away from their synagogues as well as the temple what would religious rulers then do for the paying participants?

Now it is that upon taking in all the material previously mentioned for consideration many different matters were covered of which touch upon such matters that range from people's faith to their own ways of thinking. Perhaps being the beginning even more matters of faith and thinking follows. And then there are the affecting circumstances that were beyond their control. John the Baptist was helping the Christ and not them. But where to start, as either one of the matters could touch upon one of the others. Then what would remain, nothing but chaos?

The Great Excitignly Holy John the Baptist

What a time it must have been for the civil rulers attempting to keep some resemblance of order?

What a time it must have been for the ruling high priests, as they tried to maintain their subjects keeping them from going astray. And then there were simply the poor oppressed people. Were they not trying to do the right thing? Whether it was the Levites, Pharisees, Sadducees, Scribes and the Baptist were they all not about the same Lord God? Suddenly came along that stumbling block, as the Messiah had arrived where God having taken human form by manifesting himself as Jesus Christ the Lord.

All at once there was simply too much confusion. Human limited intelligence combined with not being of the spirit, it was that the people as well as the religious authorities were unable to understand precisely what it was that John the Baptist kept telling them. Wow! What a most challenging time for the Baptist with all those closed minds, however without their knowing it was that the religious authorities were actually fulfilling the written scriptures of the prophets. He must have found those days being embroiled in arguments and disagreements. For sure his days were not only challenging but full of fascination. Why not, as being confronted with the rigid minds of the people surely some of them must have made his day. Even in the later years of modern technology, people still remain in the dark ages of human limited intelligence. Then not being of the spirit, to them materialism still reigns as the big decision maker.

It's all about money along with who has the bigger boat or the newer car. Then too there's always who has most valuable company or the most money. But all the money in the world cannot replace truth. Sure, it can buy the elimination of those who speak truth. But it is that the truth still remains.

Deceit and lies can surely win but what remains afterward? And void of truth or where truth is disabled, there remains only chaos.

So it is that with all of the chaos, deceit and lies, truth remains and what was first written or originally written cannot be changed since in fact it is the truth that the Baptist going before the Lord God was the only great and excitingly holy messenger.

CHAPTER 16.

How Well Did the People Really Listen to the Messenger?

Important to remember are the words of Isaias, where, as is taken from the written record it states, "the voice of one crying in the desert". And this should be added to in combination with the other portion of the statement. Now it is that the continued portion of the phrase is the most important part as it gave the people direction as to what they were to do. As taken from the written matter the last section states, "prepare ye the way of the Lord, make straight in the wilderness the paths of our God".

Most surely this shows that John was directly telling the people that they were to make their paths straight. In effect the phrase meant for the people to get their hearts straight honoring the Lord God who had already come into their midst. Amazing it is how people twist what they hear or see to fit their own imagination or preconceived ideas. What verbal and mental abuse John must have endured cannot even be imagined. But some consideration of how cynical and full of erroneous assumptions people are may help. Perhaps even a little bit of thinking about such, may allow some credible comprehension.

What most people seem to miss is that from those words, it also reveals the obligation of people that followed in the later times. There was no mention of any next days or next week, or of any suggestion of the following year. So, if there is belief in the Lord God, but yet limitations are put on how long to prepare, what does such thinking bring about? This may all leave a very big question. How well did the people really listen to what the messenger was broadcasting? Did they fully comprehend what John the Baptist was fully alerting them to?

Now it was that since His messenger the Baptist was spreading the word of Him the Christ, it riled the rulers even more. In the record it is found by the apostle John, just how much the Baptist caused an up roar with the religious rulers. According to the written record, the apostle

The Great Excitignly Holy John the Baptist

John in chapter 1: 19- 27 depicts how persistent the religious leaders were. As taken from the written matter it states, "Jews in Jerusalem sent to him priests, some of which were Pharisees and Levites to question the Baptist". Meeting him at Bethany, a place beyond the Jordan was where John was Baptizing. Yet when asked who he was, John replied that he was not the Christ. Then when asked whether he was Elias he responded that he was not. And when further asked whether he was the prophet he answered, no.

So, with the priests and Levites knowing as much as when they first asked any question, they showed how they were under pressure to get more information. Those lower ones advised the Baptist how it was with them where they needed to give an answer. They were under pressure to provide answers to those of the higher lever that had sent them. Amusing it is, that those that had sent the lower ranking persons didn't even have the courtesy to go ask the Baptist themselves. Maybe it was that they didn't want to be seen by the people. Or perhaps, were they concerned that the crowds would have taken their questioning methods as giving him a hard time? Then to, they may have thought that if they did go, perhaps the people would have taken their presence as actually giving John some respect.

Certainly, it must have been where the last thing that those high priests would have wanted would have been to give the people any false illusion, that they had any respect for the preacher. So, the Pharisees pushed further as they pressed him as they inquired who he was, and for him to say so of himself. It is shown in the record, according to the apostle John where he replied, "I am the voice of one crying in the desert, make straight the way of the Lord". Would not now be a good place to recall what the prophets Isaias and Malachiah had foretold. It was that they both prophesied what the messenger would have said. Refer herein to chapter 5 to refresh what they foretold. Also as taken from the written matter it was that the small band of questioners asked why he baptized since he was not the Christ, nor Elias nor the Prophet.

Amazing how the records show that they were in fact asking the right kind of questions. Such means of requiring some sort of identifying indicates where they had contemplated so much on what they believed as well as what they had been told.It is shown in the record where the Baptist at all times provided answers that were complete and straight forward leaving nothing to guessing. As taken from the written record it depicts how he replied, "I baptize with water, but in the midst of you there has stood one, whom you do not know. He it is who is to come after me, the strap of whose sandal I am not worthy to lose". Did his statements cause a sudden uproar? It could not have been taken any other way of what the words spoken by the Baptist intended.

Tis a shame, but the nature of people is always such a negative, where they must find fault with every little word or every little act that is except of their selves. Most likely John's words struck hard, especially where some actually understood. His asserting, that the Messiah was already in the midst of them was strong words. So strong in fact they must have caused a lot of genuine antagonism. Then those along with the words of, sandal not worthy to lose, fully indicated his intended message that Christ the Messiah was already in their midst. Clearly those words eliminated any possible misunderstanding about John being the messenger. Also clear it is that he was not talking about that of the future years or some distance time but in fact of the then present day.

Also, there were his words regarding being a voice of one crying in the desert. Those few but meaningful words need to be fully considered. Fully it is about what they reflect on what the prophets Isaias and Malachiah foretold. Plus, it is that Luke 3: 3- 6 and Mark 1: 6- 8 as well as Matthew 3: 1- 3 along with 3: 5- 6 show similar words. With so many people reporting nearly the same it takes away any thinking of any coincidence possibility. Unfortunately, people tend to forget that back then there were no tape records or other instant means of recording what was stated. Common sense must be applied to understand that there was much more spoken than recorded. After all most of what was written was drawn from memory.

Even if there were two or three telling the writer of what took place none of them would have been able to recall every word. Nor would they have been able to recall every instance of responses that were made to the people. Then there was the place that by such not only supports but confirms what the apostle John reported in his written matter. By all of this it can only be taken that John was not to be just another person that became or was a prophet. What if, the words about the desert were only coincidence?

The Great Excitignly Holy John the Baptist

After all, wasn't it a territory where the entire land region was made up of desert areas? Wasn't such the reason why communities were built around the rivers? Considering the mind sets of the people during that period why could not the phrase, "the voice of one crying in the desert", also meant to be about the minds of the people. For sure John the Baptist was not some lunatic out walking around in the desert howling at the moon. Nor was he out there panning for gold or collecting souvenirs. No, any relating of the Baptist crying in the desert was not only about the sand or the soil but also was all about him actually crying by shedding tears in his voice. They had Moses and the two stone tablets as well as the prophets.

Such was about the Baptist of his knowing that the Messiah was there about their area but also was aware of their hardness of heart. Such it was where the people were too blind to understand what he was telling them. Yet through his preaching he kept repeating as he told them over and over as well as to anyone that would have listened. And it is those matters must be taken together, where they can be put in context. Such matters can only support the truth that the time had come, where John was originally of heaven directly sent by and from God himself. Lord God the Creator had personally sent the Baptist on a holy mission.

Of course, what most people do is turn away refusing to consider such truth. It is much easier to listen to hollow words that call him a lunatic or a simple prophet. Without any doubt it can be seen by reading in detail, that John was sent for the sole purpose of being the bridge between the Jews with the already arrived Christ Jesus. It was that Christ was the Messiah, of which the Jews had been praying for with John being the telegraphing connector between the Jews and Christ. Should such description be taken as accurate?

Such can only be taken as accurate since one matter is that both John and Jesus were both around during the same time. Also, it is that the matter is proven, since both had been born only less than a year apart. Plus advising those that questioned him about such John told them in so many words. Those matters should be combined with the fact that it was even by the prophets' foretelling of John's duty of him to announce and bring the people to Jesus. John was not some prophet of the future as some wish to press their belief, but in fact was a messenger of the then day's news. Full consideration must be given to what the prophets some time before hand had written.

The Great Excitignly Holy John the Baptist

Then the same must also be combined with what the angel had stated to Zachary, that he himself will go before Him. Go before whom? Certainly, he would not have been going before any of the Pharisees or Levites. Therefore, without doubt it was John's purpose to broadcast the already arrived Messiah.

Read in comparison the previous immediate paragraphs. Of course, there are those people that choose to keep closed minds as only reading what they are directed to. Also, there are others who may only read a couple of lines of one, then the same of another. But then they lose interest, because, by denying themselves the full scope of the matter they fail to understand the substance of what they are reading.

Then there are others that may become confused so they stop. In such a hurry they all are that they only read the material once. Since they believe what they only know, there is a mindset denying any objective reading. Such persons erroneously expect their intelligence to comprehend while simultaneously impeding any understanding. Also, there are those other persons that refuse to read other material in other religions, because they are prevented under force from having such in their possession.

And then there are those that choose not to read because of intimidation or being disallowed by their religious friends. Such it is that those persons are being denied educational benefits. Especially it is that those persons are denied the opportunity of comparing matters which would provide them truth. But then who in the modern times is concerned about truth? One thing for sure as can be realized from the tone taken from the statements shown in the record, it is that those around him certainly had interesting days. What may add better meaning of enabling some understanding would be to combine such various matters. Then with memory of the ancient living conditions they might perceive of how people may have reacted in such situations.

Perhaps those persons attending John's preaching may have not even considered those of authority asking questions. Maybe they thought such may have been done so, intentionally only to be annoying. Then also maybe they would have even thought that the band's persistent questioning were actions of intentional disturbing measures for purpose of creating some sort of distraction. Such could have been taken as interrupting the service on purpose as well as confusing the preaching of which John was providing. Then too, perhaps some of the authorities may by their actions have even found some amusement. Maybe at times they even found John's actions as being of some humor.

Then reading in between the lines it even seems that such questioning sessions happened frequently. Such may be concluded as it was that four apostles give separate accounts yet each being void of any authority having anything good to say. Since each of the separate accounts amounted to the same thing they were mostly often of different situations. Now it is that certain types of situations may have only occurred once and there it is highly unlikely that all four would have written about such. Yet an interesting item is that the places of which each apostle speaks of appears as being similar. Perhaps they were not the exact same spot but only close, where they would not be discounted. However, it wasn't the places or the time of day that was of any significance. Rather it is obvious that the apostles certainly felt that what John was preaching along with his actions had to be substantially important. This is clearly evident since each wrote about the same kind of matters.

Then too, the people that went out to see the Baptist must have felt that they had cause. Their continuous going out to see John was so done because they must have seen something in him. For sure it wasn't his looks or his guitar playing. They must have truly believed in what he was saying along with his actions. Such actually makes sense, for if not, then the word among the people would have spread about him just being another preacher. But the crowds kept growing, and then too they even grew rapidly. Such was even to the point where the growth actually caused the authorities of the Jews in Jerusalem to be more than just concerned. Naturally as at any event where police or other authority interrupts a proceeding people become annoyed.

And so, it must have been back then when authorities came around did the people not react? Much notice about these events should be considered. For sure the religious authorities may not have participated but only provided some interruption. How would such not have caused more resentment by the people of them? Of course, as his fame among the crowds grew surely the people listening along with following John became a problem. But it was where the people respected his teachings. However, what he was preaching along with advertising about the Christ directly conflicted with the religious as well as the civil authorities. Most especially though was his rivalry with the religious authorities due to him spreading the word of the messiah being in the area. Especially where Christ was performing miracles how would such not have further conflicted with the teaching of the religious authorities? Obviously, they had real material problems. Then also maybe the crowds following of John not only took time but also caused a diminishing of the funds.

It wasn't that the people were taking money out of the synagogue or stealing from the temple. But rather by the people not attending common sense dictates they were also not giving their usual offerings. And for sure it was that the people not giving must have deprived the religious authorities of what they were accustomed to. If it was only one, the rulers probably wouldn't have had any trouble removing him. But there it was where both the religious and civil authorities had to contend with coping with the two of them.

Considering the existing situation at the time it must have been fascinating. Were the two sides of authorities not preoccupied with watching each other? Were they not waiting for the other to move against John or the Christ? Such would then mean they could then also move against him as well as the other. But the actions along with the preaching by Jesus got to be so popular that he actually started to take followers away from John.

Christ over time was quickly gaining his own following. Although John still had his following, the numbers were quickly dwindling. They were leaving him to follow Christ, and why not, as John was not performing any miracles. Plus, it was where he was constantly broadcasting about Jesus anyway. Although there were only the two, their constant gaining of followers was steadily taking away from the following of the religious authorities. And that was not good as it was detrimental to their preaching with authority in Jerusalem.

Now, since John was preaching about the good news of the Christ who was already in the area, would such word not have spread that would have given those that followed Jesus at least a feeling of more credibility? Perhaps the religious powers of the time were able to actually notice their normal following being hindered. Then to, with the overwhelming personality of the Baptist, the apostles of Christ soon found it necessary to question Jesus as to who were they to follow? Meanwhile, Jesus actually took it upon himself to demonstrate that John was due respect. This he did when He himself went to John amidst the public to be baptized.

Now it is that those matters of the two meeting are found in the record of Matthew. As taken from the written matter in his chapter 3: 13 it states, "then Jesus came from Galilee to John at the Jordan to be baptized by him". However, if that was not enough to give John credibility of his holiness, then what happened next most assuredly did. It is extremely substantial of holy significance to comprehend the meaning of what took place. Such it was where John demonstrated his being aware of just who Jesus Christ was.

That most important matter is also shown in the written record of what John stated. In Matthew 3: 14 as taken from the written matter it states, "it is I who ought to be baptized by Thee, and dost Thou come to me? But it was that Jesus simply advised him of what was necessary to be right and correct to be done for his Father, God's sake. And what was that all about, as what was meant? Awesomely critical was the reply of Jesus as he acknowledged the significantly importance of the Old Testament.

But who cares about what was written in the past? Yet it is of how Christ answered is also depicted in the record. As taken from the written matter in Matthew 3: 15 it states, "let it be so now, for so it becomes us to fulfill all justice." Of such power was the one sentence that it not only clarified what Jesus often stated, but why. It was that which Jesus kept telling people such that He was merely fulfilling the scriptures of His Father God. And was His Father who had allowed to be foretold through His prophets.

As the records show, Jesus was baptized where such is depicted by Matthew the apostle. As taken from the written matter in Matthew 3: 15- 16 it states, "then He permitted him and when Jesus had been baptized he immediately came up from the water". Also, it is, that in Mark 1: 9 the same event was reported. It is as taken from his written matter it states, "and it came to pass in those days, that Jesus came from

The Great Excitignly Holy John the Baptist

Nazareth in Galilee and was baptized by John in the Jordan". So also, it is that the same important event was recorded by Luke in his chapter 3: 21. Important it is, to note how Jesus stated the fact of their spirits. All the while it was that John fully aware of who Jesus was, he was all the while knowing of his own demise. Such is realized by comprehending His usage of the word, "us".

A must for taking notice is that Christ did not say, I have to, or it is me that must, but rather Christ stated, "us". This little word, us, as used between the two clearly evidences that John was more than just some man doing some preaching. Such a term of His using the word us, fully indicates that John was of a heavenly blessing. Now it may have been where each of their human form had not met before on earth it is evident that their spirits knew each other.

To be considered is that John was of a mortal mental personality. This could reason why he was not fully aware of exactly who Christ was in the human form but his spirit knew. For sure John did know the reason of His being there. Furthermore, by Jesus stating the fulfilling of all justice, clearly indicates that they were fulfilling truth. Not only was the reason given but it was completing what Christ's Father had spoken through the ancient prophets. It was they who had foretold of both of their coming. Also, it is the baptism of Jesus is also shown as recorded by Mark in his chapter 1: 9. Plus the two being together at that time is also shown in John 3: 26

It would be most foolish to take only one phrase, then skip all the rest thinking that all is understood. Rather it is most important to take each item, then to, along with what each and every apostle had stated. Such would enable to be realized the full meaning of what was done. Then to, what was said is even more important. Therefore, to omit or eliminate in part or whole, one or more of the other sentences or phrases may deprive a person from fully understanding what had transpired. Yet most important is that it would deny the person of fully comprehending its full meaning. Such combining what each said is relatively a simple way of grasping what happened.

But most important is that it would allow the full recognition of the significant item of importance. What this all signifies is that Jesus was fulfilling what his Father had spoken through the prophets. And then also, and most important is that the act of Baptism by John, of Jesus, was the complete establishing of the basic physical foundation. Such foundation was fully enwrapped in a religiously sacred covenant. It was that the act actually put into action a belief in the new spiritual faith. Also, it was that the event was a highly spiritual matter.

By Jesus Christ being baptized, when surely, he didn't need to be, it was the final means of establishing the very physical as well as spiritual foundation of what they were teaching. Yet, it is also highly likely that back then that with all of the discord the people didn't comprehend the full significance of what it was all about. Oh sure, people got baptized, and maybe their family did to, as well as some friends. But whether they truly understood what it all meant, such may have been beyond their understanding.

Perhaps it may have been something like being unable to realize an unfamiliar game's action. Especially when being there at the start hearing what was contrary to what the religious leaders were preaching. There were the words along with the action, but were the people truly able to understand the sacredly holy intent of the short event?

Meanwhile, while everything seemed to be going along fine, it was that John found himself in a position where he needed to back up his words of teaching. Although he was aware that the religious authorities were looking for some type of excuse to get rid of him, he could not avoid the bigger trouble that was to be set upon him. Perhaps it only started slowly or in drips and drabs but surely, he was drawing trouble. It is in the record of John's troubles really beginning being during one of those times when he was among a crowd.

Such occurrence is shown in the record of Matthew where John had a real serious confrontation with the religious authority. In Matthew 3: 7 as taken from the written matter it states, "that he saw the Pharisees and Sadducees coming to his baptism". Now it had to have been that they must have said something most annoying, which caused John to respond. Such reasoning behind this can be found by the tone of what he spoke. Of course, his tone really can't be actually heard from the written matter. However, his response clearly does not appear to be one of a happy welcome which surely can allow a relating to what the tone may have been.

Contemplating such a course attitude can be ascertained from a person attempting to speak the similar words. It is those words he spoke depicting anger are shown in the record of Matthew. Such is taken from the written matter that states, "brood of vipers, who has shown you, how to flee from the wrath to come"? Then as depicted in the record John didn't hold anything back as he really lowered the boom. Boldly he lets them know the matter of their practices being wrong. His instructions are depicted by Matthew in his written record. As taken from his chapter 3: 8- 9 it states, "bring forth therefore fruit befitting repentance, and do not think to yourselves, we have Abraham for our father, for I say to you that God is able out of these stones to raise up children to Abraham". As it was, the problem was that the rulers over time had actually moved in their religious thinking. They allowed their faith to be moved into honoring Abraham. Abraham was not their God and they were misleading the people.

Such custom that had been started was a direct insult to their God, who was the Lord God. Wherefore it was that John in so many words had advised them how erroneous their thinking was as well as their teachings. But of course, to them what did that simple preacher know? Knowing how power corrupts, does it take much thinking to understand what the high religious authorities must have thought? Then too would their thinking not have always been about being self- righteous? There was this person who they considered as nothing more than a beggar yet it is that he was actually advising them that their religious teachings were all wrong as well as behind the times.

Surely it was, that nobody before was ever able to correct them, especially in front of the people. Just who did he think he was, they must have wondered? Then to, how much of his nonsense would they take? Also at the same time, he had been warning them that it was where the Messiah was right behind him in their midst. Such extremely important matter is also shown in the record. Clearly explained in detail, Matthew shows how John told the people as well as the religious authorities in words they would understand. As taken from the written matter in his chapter 3: 11 it states, "I indeed baptize you with water for repentance, but He who is coming after me is mightier than I whose sandals I am not worthy to bear. He will baptize you with the Holy Spirit and with fire". Whereas he was giving all of them the full message, they of self-indulgence were not paying attention.

The Great Excitignly Holy John the Baptist

It is important here to note what he did not say. At no time had John stated anything vague, such as would have, or maybe some time later. Nor did he leave anything to guessing such as if He was around. Rather he clearly indicated the Messiah's presence being in the vicinity. His defining words of, am not worthy to bear, clearly indicates the then present tense. Such is just as clear as when he had said about the Messiah actually walking in their midst.To this matter John couldn't have done more, even if he waved flags while standing on his head. That situation of confrontation is also shown in the written record of Luke. There in his chapter 3: 7- 9 he noted of the religious authorities being about themselves.

Such written matter depicts an identical kind of phrasing with even the words being close to that shown in the matter aforementioned. Such was stated by Matthew 3: 8- 9 where it may be considered that at that point the final dividing line had been drawn. Also, it should be considered that there were probably many other words spoken between John and the crowd but not remembered. But it is, that those words were sufficient as clearly portrayed where each stood.

As the crowds grew in size at the places it showed how they believed in what John was preaching. What exciting times he must have had, finding people being receptive. It was that they had always obeyed the authorities of the Jews. Whatever they ruled or asserted the people believed and followed. But then there was someone new preaching a new and different way. No doubt it must have been that the discord to the authorities presented much controversy. And it is that such noting is found recorded, where the common people even asked John what they were to do.

In the record of Luke 3: 10 therein as taken from the written matter it states, "and the crowds asked him saying, what then are we to do"? Then too, it is shown from the written matter where the publicans came to be baptized. But it is that the Baptist was only simplifying things as preaching the commandments. Also in Luke 3: 10- 14 it shows even the religious asking the very same question. Even the soldiers are mentioned in the record as had gone asking John what to do. All wanted to know basically the same thing. Their question was, what could they do to live righteously? For sure the Baptist made his position known, as well as who he stood with. And for sure it was not with the religious rulers of the Jews.

However, a real big problem was that at the beginning they had grown so attached to John that overtime the people forgot the very message he was bringing. In his preaching John's message was all about Christ being the Messiah. Though such sound simple, perhaps they were unable to hear. Why? Because in their humanity, the people had become overly much used to him, where his purpose in fact had been taken for granted.

Fact of the matter was that they had gotten religiously attached. Crowds can't grow if the people stay away, so it must be taken that the majority was grown by those that returned. So powerful were his words that he had almost become a household name. Meanwhile, it must have been that whenever the authorities had their meetings there was always one subject. How would it have been that John was not discussed? There had to be bitterness, especially since he had embarrassed them in front of the people.

Unfortunately, John having his own problems was not only just with the authorities, but soon it was with the people that the authorities had stirred up against him. And sure, it was that stirring up discord against John would not be a problem that would go away. Actually, such undermining became easy because the rulers were the law. And when the ruling law speaks what do people do but assume. Even when knowing in their hearts of a specific rule or law being not morally or ethically correct people find it easier to simply follow.

Maybe while being led the people think of what is correct yet even if such rule or law is wrong they will still follow. Plus, since the authorities had the money, if anyone was willing the same authorities also had the means to reward such helpful action with pay. Perhaps, it may have been only one thing that he said at the beginning, but then as time went passed it finally became everything that John said, or even did. Then to what may have helped them was the way he spoke or replied to the Jewish leaders. And of course, there were people playing both sides.

Also, there were those remaining faithful to the Jewish authorities. For sure some consideration must be given to the amount of intentional abusive verbiage they must have thrown at him. Such situations may have been where at some point he may have even returned some of their arrogance. No, maybe it wasn't by the same language or arguing but by refusing to engage in their action. Then to while also refusing to bend, he raised his voice while asserting the correct matters. Perhaps, it was also how they were seeing the kind of people that were listening to him. Certainly, standing around they were able to watch just who was being baptized.

Surely that was enough, after all, who else would have dared to show up after it all started? Such it was they must have thought, especially with them being the authority making a presence. Bad enough the people were flocking to see as well as listen to him. The growing numbers was getting to be too much. Then to see other types of authority starting to show up, wow, how they were surprised! What next, they must have thought. Would such persons not have caused those of the priest order, especially the high priests more aggravation than they wanted? After all, to their surprise it is recorded where even the Publicans started to go to John seeking guidance. Not only did they go to watch and listen to him preach, but also they soon started getting to point where they got baptized.

Then also, were those same people not asking John for advice? Most of those matters are also found in the written record. As taken from the written matter it is in Luke chapter 3: 12 where it states, "and publicans also came to be baptized, and they said to him, Master what are we to do"? Furthermore, as shown in 3: 14 the written matter states, "and soldiers also asked him, saying, and what are we to do"? What could the leaders have thought? Was their world falling apart or going crazy? What could they do since they could not face the man directly? Physically there would not have been any problem as being easily able to overtake him. But it was that they lacked any credible religious responses.

With the religious leaders preaching one way and John another, what was it that the people could have done? How long would the nuisance of the man stay around? John the Baptist must have had the whole Jewish religious authority community in a tizzy. Were they afraid of him? It doesn't appear that way as, more likely it was their ego and being jealous. Then along with worrying about their power being disrupted, there was also the greed factor. Now, since it is that those matters combined do drive people to do things, how would such not have come to bare on the Baptist? Even in his human sense he must have had days that were exuberant.

Surely the Baptist had become aware, knowing how the people were learning. Not just learning from his preaching but such came to the point of the people seeing how closed minded the authorities were. To them the Baptist was teaching a new kind of religion. He was preaching of respect where they could actually feel the difference. Yet such was contrary to the ruling authorities that only preached obedience and punishment. Of course, as people are easily led so it was that the rulers would eventually have their day. Though they showed some tolerance to keep rioting down they were not afraid of the people.

But John was on a mission of which he was only concerned with fulfilling that mission. He was not interested in any popularity race or running for office as he had his duty which was of greater importance. But although he knew of his enemies he didn't give them any chance to stop him.

However, even though John was in the middle of everything, knowing full well of the unrest he was causing the man may not have been aware of the treachery that was soon to come his way.

And for sure it wasn't going to be fun out on the fairway dodging golf balls.

CHAPTER 17.

What a Mess of Confusion the Two Must Have Generated!

Not to be taken out of context, but merely as some humor, it was that the previous chapter reminded the author of the old-time western movie serials. Such were times where the good guy shows up seeing the bad hombres have taken over the town. Then just when the story got interesting with the film starting to get exciting, of course then came the bad news. Everything came to a standstill as a sign flashed on the screen, "tune in next week for the following exciting episode". However, unlike Hollywood, the religious matters of the time period in discussion were not staged for advertisers or practiced as some serial.

Considering the hardships of the times certainly the apostles didn't write all they did simply because they had nothing better to do. They must have written such not only because it was what they had seen or heard but what was also told them from reliable sources who they personally knew. Plus, and most important was that they had fully understood the high significance of the matters they wrote about. Also, it is to remember that the apostles were there during or about those times. So, there shouldn't be any question as to how it was that they did know precisely what they were putting into the recorded written matter.

With them it was all about writing factual matter as they heard about or saw it happen, or overheard what was being said. Also, it may have been information from who they had received from other reliable sources of first-hand instance. This can really be appreciated by the shortness of the various statements made as well as the paragraphs. Those leading but fictitious statements normally found in novels are nowhere to be found in the gospels. Rather, what is shown of the matters written about is the simple descriptions of what occurred, all without any of the frills or long-drawn-out pages of literary composition.

So now it is to move on further in the life of the holy, John the Baptist. It was a time period where the Jewish religious leaders over time had become more and more leading toward praying to Abraham. Such was a religious error in the eyes of God. Of course, the sacred part of it was that their creator the Lord God was being slowly overshadowed. Then to, during the same period, the people were being squashed by the Romans. While enforcing their rule they also pushed their laws which certainly caused much controversy as well as hardship.

With the Romans it was all about their worshipping Caesar as their god. Following him as the basis for all laws, such had the conquered Jews in a box. While the Jewish religious rulers were doing what pleased them, they also pacified the civil rulers. Did the religious authorities knowing they could not push the Romans out originally think to start worshiping Abraham as a trick to full the Roman rulers? Perhaps because Abraham was a known figure they thought such might help with dealing with their rulers? Either way how did such actions not leave the people in discord? How were they not out in the cold with no real direction?

Now it was that Jesus was gaining in popularity very quickly. Then John, though preaching the same message of salvation was also completing his mission. Teaching the people of the Messiah being the Christ, it could have only directly provided credibility to which, helped the cause of Jesus. Then with Christ stating who He was along with John advising the people that Christ was the one, must have given the people some hope. Actually, there were people following the Christ from the very start. But also, there were those who had changed from following John.

So much was going on with more people following Jesus, as well as switching from the one to the other, that it even made an impact on the apostles. Concerned they were, because many of them had originally followed John. So much so was their seeing over time the various occurrences that had been happening, choices came about that had to be made. Such matters must have been felt as important since they are shown in the written record. Portrayed by John the apostle is some of those situations.

It is where the author feels that considering how people love to argue there seems to be much information missing. Such is especially noted when taken from the written matter in chapter 3 of John's record. Those several words stated depict what the apostle's attitude may have been.

The Great Excitignly Holy John the Baptist

Such can be realized from the questions they directly put to the Baptist. Now, although it is recorded of the words they used, what is not shown is their insecure position along with their doubting tone. Such attitude can be realized by contemplating what was expressed by them.

Also, it is the same of John who would also have had tones of expressions. To have seen them pleading while also hearing the substance of such conversations would have been most interesting. But hearing of how the men questioned John would also have been most fascinating. So now it is as taken from the written matter of John 3: 26 it states, "Rabbi, He who was with thee beyond the Jordan to whom thou hast borne witness, behold He baptizes and all are coming to Him." Wow, what a mind turning experience.

One can only imagine how the apostles must have felt especially after having found someone like John that they could believe in. Then after having placed their loyalty with the man, they came to a time of trusting indecision where they had to make a choice. Yet things were actually made somewhat easy for them. It was that John of who they could listen to had actually provided some direction. What may have helped them was that they were again reminded of just who John was. But most important it may have been when they heard of who he was not. Such substantial facts are shown in the record of the apostle John. There in his chapter 3: 28 as taken from the written matter it states, "you yourselves, bear me witness that I said, I am not the Christ but have been sent before Him".

Wow! What a statement! Such a phrase clearly depicts how they respected John where they had no idea what he would have told them. Of course, he would not have had any idea as to how they would have reacted. What a mess of confusion the two must have been making.

There was Jesus the true Messiah along with John His messenger. Yet important it is to keep in mind is that during that time period there were no phones, telegraph or newspapers to daily inform the people. What those meant was that there was no daily or even weekly news. If any kind of news was not spread by word of mouth it just didn't get around. Yet, while he was preaching and baptizing simultaneously John was also announcing that the Messiah's presence was already among them. Wow, and then with both speaking with such authority. All the while it was that John kept telling and preaching of present tense.

The Great Excitignly Holy John the Baptist

John spoke to both the apostles as well as the Jews just who should be followed. But after coming to believe in John then respecting him as being a holy person, how could the apostles as well as the people change their hearts? At the places where John had started as well as been preaching, once his mission got under way there must have been a steady growing of unified faith. Oh, sure it was that they all listened while hearing, but hearing what? Hearing what they wanted while also turning a deaf ear they just didn't understand the message of the Messiah already being among them. One could almost feel the exuberance of John as he transferred some to the people as he spoke.

And then along with his preaching there was the performing of the baptisms. So not only was there the mental connection but also the actual physical action of the baptism which would have provided some physical connection with the spiritual. With all of that to look forward to, there must have been at least some feeling to celebrate. Would there not have been much clapping and singing showing the joy of the people? Then to perhaps even some dancing may have taken place. Such were the times and place where not only was the people's faith strengthened as believing what John was preaching. Also, there must have been the feeling of being free of the rulers browbeating.

Yet with all of that, John was lacking what Jesus the Son of God had. It was that the Baptist didn't have the power to work miracles. Sure, it was that Jesus was working miracles but as it was, such was not for John to do. His mission was totally different where he didn't need to perform such things that others could not do. Just as he had been doing, his sole purpose was to spread the word that the Messiah was already in their midst, following right behind him. So, with all of that, along with the Jews starving for hearing truth, it was that John was pushing them toward the Christ. Such situations could only have generated times where hard decision times arrived.

It is just that while people maybe stubborn, as well as others being of a closed or one-track mind, they do have soft spots in their hearts. Then too, once some people decide on something is it not hard for them to change? Minds of people may be a real challenge while making decisions, even when shown the correct way. Perhaps it was the same with those people back then. But also, it was that over time, John had been going around preaching as well as Baptizing. Such it was that his followers had not only grown to believe but most important was that they trusted him. Most amazing it is that there is no record of anyone that was able to convolute what he was preaching.

Wow! What a time for the people it must have been. Not just coping with the poor living conditions as described in the beginning chapters of this book but being oppressed by their rulers. Yet the religious and civic authorities were unable to convince the general public to stay away from him. Such is depicted as when they asserted their authority along with use of force. Surely the authorities were successful in breaking up the crowds from time to time. However, it was too, that the people simply returned the next day to the same place or at some other location. Of course, it was that the harassment by the religious authorities only provoked the crowds even the more.

Surely the Baptist was having success spreading the word of the Messiah. Then too he must have been somewhat aware that his mission was soon to be ending. It was his job being the messenger of God to alert the people that God's Son was already in their midst. And this it was which he had been doing. So, does it not make sense that since he knew who his message was about and as such was aware that his purpose was limited he would be aware that his time was drawing to an end? Now it was that Jesus had already been gaining in popularity which indirectly affected His messenger. Now it was but not specifically stated as such was that the Message from the Baptist was spreading even before the Christ was physically seen.

Then with John mentioning the matters regarding Christ to the people it could have only created a big problem. Perhaps for the people there was a lack of communication understanding. It is that John was led by the Holy Spirit moving according to his spiritual mission. Yet it was that the people were moved by their human nature. Perhaps some failed to comprehend John's full message while others had a difficult time believing him. Some of those matters can be found in the written record where the substance then may be realized. By combining what Matthew stated along with what the apostle John had wrote it may present a somewhat clear picture.

In Matthew 3:11-12 as taken from the written matter it states, "I indeed baptize you with water but one mightier than I is coming, the strap of whose sandals I am unable to lose". Now it is such can also be found in the record of Luke in chapter 3: 15- 16 where the apostle depicts basically the same similar matter. Such words are too significant to notice that the Baptist speaking, "unable to loosen", was in the then present tense. Certainly, important they are because they fully indicate being of the then present time. Clearly it is, that eliminates all possible suggestions such as referring to the Messiah as someone ten, twenty or a hundred years later.

This matter is shown in John 1:29-31 where the Baptist spoke of the then present time, with the Christ being in the same location. Such it is where John continued, "he will baptize you with the Holy Spirit and with fire". But even with all of that, the people didn't understand fully the message of the holy messenger. However, the most important matter is what the apostle John had recorded. Such matter clearly explains the message of the Baptist.

In the chapter of John 3:28 as taken from the written matter it states, "you yourselves bear me witness that I said, I am not the Christ but have been sent before Him". How much more explicit could the Baptist have been? At that time, he fully admitted as well as instructed who he was not. Then also he advised who he truly was. Yet important but overlooked by many people is that he also instructed as to what his mission of purpose entailed. Then in critically defined words the Baptist was recorded of how his duty was being fulfilled.

Recorded words of John the apostle makes clear the sure function of the mission of the Baptist. However, it is in other words of the Baptist that really explodes with defined meaning. In John 3: 30 as taken from the written matter it states, "He must increase while I must decrease". There for sure the Baptist was telling of the then present time. Also, indirectly it clearly evidences what his purpose was meant to be. For sure such words were providing what John's mission was, but perhaps they were also meant to be over taken by how inspiring he was preaching the new way. It was certainly a fairly confusing time not just for the common people and the apostles but also for those of the religious authorities.

During the same period of time there they were the two of them, the Messiah and his messenger.There was John, who was the last of the voices of the Old Testament, Law and old covenant. While he was bringing in the news of the new, at the same time there was Jesus Christ who was in fact the New Testament, Grace and new covenant. But who knew, as well as how could they have known? Such a lack of understanding by the people of what was going on at the time can be appreciated by reading what Jesus Christ had to say regarding just how holy great John the Baptist was. Those stated acclamations can be realized from the written record of Luke in chapter 7:24-29. But especially it is where such is depicted in 7:26-28. As taken from his written matter it is that Christ stated, "yes I tell you, and more than a prophet. This is of whom it is written, Behold I send My messenger before Thy face, who shall make ready Thy way before Thee."

Full notice must be given to the most highly significant words, I send, then also, my messenger. Such could only mean that John came directly from, as well as was sent directly from the Lord God. Nothing more can or could be said for it is that those that have faith and believe they understand. However, for those who chose not to have any belief any other or additional words would be useless. Of such gravity was the statement that it could only mean that he was in fact, of the spirit and not simply any human person or just another prophet.

Then continuing in a more defined statement Christ asserted, "I say to you, among those born of women there is not a greater prophet than John the Baptist". Wow! How powerful is that statement, yet people are drawn then focus only on the word prophet. Failing to combine those two phrases with what had been previously said can only impede full comprehension. Wherefore it is, by stating those words combined with, I send my messenger, it can only be taken that Jesus was referring to God himself sending John directly from the spirit world.

Furthermore, to add to that acclimation, Christ put His final elation of John. In a phrase from Jesus which told the people just how holy John was, such high praise for John is found in the record of Matthew. As taken from his written matter in 11:11 it states, "amen I say to you that there has not risen a greater than John the Baptist". Then Jesus concludes, where it is shown as taken from the written matter at 11:13-14.

There it is stated, "for all the prophets and the law, have prophesied until John. And if you are willing to receive it he is Elias who was to come". There it was just what the people didn't want to hear. Contrary to their thinking Christ had laid it out in a clear definition for all to know of just how holy the Baptist was. He had clearly defined that the Elias they were hoping for was in fact in the form of John the Baptist. What in effect He had stated that in fact it was that John was not Elias but rather, though another being was just as holy as he had come in the holiness form of Elias.

Such was the power of the statement by Christ that it was final. Christ's words dispelled all thinking which in effect rejected the idea that Elias was still to come. Stunned the people must have been when hearing such that was stated in a phrase from Jesus which told the people just how holy John was, of which such praise for John is found in the record of Matthew. Similar clarification of John's holiness is also shown by Luke. It is in his written he depicts the same clarity. In the chapter of Luke 7:24-29 it states very similar almost exact words that are written in Matthew's chapter 11 as shown above.

What in effect Jesus had told the people, was that their understanding of Elias to come was not the same as what God had in mind, nor intended. Yes, it was that the ancient prophets' words were to be fulfilled, but not in a way that the people were praying for or had hoped for or wanted. Rather it was what the Lord God wanted which was stated by Christ. God in the human form of Jesus Christ had clearly laid out the factual truth. Most difficult it was for people at the time to accept the words of Christ that John was the Elias that the people had in fact expected. However, with the closed minds of the people they could not recognize what Christ was telling them.

Contrary to the prophets as well as what Jesus had told them they had preconceived ideas as to what Elias was to act like. Also, it was they couldn't get past the name of John, even though it was where God the Lord himself had advised them. He actually spoke directly to them one on one. Not as He had done through other earthly human prophets but Christ had clearly explained how it was actually that John was sent as His personal messenger. But then who was really paying attention?

In effect John was broadcasting his message that was to be spread of which had been directly sent from the Creator. Yet it was where John could only do so much. No matter how hard he tried the outcome was always the same. Sure, he was speaking of religious matters as well as instructing the people about the Ten Commandments. But his message was always the same which contained the same Messiah matter. Yet it was that those same people that were listening as well as following him had the mind set of old.

So easily taken in the people were by worldly things such as false assumptions, preconceived ideas and gossip. Then too, they also had to cope with the propaganda of the Romans as well as the religious authorities. Not only had the people been raised in it, but also were taught about the Old Testament. Having been taught then raised in custom and traditions it was difficult if not almost impossible for the people to fully comprehend the Baptist's message. How could they turn the hearts and minds when raised and trained for years in the Old Testament ways?

Jesus Christ the Messiah who was the New Testament though totally found in the prophets of the Old Testament was contrary to their understanding. Regardless of what John or his disciples may have said for sure there was the gossip or untrue rumors. Those kinds of vicious or untrue things that sounds real are usually so easy to believe but lack credibility due to either added falseness or omissions of truthful facts. Perhaps some may even cause people to detour, especially where they may have been spread by John's public authority enemies.To be considered is that where he was of religious and moral matters, it was that they were of the law.

And who wouldn't have believed what the king or his wife along with the religious authorities may have stated or asserted in gossip? Then there is where a government being of law, with its peers yet void of religious conviction does it not enforce its own laws? Then with the advantage of using oppression how would they not have suppressed any religious beliefs? But then even if there is a religious belief, being the authority of law can they not due to the religious traditions and twist as they please?

Even during modern times of instant communication, higher learning and technology similar situations can be seen from the news across the media. How much then was it of the way of government back then? Is it not almost seen the same in today's government? Even after what all the fathers of the country gave up to establish the constitution it has been distorted by people lacking true morals. But it is those in authority void of character that done the most harm by allowing such.

Anyway, it was that John's time had slowly reached its potential where he had completed what his duty was. In those several statements made by Christ He had let the people know that there was to be no more prophets. Clearly Christ gave the signal that the Baptist was the true end of the line for all prophets. Now it was that John's mission was soon to come to an end. Unforeseen, as well as unwanted it was where the Baptist got himself entrapped in a situation that was beyond his control.

Tangled up with the civic authorities John was to find himself in a situation where law was the ruler. But even more than that, it was where the rulers were the law. Then he not being a part of their arena was nothing more than just another subject. He was matters of the spirit and truth while they were matters of ruling self indulgence. They're being the domineering rulers left John truly on the outside looking in.

Of course, they often gave the impression, if it was to their benefit, as respecting or even assisting the faithful ways of the Jews. But in reality such was only shown where it was they could use their actions to help further keep the peace. Such made sense since it made their ruling time easier. Of course, with the people all complacent nothing would change.

And for sure John the Baptist with all of his preaching wasn't about to be allowed to cause any change. So it was that John was to find out the hard way. When he stepped on the toes of one having civil power he created an enemy that simply would not go away without having revenge. Yet, it may have been that the Baptist probably had more days of joyous excitement than any two religious preachers have in their life time.

Of course, such would not have happened had he not been able to endure. And endure he did as not only the onslaught he received from the civil authorities but also from the religious authorities of the Jews. However, it is proven by the record that John the Baptist did in fact have his mission plus and most important is that in fact he did complete it.

PART X.

WOMEN, POLITICS, BAPTIST AND LAW!

Chapter 18. Especially for Herodias Since it Made her out to be a What?

Let us return now, to those thrilling days of yesteryear when from out of the past comes the thundering foot beats of the great queen. Seated high with the speed of authority, glasses of wine and with her faithful adulterous husband at her side the daring and cunning Herodias plotted onward! Found in the record it is where King Herod Antipas was having fun using his authority. While enjoying his authority he had an affair with the wife of his brother.

So, while such things occurred it was that Philip, the brother of Herod Antipas, was still living. This can be deduced since Herod Antipas divorced his wife then married Herodias while Philip was still alive. Such matter is found in the places of the record where John verbally rebuked them. One of those places is in the record of the apostle Mark. There as taken from the written matter in his chapter 6:18 it states, "it is not lawful for thee to have thy brother's wife".

How many people were those words spoken in front of? Of course, there was most likely many other things stated as was probably an argument. But it was like a person that goes some place where authorities are speaking. And if there is no recording device or paper and pen taken to write exactly what was said, does it not leave all to memory? And who can recall all of those phrases stated the next day? So, it was back then, for sure where all writings of what was said by whom would have been made by memory. Then considering the difficulty in writing who would have wanted to write matter simply for the sake of writing? That is why everything is short depicting only significant matter. But it does get the intended substance across.

Wow! Had John put Herod in a highly unexpected, controversial spot? How did such not cause a moment of huge embarrassment, especially for Herodias? Surely it was that she had taken offense. Yet at any other time, perhaps such matters would not have been a problem. Maybe such personal matters would have even been kept within the walls of the ruler's house. From out of nowhere came this holy man all alone boldly confronting, not someone working in the field, but the person with the highest authority.

But as it was, the Baptist had opened the door expressing religious matters relative to their behavior. There it was where John was preaching all about the intended meanings of the law of the commandments. As such he must have also been stressing the points of what was religiously and morally correct. Of course, as it was what Herod did was totally contrary to what was morally right. But most important was that their actions were definitely contrary to the commandments. And it was where John had been preaching those very same points of morals.Of course, John could have acted like the others where he could have simply looked the other way. Such as what people do in politics by those that only follow. He could have been like the happy politician that simply overlooked the matter along with simply ignoring the situation.

Now as far as the people, well as it was that they were following his preaching. Then to, due to his teaching they had become well versed in the commandments. Perhaps it was a situation where the Baptist found himself needing to show that he strongly believed in what he was preaching. Would there not have been some of his followers that even asked the Baptist what he was going to do about it? Maybe he was totally confronted by the unprepared for situation, yet as it was the ruling couple was living in the state of sin. Highly important was that they cared not who knew for they were the ruling party.

Now, since it was that the couple was the ruling government, who would dare to say anything? Also, it could have been that along with Herodias being married to the civil ruler, she probably flaunted her position. Such would deserve attention especially understanding her love of power. Therefore, in considering those matters there must also be some thought given to how most well to do people look down their nose at the poor. Then it is, where with all of those matters combined only then can it be imagined how their actions affected the public. Void of any doubt the couple must have irritated the common people. Especially it would have been Herod since he even attended some of John's preaching.

The Great Excitignly Holy John the Baptist

There it was John teaching of the commandments with the people trying to follow. Meanwhile the rulers were doing as they pleased living a double standard. Not only were they violating the commandments but also were bashing all morality. How would such matters not have created a tense, explosive atmosphere that would have drawn John into the scenario? After all, if John didn't say something to the couple what would the people have begun to think? Would rumors have started regarding the Baptist and his preaching's value?

Would not the people slowly have started to doubt his holiness? So, if the Baptist did little or said nothing, what then? What would have been assumed, especially by his closest followers? Would the people not have thought how he was teaching them one way but the rulers another way? Then to, would it not have been considered that what John was preaching was not credible? Surely if the Baptist didn't speak out against the actions of Herod and Herodias, such could have eventually been taken as an acceptance. Then too, if he didn't speak out loud enough or often, why would any of the people later listen to him? Would he not have lost all credibility? Especially it would have been at times when John spoke on the subject of marriage, how would his teaching not be questioned?

Would they later, not have gathered doubt maybe thinking how John preached one way but acted another way? Or would they have thought where he taught one way, yet spoke different when teaching civil authorities?It was recorded by Mark what John said to Herod regarding his sinful marriage. In Mark 6:18, as taken from the written matter, it states, "it is not lawful for thee to have thy brother's wife". Had he only pressed about the rulers' unlawful position perhaps it would not have caused such a ruckus. Especially, had he not stated the words which identified who the wronged party was, perhaps things would have been different.

Maybe if the Baptist hadn't mentioned the fact of the ruler's brother' wife things may have gone more subdued. Wow! How those words in front of other people by John would not have questioned Herod's authority? Even if only a few people, knowing how gossip spreads, such was not what Herod wanted to hear. But as it was, the worst was where the outburst caused a moment of huge embarrassment. Especially for Herodias since it made her out to be a what, certainly not the usual person. What could be imagined, as to what he was thinking? But more important was what she must have been thinking! That kind of verbal action by John may have been bold beyond the norm when considered the means of normal people but the ruler's response may have just been the norm.

In those days the oppressed people were probably not beaten so much unless situations called for it. And for sure it was where the words used by the Baptist in front of other people was a direct attack against the ruler's integrity. Certainly, such vocal action against the authority was a situation that called for an immediate response of action. About then perhaps the king displayed his normal authority when appeared several soldiers on horseback responding to the king's signal.

Maybe as the soldiers rode through the crowd they displayed the king's sentiments. Slashing the Baptist along with the other people using their whips while hollering outlaws or criminals they would have showed the king's anger. Such was the kind of John's language of which the leaders could not have allowed. Had it been anyone else most probably the person would have been killed instantly, if not the next day except for the king who liked the preaching of the Baptist. However, as it was all of the people were afraid of the civic ruler, especially knowing of Herod's mind for power. In reality they could have cared less for what the king thought about John.

It is, that such matter regarding Herod's thinking is found in the record of Matthew. As taken from his written matter in his chapter 14:5 it states, "and he would have liked to have put him to death, but he feared the people because they regarded him as a prophet". Also, there is found in the record of Luke, the same matter but only similarly described. Such was the situation where it is found in Luke in his chapter 3:19-20. With the people being even more afraid to say anything probably grew leap and bounds by the day. Of course, what such meant was that John was all by his self.

Yet it was that Herod wasn't about to really do anything about John. For sure it can be taken that the ruler respected the Baptist. Also, he knew that most of the people considered him a religious person as other thought him being a prophet. Then too it was that the king was aware that some people even regarded the Baptist as a most holy person even more than a prophet. So, with all of those thoughts in mind Herod must have felt that it would be better to leave the man alone. Of course, such were only his feelings, but in fact it was that they were in discord with his wife.

Now it was that the very person that Herodias hated was the very same person that her husband respected. Wow! Could there have been a ruling party of fun time discord? Those matters shown in the record of Mark surely deserve some thought. As taken from the written matter in the chapter of Mark 6:20 "it states, for Herod feared John, knowing that he was a just and holy man and protected him". Then also there are the words which describe the depth of how Herod thought.

And it is such matter is also found in the record of Mark. In the same place it is shown where the apostle continued as he stated, "and when he heard him he did many things". Those few words clearly manifest their effect on Herod to the point where he often reacted. Upon reading the statement it can easily be realized that Herod did more than just hear about what the preacher had said. The fact is, it means that Herod actually must have gone out to listen to him. It shows that Herod not only paid attention to what John was preaching but in reality actually had good feelings about the Baptist. Such also indicates that the king must have also accepted what he was teaching. Such were his feelings that they had even reached the point of fully respecting him as a holy person.

However, it is plainly evident when considering everything in the records it can only be taken that Herodias felt differently. There must have been some interesting debates in the Antipas house from time to time. Then too maybe as the days past there were even evenings of outright heated arguments. Had Herodias become not just a person full of ego but then one of vicious contempt? How filled up with hateful revenge had she become is a question to be asked? Evidently the words spoken by the Baptist against them went past the mind directly to the heart. Either way, it must have been for sure that Herodias worked on her new husband pitting him against the Baptist?

Did his staff bring the matter up from time to time reminding him of her actions as the days went by? Did they drop hints or make comments, even between each other of which the couple would have overheard?

The Great Excitignly Holy John the Baptist

For sure it was that Herodias wanted to have her revenge! But how, since she was only a queen? With Herod being the ruler what could she do? Being subject to her husband who was also the ruler, without his cooperation what could she have done?

Meanwhile with him being the husband as well as the king, then especially with him actually liking John, for her it was to be no simple task. What could she possibly do, as it was a huge obstacle beyond her capacity? Yet she was determined to get even with the Baptist. No matter who she was and would have liked to have had done the woman would get her revenge. Then too, no matter what she would have been able to do she was forced to wait. But no matter how long it would take she was determined to have her way.

Time as it was, was on her side. Yet, as days passed by, it was where as they did, her hatred for the Baptist grew and grew as it constantly with every thought ate at her. Inside the mind, Herodias must have constantly dwelled as her thoughts must have fed the hate. Then too, heated up by being forced to accept not being able to act could only have added fuel to the already burning desire for revenge. Perhaps it may have had such a hold on her that she had been acting like a boiling pot about to explode

So consumed she was that it was eating her up inside to the point where she couldn't contain the hate inside herself. But she was after all, an anxious female with a cause. Driven by hate while being cunning she plotted her schemes. Then adding to the fire had to have been John not changing his mind or his tone. Perhaps, had John not pressed the matter relative to her husband's brother it would have quieted some. But even then there were the rumors that got back to him. Maybe if it had been anyone else the situation would have even been swept under the rug, without much ado. But John wasn't much for taking a back seat, especially when such matters were publicly known. Then along with the scenario being talked about while being heated by all of the gossip, surely John was thrust into the matter.

For sure the Baptist must have been questioned again and again by the people during his preaching. And how could he have answered any different. Certainly, his actions could not have been different from what he was preaching? Being the center of attention, then because of the fiasco, he must have been quizzed as to how could Herod do such? Then also, he was probably asked whether it was ok simply because the woman was then married to a king? So, had he responded how it would have been ok simply because he was a dignitary then would the people not have asked why they couldn't do the same? Also, could John not have responded how it was ok since the man was the state authority? But then, what would the people having heard such difference, have stated?

Would not the people have claimed how they were part of the state and should be allowed to do the same? But, it was that John had already shown his position. It was that he had told Herod without any ifs that he could not have her. And for sure he couldn't simply decide to change his position. Initially perhaps he could have ignored the whole mess, as stating that it was none of his business. But then, how would he have explained such a contrary attitude to the people?

Now it was that Herod didn't want the matter to blossom into some sort of out-of-control situation. Being the king, he couldn't simply wait around then allowing the matter to get to the point where the people would have been rioting. Then to, maybe he had an even larger problem than the people. It was where he did have his new wife to contend with. Oh, how attractive, pleasant and resourceful his wife must have been. Then also ruthless as she was, Herodias probably played her husband along until the right moment.

There is no doubt from her actions that Herodias knew full well that she had her husband in a box. Now it was that she hated John for what he had said and did. But then too, she was angry with her new husband. Not only had he refused to take immediate action against John but also he even blocked his wife's subsequent schemes. So it was that she was left with just more time of waiting. But as it was, the woman was a person of power who was not used to being forced to do against her will. Such must have only fed her fires of hate. However, for the right opportunity to demonstrate her shrewdness she would be patient.

As can be detected from the written record Herodias was extremely determined to get even with John, no matter what. And most important it was that no matter how long it was to take she would wait. Sure, it was that she made several attempts but all were denied by the king.

The Great Excitignly Holy John the Baptist

It doesn't take much thinking to imagine the gossip that must have been going around. Of course, there would have been the normal talk among the people which happens over every little thing.But that matter had potential for being explosive, especially by those that only heard rumors. Plus, there was the talk among the religious leaders.

But then, surely there must have been those others like in any other civil arena where many of the players wear two faces. Although they put on the act of being a part of the king's team, they were not known to be truly friendly with Herod. Also, there were those concerned about their life. If Herod decided to take action against them where they had ever shown any agreeing with John their heads would have rolled. Then also there was Herod's royal family and their friends.Plus, there had to have been other public figures of authority that had been associated with him, of which would have said nothing.

Such was his reputation that regardless of what the king did they would have said nothing of which could have been taken as contrary. Now it is where they too must have had their own type of gossip. How would such not have easily expanded into the ugly, vicious jokingly kind? Would that type of gossip, not also have been directed in a fashion about his wife? Would there not have been the jokes and gossip that made fun of the king's wife, as well as the king himself? Now it was that even though such talk may have been in fun, as it got back to Herodias certainly she wouldn't have found it amusing. Would such derogatoriness heard only indirectly have added fuel to the heat of her hatred?

What a hot time in the town some of evenings must have been in the social arenas. But who was the person that got more talked about? Was it Herod that did the wrong or his wife that caused the wrong? Or was it John that called to the surface their wronging? Either or, consideration must be given the high level of public officials involved. Every day that passed such matters must have stimulated some quite amusing conversations in the social arena. Was the king going to act? If so what would he do? There was no doubt during that time quite an explosive situation existed where tempers often flared up.

It is construed by most that what John had said was directed at Herod. Such were the words used that they were strong and direct. Yet along with the manner in which they were used, how would they not also have directly affected Herodias? Surely, she would have taken such as affronts on her person. Especially it was her being unlawfully married to the king with everyone then hearing about it. What was she thinking? As a woman caught in a triangle of religious adultery what could she think? What hateful thoughts must have run through her mind? Then also the same would have been thought by Herod.

Would she ever take matters into her own hands? How often did she act in some forceful fashion contrary to her husband's position? These may have been some of the gossip questions going around. But whether there was one or two, what difference did it make? For sure all of the innuendos, slight remarks and gossip somehow found their way back to the team of Herod and Herodias. How would such talk not have bothered her? Then to, there was her daughter.She probably helped to feed the hate as she agreed with whatever her mother said. If all of that wasn't enough, there was the rest of their family and friends to contend with. A heated circumstance it must have been that was soon to boil over.

Day in and day out the king's arena must have been more than just a conversation area. As it was, with all of the wide spread talk being exaggerated, the daily tempers of each must have been soaring. Then too with nothing else to rival the matter their tempers may have even reached all time highs on some days.

What would the type of talk at the synagogue and temple have been like? Would such have been similar to casual type heard in the shopping areas? Maybe such had been the worst at the temple, for there it was where everybody was about everybody else's business. Why not, as although Herod was the king his action was also one of religious content. Then to there may have been the ugly stuff where their daughter was drawn into the gossip. Then also there would have been much discussion between the various close by neighbors. But it may be taken as most probably at the market places, where the big gossip centered. Yet those ugly rumors seem to find their way around even the most unlikely places.

Whether Levites or Publicans, Pharisees, priests or common folk everyone had to eat. And where there is found food and beverages are there not found people who just like to be sociable? Don't they enjoy the simple pleasures of talking while spreading gossip?So it is that where there is talk there is sure to be found the usual exaggerations and even added little twists. So, with important people to talk about, such must be combined the matter having religious importance, New or twisted old gossip must have found new waves every day.

With the atmosphere in the area all a buzz, a person could probably have even felt the tenseness that was surely building. Even where there was talk about other things, no matter how significant the item the matter of the ruler's adultery had to find its place. If information related to the couple, for sure it got talked about. And whether it was a small matter or trivial, correct or incorrect it probably got blown out of proportion. There were no newspapers or radios to spread the word.

So, as it was, talk and discussion was how the word got around. And for sure people just love to talk about others. Especially it is when the subject matter is juicy. And then with their having a daughter all is left to the imagination of just how low some of the gossip got. Yet, those type of subjects as well as the subject matter were of a different nature. During that time period such was not the normal type of subject matters found in daily conversations. Those were hot matters about high people in authority of high places. So, with the matter being such a hot subject, especially among the common folk, why would there not have been the talking about whether there was to be some kind of action by the people? Then too, would they see Herodias have her day? Or, would they all end up rejoicing in seeing John have his day?

Would Herodias find a way to assert her full-blown hatred? Then too, would she so connive as to show her husband and king, who was really the boss? And then as far as Herod was concerned, would he find himself in a situation where he would be forced to act? Even where such action would be against his own will? Of course, John was just going along day to day preaching as if nothing out of the ordinary was going on. Why didn't the couple simply listen and make things correct according to religious custom and traditions? Was there that much ego mixed with her hatred?

Meanwhile the Baptist wasn't the type of person that had any time for gossip or arguing about civil matters. Also, it was that political gains or position was not of his interest. Continuing his mission for the Messiah was the only path John was interested in following. Now it was that Herodias was the granddaughter of Herod the Great and being a party to the civil leader would she not have been spoiled? Then also it was that she was the daughter of Aristo ulus. Being of high stature in Egypt with her being the daughter such may have led her to develop big aspirations. But maybe as time moved on, it played on her mind of her getting older. Such may have been where it affected her where she could have really gotten impatient.

Young and pampered, would Herodias not have had dreams of being a queen? Perhaps some ego became mixed with her being impatient. Then especially when having all that royalty around while she was married to her uncle, her desire for power must have really soared. For sure, upon some consideration of all of those rich relatives she had, there could not have been any want for anything. Especially when added their high political positions. But when people have everything as far as having all the worldly possessions, where does it stop? Does it just drive the person to crave for more power or money? Could there not have been a heavy driving need for an influential position of authority?

With her mind set, had vanity taken over? Had she become obsessed with an overwhelming desire for power? So, what was lacking for this woman out to set the world on fire? Well, as it was she was a person that needed attention but most important she needed a position of more than direct influence. However, her uncle though of influence was not of the elite kingly ones leaving her still on the outside. In fact, he was not even one of the high-ranking type officials that could have provided the luxuries along with the power she craved. Wow! Such a change of status for her must have been a really big letdown.

Even though her husband Philip had his responsibilities such just didn't open the kind of doors she was seeking. So, what was it that she could she have done? Well as it was, there came the time where her big opportunity presented itself. Suddenly out of nowhere her rescuer was on the scene. With a white stallion, a king's crown, out of a cloud of dust and hearty hi you reigning, her hero arrived. So as not to leave anything to chance, while also not wanting to waste any time, the woman of ego distress quickly grabbed the chance. Of course, what it meant was ruining the life of the man she was already married to. But then since she was of such royalty, perhaps she didn't care anything about the really important things of her marriage. It was that the woman had her eye spent on someone with position of real power.

So, it was not to waste any time she moved to take advantage of it. Of course, unbeknownst to her was that it would be where Philip would eventually see to her down fall. But that was not to be until many years later. And so it was that Herodias finally found her way to the big time.

Her big move came when she married into the royalty of Herod Antipas. He being the son of Herod the Great had plenty of power along with all of the prestige that went with it. However according to Jewish law, he had acted in direct violation of their law. As it was the big problem was that her first and real husband was still alive. Not just alive was he, but the man was healthy. Of course, with her not caring, why should her future husband show any care? Her position then getting married to one of ruling authority was the big move she had waited for. And as it turned out it was just the kind of power position Herodias was looking for.

So it is, as the matter goes, the royal couple lived happily ever after. Well, almost, that was until the Baptist came along. So, there it was and such a small problem he was. At first they probably attempted to sweep it under the rug making little of it. After all, she had only married that Antipas fellow, all the while knowing that his brother was still alive. But the problem really wasn't so small as such an act had been done not only against morality but against the religious laws. Now it was that the Baptist had raised the level of the problem as he had pushed it out from under the rug to being very big. John's direct personal actions caused the couple to have such a situation that it was broadcasted across the country side.

Such was it a wrong, that the situation can even be found in the record of Mark. As taken from the written matter in his chapter 6:17-18 it states, "for Herod had sent and taken John, and bound him in prison, because of Herodias, his brother Philip's wife, whom he had married. For John had said to Herod, it is not lawful for thee to have thy brother's wife". Now it is where the situation was considered of very high importance. So much so was their situation noted important that very similar words are also found recorded in Luke at 3:19. Then also the very same can be found as recorded by Matthew, where such matter is found in his chapter 14:3.

People are always in a hurry to grab whatever it may be that pleases them. So also, it is they do when reading where such action may even be reckless. Tending to skip over things that don't seem important, they may miss the emotion or feelings of individuals at the time such matter was written about. Such exercise may have been extremely substantial as causing the missing of any comprehension of the feelings or emotions also disables from understanding mind sets. But once the matter is skipped over, such critical matter is lost. Even if it is about people that may have been close to them people just don't pay attention.

If flags are not waving and guns are not going off or other exciting action is not happing readers seem to move over matter. What that all means is that if there isn't anything that seems really exciting, people would simply pass over the matter It would have been almost as if the matter or situation wasn't even there. Tis a shame, as they may gain the story, but lose the substance. But then each person reads differently looking to realize different objectives. It is here to, where people pay little, if any attention to the short phrases

Wherefore it is that if people tried writing with the type of means that was available back in those times, perhaps there would be more understanding why there aren't the long literary innuendoes and descriptive wordings. Also, if they were living under the same kinds of conditions, maybe those persons would have even a little more respect for what was written. So, it is here, that reading between the lines is not only helpful but absolutely essential to gain full comprehension.

It is understanding what the apostles may have been trying to tell. Such is exemplified by taking in the phrases available which may portray a good picture of Herodias. Was she very attractive? Perhaps there is no written description of her. But, considering in depth the circumstances such may provide a good clue. Since she was taken from one brother by another such must suggest that she must have been at least good looking. Especially, such must be considered since the brother whose wife was taken from was still living and healthy.

Also, it was where she must have had a way with words. Then to, maybe she was also highly devious. Those matters, although not specifically stated may actually be realized by putting together what is shown in the records. Written matter by the apostles, in their gospel's information is provided in the records. However, such written matter is not all substantial enough for that first visual. A matter of combining what was expressed with other depicted matter is necessary.

Then along with that matter using some thought process applying reality should allow a good understanding. In the record it is depicted where Mark tells of just how much hatred Herodias was carrying around. In his chapter 6:19 as taken from the written matter it states, "Herodias laid snares for him (John) and would have liked to put him to death, but she could not". Wow, such words of power would hardly apply to a person that had feelings of only feeling bad or throwing a temper tantrum. Rather, it is that those were words which can only be taken as expression of much hate along with revenge seeking.

Unfortunately, there isn't a lot of written detail to go on in the record regarding the personal relationship that existed between the king and his wife. Wherefore it is that without such detailed information it is most difficult to arrive at a true and clear picture of the couple's relationship matters. Such personals as trust and respect they may have had for each other would have greatly been a benefit. But then also the same applies to matters of distrust along with just putting up with. And in considering the situation at hand such things matter. Therefore, it is that any and all information that can be found must be used in a manner to combine it in order to realize a truer understanding of what the apostles were describing.

Fair attention must be given to the fact that those were very hard and difficult times and to do any less would not do the writing apostles any fair justice. An example is the word snares. It is not just the word itself but rather the significance as to what it implies. Also, what helps is that it is stated in the plural which directly signifies determination. Not only that it implies more than once but in the context as used it manifests the implication of many times. Most important is that the word shows where there was intentional planning and not just some whim that happened at the moment. Those matters are most important because they provide a reasonable picture of just what kind of people the couple was.

The Great Excitignly Holy John the Baptist

What would have really helped would have been the noting of some remarks from some of the people in the groups or crowds along with the kind of persons. Such would have provided more clarity as to what the people in general were thinking.Not only thinking about each of the rulers but also about John. But considering the lack of writing material available it is in today's world a lot remains to the imagination. Highly significant is how the word in the plural clearly manifests what type of people John was up against. Yet, what would have really helped would have been the noting of some remarks from some of the people in the groups or crowds along with the kind of persons. Such would have provided more clarity as to what the people in general were thinking not only about each of the rulers but also about John.

Considering the lack of writing material available it is in today's world a lot remains to the imagination.

CHAPTER 19.

Would She Spring Like a Cat, Out in the Open Attacking a Mouse?

About that substantial information of one phrase found in the written record of Luke. As taken from the written matter in the chapter of Luke 3:19 it states, "but Herod the tetrarch, being reproved by him (John) concerning Herodias, his brother's wife, and concerning all the evil things that Herod had done". For sure it is, that the statement provides not only a substantial amount of detail but that which is significant. Though only of a few words, it is that those few words in the phrase are most sufficient.

One must take the time to put them together, then compare in perspective with the others to realize how strong enough they are to allow a clear picture. First, there is the fact that Herodias was able to latch on to Philip's own brother. Then there are those substantially descriptive words, "evil things that Herod had done". Then it is that notice should be taken at what Mark in his chapter 6 did not say. It is that the apostle did not state such things as, tried to trap in conversation or attempted to embarrass him. Nor did he apply any other words that would have indicated only a one- or two-time effort. But in fact, it is, that Mark clearly used those words, "laid snares".

Those two words could only have meant at least several times. Plus taking in context the way the two were used they clearly establish intended planning as opposed to just some hit and miss attempts. Furthermore, it is that he clarified just to what extent the word snares fully meant. Such is in his other words of the same phrase. Notice should be taken where in the very middle of the phrase what Mark stated. Highly significant is the phrase as taken from the record of Mark states. "and would have liked to put him to death." How much more defining of an attitude could he have written about the couple than what he stated?

In referring to Herod's term, "putting him to death" the words make clear what the meaning of snares, in reference to Herodias was. Then if not, what else could have been stated to emphasis the couple's attitudes? However, with regards to what Luke wrote, it may be a little harder to grasp. However, when it is that both phrases are combined it sort of completes a picture. At first read it could seem that what Luke had wrote in the simplest of words, "but Herod the tetrarch, being reproved by him concerning Herodias, his brother's wife", may be only a little.

Actually, the simple sentence by itself in its contents could actually be taken out of context as mediocre. However, when combined with what Mark stated it is easy to see how it paints an interestingly strong picture of hate. Reproved, as stated may be easily overlooked, yet, when considering the sentence, it is that it strongly engages over time bent up emotions. Now when that is added to with what Mark stated, the word reproved surely takes on a much very strong intended meaning.

Excitement must have stirred around the throne when it was where Herodias was finally able to show her fangs. With only herself in mind she reached into her daughter and husband's heart. So much was her cunning that she was able to cause the king to be in an uproar. But it would be his own loss of control that he would regret the rest of his life.However, it was that Herodias was to have her day, regardless of her husband's feelings. Maybe some women would have just ignored John, putting his actions behind them, as mere part of the lower people. Perhaps other women may have told John not to bother them and go preach somewhere else. Then perhaps others may have tried to pay certain guards to escort him away along with a threatening message.

Maybe some women would have even cared for their husband enough to give more understanding of how much discord he would have caused them. Would they have not considered that they had better things to do rather than get involved, arguing with just another person? Especially a person who was actually one of their king's subjects? But with Herodias, such was neither of them, as she was married to the king and it was that her royal fangs would be felt. Was not the sinfully life style matter of the couple more than what John had been preaching? Did the Baptist say anything to them in any of their public meetings? Did he ever meet them in private where he may have really upset her by relating her to paid for types of professions? And then did he chastise Herod for abusing his office while enforcing his will among the people?

The Great Excitignly Holy John the Baptist

Surprisingly it is, yet the fact of the matter is that as found in the record, Herod actually enjoyed listening to John during his preaching. All of this matter may be really very interesting material. Such may be especially fascinating since it was that John the Baptist was only supported by the commandments. After all it was those of which he had been preaching. Now it is there is no record noting of how or where from, John received his learning. So how was it that he had so much knowledge that brought crowds? Evidently, whatever it was that he had it was so powerful that it was more than sufficient enough to denounce the royal couple publicly. Then too his verbiage must have been not only capable but also powerful. This can be deduced since the couple evidently was unable to refute any of John's words.

Yet it is that in all of the written records there is nothing that depicts where any of the Pharisees or Sadducees rendered any assistance to the Baptist whenever he had confronted the royal couple. How would such earnest feelings for John by Herod not have ballooned his wife's antagonized hatred for John? Oh, how at the same time the queen's attitude regarding John must have catered a steady feeling of anger against her husband. Another way to look at it is whether she would have liked his good feelings about the Baptist? Even more so, how it must have been especially when John would have criticized the king while also his wife was present. After all, such measure would have plainly put her in a most highly embarrassing situation.

Direct strong words by the Baptist may have only have left her being labeled as a hoar. Then too, what may have been asserted, was it in front of a group of authorities or while standing with a crowd of people? Either way, there must have been at least one situation where John had been forced to say something in public. Not only where one or two people were around but actually where there was more than half a dozen.If the Baptist had unexpectedly screamed loudly his words, would such not have created a surprisingly alarming situation? Such it was that particular time where it had embarrassed the king's wife before the public.

What elevated the alarm to her was that she was not one of the usual people of the town. Herodias was the king's wife and as such she couldn't allow being addressed as such. And who was he, some poor preacher? Most likely after the first occurrence, any contacts between the three must have turned any disliking by her into a deep hatred. Of course, there was her ego and self righteousness, but then it was that in her position she was allowed to carry any attitude she felt like. After all she was able to enjoy the status of being attached to the king's throne. Such was not her being as a mere relative or servant but in fact she was the man's wife.

No doubt it was that from that time on she would use her position to the maximum. It was where she took every advantage of every moment she had for playing on her husband's ego. Would she not have constantly reminded him of his authority? How often would she have mentioned his high status, then being insulted by that raggedy old man? Such may have been her strategy as hoping to be able to coax her husband into confining John. Then too, if she could perhaps persuade him even to dispose of the Baptist. Maybe eventually it would be through his will directly, but if not, then perhaps it would come down to her using other means. Then too, maybe it would be where she would use her skill to cause his action.

With those things constantly on her mind would it not have been just a matter of time for her to act? Truly it was that Herodias was determined, but in her intelligent, yet hatred way she was patient. Daily she bided her time waiting and watching for that right day. And then, when the right situation presented itself, she would spring into action.

Like a Hawk going after its prey, she would pursue as she would make her move one way or another. With her it was all about her being able to entrap her husband in some sort of a scheme. After all he was the king and she needed either him to use his authority or give his cooperation. Would she spring like a black widow out in the open attacking roach? Or would she carry out some plan in secret that might even involve others? But, whatever type of plan she could find to work she would execute. Now it must have been that as time went on she must have realized that in order for her to be get satisfaction it would have to be where she would be able to demonstrate her hold on her husband.

Therefore, it was where the set up would have had to have been of such thorough entrapment where it would actually force her husband to act against his own will. Meanwhile, it was that John must have been aware of her feelings. Surely if the Baptist didn't recognize them, his followers that were aware would have warned him. Now it was with John being void of any religious authorities backing, along with his having no political ties, he truly was all alone. All by his self there was actually nothing he could do. Void of any civil authority the Baptist could not have taken any kind of legal action. His direction though was solid as he maintained his position regarding the couple's illegal married state. All the while he carried on his mission spreading the word of the Messiah.

Wherefore, since John was preaching the commandments, which included matters pertaining to marriage, questions from the people must have constantly arisen. Also, if it was that his teachings were about the matter of loyalty to one's partner how would the crowds have reacted? What would he have said about the ruling couple? Did Herodias not owe some loyalty to Philip? And then, should John have been questioned by the people regarding the matter of morally staying married to her partner, how would he have answered? Then especially when he would have been preaching the subject as from the commandments, what then?

John could hardly have been teaching those things to the people then going to give a blessing to the royal couple. Such would have been contrary to all morally ethical teaching. Wow! What a position he was in. And for sure, Herodias must have been fully aware of the boxed in position John had gotten himself into. So, it was from then on, it was that all Herodias had to do was just wait. And wait she did watch for the right opportunity to strike. Oh, how the days around her must have been long and tense. People purposely must have walked long distances around her just to avoid being in her area. What kind of thinking could be attached during that period of time to the royal couple?

Would Herod have had any similar type of edgy feelings that Zachary had encountered knowing what his wife didn't know about the forth coming pregnancy? And then what about Herodias, would she have been as bitter about her husband as Elizabeth was about hers? Was she not extremely bitter at the time when Elizabeth first realized of her pregnancy? What a time it must have been in the Herod home life as Herodias was often impeded by her husband. But such matters regarding the Baptist certainly didn't matter to Herodias. As can be determined from the record, for sure it was to be where she would have her day, and that was all that mattered.

On the right day at the right time, she would act where she would show her husband just what she was made of. Also, it would be where he would find out just what kind of a person she was. With every day passing, had her hatred grown to such limits where it ate at her so bad, that she couldn't even speak decently to her husband? Meanwhile such attitude had to have been easily recognized where it affected those around her. So, what was the daughter learning among such organized mayhem?

Now it was that time had quickly passed to the point where John's misfortunate time came about. Those matters of John's demise can be found in the written records of several parts of the various gospels. Such matter is shown recorded in Luke as well as the others. However, it is that he provides substantial matter that allows a good beginning. Though the paragraph is short it contains enough descriptive that can be built upon with good thinking. As taken from his written matter in the chapter of Luke 3: 19- 20 it states, "but Herod the tetrarch being reproved by him concerning Herodias, his brother's wife, and concerning all the evil things that Herod had done, crowned all of this by shutting up John in prison".

Now those words "all the evil things" are of substantial intent and meaning. They can only be taken to indicate that there were other matters of significance which Herod had done. Then there is the applying of the highly significant word "evil".Such word of power clearly indicates that the king's matters were way beyond that of being mistakes or simple wrongs. Calling Herod's other actions, beside that of lying with his brother's wife as evil, raises the man's wrong doing beyond what would be considered as mere simple mistakes or easy errors.

But of course, it was that John was speaking from the religious side of law. Evidently as can be understood by the record, Herodias had no interest in such. As far as she was concerned there was only one way to be, which was to be her way. Choices were always many as either it was her way, no way or the highway. But with John being all wrapped up in prison it posed a problem. Her long-awaited opportunity must have seemed as if it was getting further away as no one had brought any serious charges against the Baptist. And wow, was she angry. Stymied and forced to wait, yet she was ever ready to take advantage.

Anxious the queen was where it would only take the right kind of moment.

The right time it would he for her to make her move. Well, it is as shown by the words depicted in the written record the determined woman kept on trying. But her past efforts resulted in no success which must have only magnified her hatred. With all of her previous attempts having failed, would her hate not have grown to high levels? Now with all of the bitterness growing by the day embroiled in her anger from her disappointments with her husband what would Herodias have been thinking of? However, as things go it was to be nothing of what she had planned. Rather it was that fate would lend its ugly head.

Such hate and bitterness had overtaken the woman reaching an extreme level. Such was where Herodias the mother even brought her young daughter into her vicious web. Of all the times it was that one period in time, when it was Herod's birthday. For whatever reason there was, the king decided to do something big. So it was that he wanting a really big event Herod would have it as not a simple man celebrating his birthday but rather, as the king throwing the party. Evidently, he intended for it not to be the usual family and immediate friends gathering. No! Being all happy about something he wasn't about to stop there. Nothing in the records could be found to indicate where there was any significant reason for the exceptionally large affair. So it must be that the king just had a spur of the moment idea.

Rather than the usual family type party Herod was to have a big occasion where he would splurge. He would have the most of authority type people invited along with the best of entertainment possible. His wife was probably in the midst somewhere overseeing everything even until the time of the party. Then along with providing her directions Herodias would be watching out for the right moment where she could act. It was an occasion for the king where things started going joyfully as planned. Yet it is as some times the happy gets carried way, especially when the wine starts flowing. Surely at one point it must have been where Herod even got to feeling his oats. Would the merriment along with quantity of wine taken have affected the king's thinking? Just as with other people that have a little too much too soon, the king's control of his senses may have wavered. What a fun hot time in the ole town it was to be where even heads could roll.

Actually, it would be so hot in fact that the guests would never forget that evening. Most probably it was then during his weakest moment when Herodias found her heart taking control. Finally, after all of that waiting it came to be presented to her the right time where the king's wife was able to apply her treacherous cunning. Of course, she was sharp with all wits about and, it is that such matters are actually found in the record. Perhaps one line there and another line somewhere else doesn't tell the full story. Also, it may be that perhaps one paragraph there and another paragraph somewhere else doesn't give enough details for it to be juicy.

A full reading of one of the apostle's texts in detail combined with another provides sufficiently able matter. Such combined information of substantial detail allows an explicit comprehension of the horror that filled the party. Also, the information fully reveals the wicked hate filled mind of Herodias. Most people think only of what she had done to the Baptist but overlook the other people and circumstances. By skipping around or not taking the time to give full consideration a lot of people fail to realize just how devious she was. No kind thought whatsoever, did Herodias demonstrate, as she pitted the members of her own royal family against each other.

Motivated by bitterness simply to satisfy her own selfish hate she grabbed the long-waited opportunity. Mark the apostle made note of just how extraordinarily large the king had in mind for the party by describing some of the titles of those who were in attendance. As such, it is by the titles is can be concluded not only that there were ones of high ranking but also that there were many. As taken from the written matter of Mark in 6: 21 it states, "and a favorable day came when Herod on his birthday gave a banquet to the officials, tribunes and chief men of Galilee". And would not those of the higher ranking not brought along their assistants? Galilee was not some road stop or a place of a few tents, but a main city.

Now when people were invited by the king there were no excuses.

The Great Excitignly Holy John the Baptist

Everyone jumped since such would have been liken to an order. Also, to be considered is that since the occasion was the king's birthday they all knew very well that only the best of food and beverage would have been served. Surely, no one would have dared to insult the king as not to show up. But then considering the refreshments along with the amount of food then being free, who would not have wanted to go?

What did favorable day mean? Is it misleading, as some people quickly jump to wrong assumptions? Such words for most people would mean that they reflect to Herod as being his birthday, but that may be a fallacy. Since there were no telephones or electronic means of sending messages quickly, such would have required the party to be planned more than just several days in advance. Perhaps it may have been better had Mark attached the word fateful, so that it would have read a fateful favorable day. What in fact Mark may have been referring to was how it was a favorable day for Herodias. There are things in the record that shows how it was not the usual every year family only affair. Rather it was a celebration which was put on by the king himself.

Even the words as stated by Mark dictated that Herod was the person that supplied everything. As he depicted in his record it was not some sandwich and beverage to go party. Rather as depicted, it was a full-blown banquet. Now it is that such descriptive word is full of intent as well as being substantially definitive. It can only mean the best of everything that only a feast could provide. So also, there had to have been much entertainment. Would there not have been many dancing men and women along with persons doing acrobatics? Would magicians able to do what they could do, and strong men displaying their abilities not also be there to perform? Then too, since it was all about the king, surely they would have been only the best that could have been found. Also, there would have been musicians playing the cymbals, drums and pipes along with the servants and guards.

So, it was the feast occurred where there would have been the best of food, meat, rolls and beverages as well as the best of everything being plentiful. Since it was the Kings birthday it can be taken that the best of everything had to be made available even down to the servants. It was to be that kind of a special day for everybody. Everyone that participated, even the guests, would have put on their best attire. Those that gave a performance would have showed their best in what they did, from the performers to the cooks to the guards. What a hot time in the ole castle it was to be for the married royal couple and guests. Also, to be present there was the daughter of Herodias.

Of course, her daughter did her best as always only had her mother's best interest at heart. Tis a shame that those that wrote about the gala didn't include the niceties mentioned in the above paragraphs. However, for sure it must have been easy for those apostles doing the writing to assume that anyone reading the matter would have understood the enormity of how it was. Surely, since the king himself was the one throwing the party there could not be any lower grades of things used or served. A party for the king thrown by the king would have only meant the best of everything.

Especially such would have been since he had important guests who were invited. Then too it must be considered that such planning was not a mere coincidence but to be of importance to cause the event. For the king it would have been a great time to make a big impression on people he needed on his side. Would such have not made sense, as for what other purpose would he have invited them? So having the best of everything being served would have at least helped to do the job.

Now, where the guests having received their invitation from the king, would not they have arrived dressed in the very best? Would not such provide an opportunity for the king to discuss matters of his secret plans with those special guests? Especially if he had of such mind to discuss political moves would the situation not present itself a favorable? So, with all of the king's good intentions along with all the king's men of making merry for so many people, it turned out to be an event beyond his wildest imagination.

Also, it became historical because the king's party having such a prize must have given all of the people in attendance something to gossip about for an awful long time. And who wouldn't spread the gossip?

Wow, what a joyous day of happy celebration it was to be. What a time in history of what history the party would make. Surely it is that history would tell that it wasn't to be like any other birthday party. For sure it was not like any other recorded birthday celebrations that other kings had thrown over the centuries. Eventually the day of cheer had arrived when all hoopla broke loose. So much was to happen that even the devil may have had his fun.

PART XI.

THE KING'S BIRTHDAY PARTY.

Chapter 20. For Herodias, it was the Type of Situation She Had Been Hoping For.

It was the time when it was that a royal event was called for. Such majesty it would have had to have ended in the desired objective which the king wanted. With all of the high officials in attendance it can only be taken that its main purpose was that of making a great impression. Perhaps he had some intention of presenting a military or civic plan of operation. However, whatever it was, the reason could not be fully determined as there was nothing that could found that suggested any mention of any specific big motive.

Yet, the number as well as the ranking of the high officials clearly indicates that there was a cause. With those special guests in attendance clearly indicates most probable it is that the king must have had something in mind. What the event included as far as people and other matters clearly manifests that the party was not simply one of a birthday, especially since the king himself was the one that required it to be. Tis a shame that in Matthew's written description he left out a lot of descriptive that could have been used.

Such extra information possibly could have helped to understand a lot of the interactions between the host and the guests. However, with his materials along with another there is enough to allow some arriving of some reasonable conclusions. An example of this is their daughter, as to whether her dancing was planned or just an act of the moment. Understanding her mother's attitude why couldn't her act have been planned?

Although both Matthew and Mark mentioned the action unfortunately, they also left out too many factors. Depicted, it is taken from the written record of Matthew in 14:6.

The Great Excitignly Holy John the Baptist

Matthew wrote, "but on Herod's birthday the daughter of Herodias danced before them, and pleased Herod". Now considering her young age, Herodias would not have told her daughter what she had in mind. Even of importance it was that the occurrence was similarly recorded by Mark. As taken from his written matter in chapter 6:22 it states, "and Herodias' own daughter having come in and danced, she pleased Herod and his guests." Of some importance is to consider the way people in authority are as here is a question that could be asked.

Is it that Salome really did please his guests, or rather, who would have spoken any words against the girl's dancing? Even if she was terrible, who would have spoken up to say so, especially since she was the daughter of the king? Perhaps it was well after the eating when the wine was flowing. No doubt that Herodias in her cunning was aware of how the minds would have been softened by the wine. Especially knowing it would have affected her husband's will. Then to, with the wine, along with the cheering of the guests how would such not have influenced Herod's thinking? Should their daughter not be having been that good, when in fact initially perhaps he felt the same, but had her beauty in mind, then what?

In continuing, it is that the record depicts how the opportunity arrived of which Herodias had waited for. It seems as though; taken from the record that she held back doing anything of making any move until the precise moment favored her.Now it was that the daughter danced before everyone. Perhaps it was more of the cheering along with the wine that got to the king. As taken from the written matter of Matthew in 14:7 it states, "and the king said to the girl, ask of me what thou willets and I will give it to thee. Whereupon he promised with an oath to give her whatever she might ask of him." Trying so hard to please everyone while a having a good time, it would suggest that the man simply didn't give thoughts to what he was saying. Surely it was that the flowing wine affected his thinking. Would Herod being the king have stated such had he been sober?

For sure he would have been generous in his sober way but at the time such was not the case. More to be considered here was that he failed to give thought of who was there to take advantage. Such matter can be ascertained by what was depicted by Mark.Shown by Mark, was not only the same, but of a little more detail. It is in Mark 6: 23, wherein as taken from the written matter it states, "and he swore to her, whatever thou dost ask, I will give thee, even though it be the half of my kingdom." Wow, who could imagine such a statement from the king?

How would such powerful wording not even have stunned the guests? Would any king in his sober mind have ever stated such in front of so many people? Yet, who wouldn't have been impressed with that offer? Had not Herod really opened the door for whatever? What a temptation it was! Who could have resisted taking advantage of even part of such an offer? Wow! Such a generous intention, and guess who was there to take advantage of the moment? There should be no doubt that Herod would have had no real intention of giving away half of his kingdom. Perhaps he said it while feeling so happy, yet erroneously under the impression that such wouldn't have even been considered by anyone.

But then considering matters of the heart, who wouldn't make such a presentation of half his kingdom, especially if it was their marriage partner's daughter? After all, would it not have all remained in the family? However, as fate would have it, for his marriage partner Herodias, it was just the right opportunity in the right place, at the right time. Stunned by what she had just heard of which had just been stated, the woman may have even felt a sense of ecstasy. Upon realizing that for a change, suddenly she was in control. For Herodias, it was the type of situation she had been hoping for as well as had been waiting for. Anxious while being filled with joy she must have been like a cat having its meal within its claws. Oh, how the exuberance flowed.

Meanwhile it was that her daughter had gotten all caught up in the excitement of the moment. Was it the excited atmosphere or her young age? More likely it was the combination of both where she may have actually become delirious. Especially, having received the loud ovation from the guests, how would such not have affected such a young person? Would such adulation not have mentally swept the young girl away into a mental bliss?

Perhaps such may have even taken her to the point where it raised her ego to new levels? Attention and more attention there was to the point where so much was Salome about herself. Just maybe it was truly where the young girl had not realized the full extent of what Herod had sworn to her. As it was in effect, what Herod had done in front of the entire crowd was that, he being the king had given his word. Not only had he given his word but then as being sworn to, that he would give her whatever it was she asked without limitations. Surely a lot of people would have known what to ask, as would have taken full advantage to advance their own lively hood.

In the normal way of things that are done with offers there is always the small print or some sort of restrictions. However, in the moment, it was that the big catch then was that there were no restrictions or ifs to be applied. Surprisingly to everyone such an offer was not to be found favorable to the person making the offer. As it was, for him it would be a big catch of loss rather than gain. Wow! Of all things not to do, it was that Herod forgot to attach any limitations. Now it is that since the king left his oath wide open stating, "anything", such could only have meant that there were no restrictions what so ever. For most people such an opportune moment may have been grabbed to be used for improving their life style.

Awesome it was, for the dancing girl's mother it was just the right words, from just the right man, at just the right time, in the right place. So, what did the daughter, who was all hyped up, of Herodias do? Was she so blissfully carried away by all of the excitement along what had been presented her that she was not herself? Could the girl have been so cheerful that she couldn't wait to allow her mother to participate? Surely, the girl not feeling greedy or selfish, while rather happy, couldn't wait to actually give the prize to her mother. After all, at her young age, being single while not owning anything, what would she have thought of asking for?

Had she been brain washed with her mother's hatred? Had she even considered such before speaking to her mother? Probably not yet, she probably made her mother happy beyond description. Maybe it may have been in the full excitement of the moment, where it even caused Herodias to wet her pants. Why not, after all of the waiting along with putting up with all of the hindrances she received from her husband? Then too why wouldn't she also not have been in a state of bliss? Wow! And there it was her daughter provided her the means. Such was the using of person opportunity she craved for. But did the daughter know what contrariness would have been in her mother's mind? Such a happy occasion and full of high merriment only good feelings were displayed.

So how could the young girl have even thought of anything that would have been sad? Yet it is where so much closeness can be determined between the mother and daughter in the written record of Mark. And it is such closeness enabled the occasion to be turned upside down as shown in his record. As taken from the written matter in his chapter 6:4 it states, "then she went out and said to her mother, what am I to ask for"? Clearly it is most obvious that the girl could have asked for multiple things that could have gone to both or anything even to have been solely for herself. But her mother being woman was in another section evidently behind a wall. However, maybe it was really without giving any thought where the girl simply acted on her emotion.

All things taken into consideration it seems as though she didn't fully comprehend the wickedness that was in her mother's mind nor the magnanimous offer she had been given. But as for her mother, well that was a different matter. Full of hatred, the female adult fully understood what had been given her daughter. Now for sure it was that Herodias wasn't about to waste such a big opportunity. As such was presented to her, all she had to do was think, then speak. Even though it meant being so selfish, but then with her, bitter hatred had to come first, even before her daughter.

It was that the hatred burning inside Herodias would take priority over everything and everyone. Whatever she could do for herself, to satisfy her lust for revenge would be done regardless of who it would hurt. Such hate she had been carrying it was that the opportunity was simply too big. Such it was in her mind that even at the expense of denying her daughter, she would have her way. But what was most selfish was that she had totally acted in meanness. Swiftly moving with the queen's adrenaline pushing hard she strived to take advantage of the situation. The event one thing, but the mother seizing the opportunity to use her daughter solely to satisfy her hatred anger!

Wow! How much was her hate built up pushed by ego? Her instructions to her daughter, was most direct, solely for only satisfying her own hatred revenge. Then as she capitalized on the opportunity that was presented, it was at the same time that Herodias satisfied her own ego. While the mother dug in her claws she prevented her daughter from realizing any type of benefit for herself. How great it was for her of how young her daughter was for surely, she must have had no idea as to how her mother would respond.

It is highly doubtful that the excited young girl would have thought of what her mother was going to do but, for sure she must have been astonished as it wasn't the normal way with her mother. It was just that quick where the king's wife didn't even hesitate. Her exuberance must have been over bubbling. Right away it was Herodias responded to her daughter with her demanding voice. Very simple it was that which was stated, but it really hit home. There were no such things of pleasant appreciations by the daughter as, please daddy, or would you please, or any other kind of nice words showing appreciation. Rather it was just the rough statement so ordered by her mother. Such personal matter can be found depicted in the written record of Mark.

As taken from his written matter in 6:24 it states, "and she said, the head of John the Baptist." Perhaps it is that such was all that Mark had been told from his source, or maybe it was that he forgot some of the information which was provided to him. But the phrase does ring of a mean intention. However, even though the phrase says a lot, it is that Matthew provides not only more, but words of better description. Found in his record is matter which provides much more detail especially when added to what Mark wrote. Taking into consideration both they in turn allow more of an understanding of the cunning as well as the hatred carried by Herodias. Plus, it also allows for a more thoughtful true consideration of the attitude of the daughter.

At her young age she would have been much more respectful of which the phrase absolutely denies. How cold, the short phrase that consisted of only a few words is. Yet it is that those few words fully depict the woman's mind set. Not only does it show her anger but also how much control she had over her daughter. As taken from the written matter of Matthew in chapter 14:8 it states, "then she, at her mother's prompting said, give me here on a dish the head of John the Baptist." How simply easy Matthew made it seem using the word, "prompting".

It must be given thought as to the natural to be considered, the feelings of Herodias at that moment. After all of her times of trying being thwarted, then along with all of her time spent waiting, most surely there would have been more substance than a thing as prompting. After all, Herodias was not holding class as some teacher providing training on manners. Nor was she a mother that was teaching her child how to curtsey. What must be considered here is the woman's total focus of hatred vengeance. It was the moment where the cat would attack its prey. That split moment must have taken all her strength to hold back her natural tendency from wanting to scream out her order. A person probably could have cut the atmosphere of revenge with a knife. Here it is shown in the record by those statements which stresses on what had been said by Herodias. There are no descriptive words noting the conduct of Herodias or the vocal tone she used, found in the record. However, it is how the phrase standing by itself demands a tone of authoritative assertion.

Would not her innocent daughter have been thinking of a new dress or jewelry? Or perhaps, she may have wanted a new horse or other things. But wow, was she stunned having received such a cruel order from her mother. Receiving the sudden outburst which was totally void of discussion, the girl must have been taken aback. Surely the little girl was not expecting of what she heard from her mother. Especially amongst all of the jolly amusing time that had been going on. Also, it is that apparently it seems where animosity had already been prevalent between the two parents.

Such strenuous attitudes are easily able to be recognized as evident by the shortness of the phrase. Plus, it was being the only statement made. Furthermore, such horrendous words as directed by Herodias were evidently only repeated by the daughter. At the young girls age she would certainly not have thought of such a statement. Especially what must be considered is that she was not the one carrying the hate. Statements by both apostles when combined, not only depicts the innocence of the daughter, but also the quickness with which the order was put upon her. Then too by her actually duplicating the words of her mother void of any of her own depicts her displeasure with what she was doing.

Was it what the daughter did or was it how she did it? No, rather it was how quick they were presented. Then too, it is all about the words formation that was used which clearly depicts coarse arrogance. In Mark chapter 6:25 as taken from the written matter it states, "and she came in at once with haste to the king, and asked, saying, I want thee, right away to give me on a dish, the head of John the Baptist". Important here is to notice the words that are used to describe the daughter's actions.

Not only did the apostle write, at once, but also added, with haste. Do not the words at once indicate speed? Then too, does not the word haste also indicate speed. More likely it is the apostle by using both which were really not necessary was indicating attitude. No doubt that the daughter only moved under obedience to her mother's oppressive will. This wording fully indicates of the daughter's wish to get the entire scenario over with. Why not, after all there was nothing there in such action for her to enjoy?

Wow! How would the guests not have been shocked? There is nothing shown in any of the records that even remotely suggests that the situation was planned where they would have been warned of such activity. Wherefore it can only be taken that there was no time of providing warnings of what was to be. Did the king close his eyes, while hoping that his daughter would go away? Was he hoping that he really didn't hear what had been spoken? There is nothing that could be found in the records, regarding the amount of time it took for the king to make up his mind. Nor is there anything written that gives disclosed evidence of the King's initial behavior.

However, there must be some good consideration given to his poorly admitted respect for the Baptist. Then also there was the matter of his putting up with his wife's attitude. It can only be assumed how his temper must have sky rocketed. And why not, was he not embarrassed by the child's demand? One thing that presents such fact of the king's actions is that there is nothing to be found in the record indicating whether any of the chiefs or high-ranking guests attempted to intervene or stop the madness. However, the record does show that authorities and soldiers in the past alike had been going to John listening and getting baptized. But then who would even think of arguing with the mother who was married to the king? Especially it was the guests were aware of the great personality of Herodias along with her known revengeful attitude.Then who would have wanted the problem of her company?

Of course, what this simply all meant was that the king was without support. In effect, it was that Herod, even with all of his invited guests was all by his self. In that one moment, he had become the true center of attention. And for sure it was that all the eyes of everyone who was present were on him. How would he act to such a heinous situation? Would the guests have been thinking how the entire scenario was part of some sort of an act or prank? Did they really think he would do such a thing?

With the guests being fully aware that John was a holy person that the people loved, as well as the king what did they think? In effect, it was that while having all authority the king found that even with all of his invited guests he was all by his self actually being the entertainment. Oh, sure his daughter had the floor along with the attention of everyone. But once she popped the demand of what her mother had ordered there had to have been an instant silence. As if a bomb had exploded the king suddenly had not only his crown but his reputation to think of. Would the guests not have given both some thought?

Wow! What a compromising situation it was, not only for the host of the party, but also the king who in effect was the host. Yet, how would it not have been an exciting time for everyone else in the old party? Over a very short time there must have been some words spoken between the various chiefs that were there. As for sure there were the unspoken words spoken between the father and daughter. Then also there may have even been some betting going on between some of the guests. What or which way would their king decide? Surely it had to be the question of the year. A person could have cut the suspense atmosphere even with a dull blade. Would he grant his daughter in law's wish in the way she had asked for? Or would he only allow such with certain conditions?

Would the king offer other things in substitution? Maybe he wanted to rule that such was out of bounds. But then the king wasn't stupid only under the influence of the wine. Surely it must have been how the man was fully aware how it was only from his wife's wicked hatred that her daughter had gotten such demanding words. Suddenly in one moment the party had been turned into something of horror. Nothing of the kind had any of those attending ever experienced such before. But also, those in attendance may not have wanted to experience such a similar horrific event ever again. Being the king, could Herod not have had the girl thrown out of the room?

The Great Excitignly Holy John the Baptist

Until his daughter was ready to ask for something sensible could he not have had her removed? Everyone knew how the king liked John. But it was also that word had spread where the people were fully aware of the king's problem with his wife. People knew that Herodias had a problem with her husband, as he had constantly blocked her wanting to do away with John. But here it was the time where Herodias was determined to show who she was. No matter what it would take or who she embarrassed in public it was that the king's wife was determined. Not only would she win over him but important was the king's wife having her way.

Meanwhile the king caught up in the situation was fully aware of all the guests watching and waiting for his reaction. Totally stressed under the pressure of the surrounding people along with being under the influence his thinking was fully impaired. But he had to do something so it was that he catered to his wife rather than show some character of authority. Those matter of how the king responds and what he does in found in record of Matthew.

As taken from his written matter in chapter 14:9 it states, "and grieved as he was, the king, because of his oath and his guests, commanded that it be given".

It seems that Matthew may have been upset by the event as only wrote what he felt was necessary. It is obvious that he left out an awful lot of detail. Yet, while the word, grieved, by itself does not portray much detail, when combined with Herod's liking of John it provides some reasonable substance. However, it is that Mark, as shown in his record, provided a bit more information. Then when taken along with what Matthew stated it provides some reasonable emotions. His notes add for a better understanding of the king's pressures.

Such matter taken from the record shows Herod's high feeling towards his family. Not only that, but such information also reveals just how much he cared for his daughter in law. Perhaps it was the combination of the family along with the daughter's consideration that was the real pressure. Maybe it was that he gave no consideration whatsoever to what the guests may have thought. In the record of Mark at chapter 6:26 as taken from his written matter it states, "and grieved as he was, the king because of his oath and guests was unwilling to displease her."

The Great Excitignly Holy John the Baptist

So here is asked an important question. Was it his love of his daughter in law or the king worrying about what the guests may have thought that influenced his reasoning? Also, it must be taken into consideration that he knew it was all by his wife's instructions.

Yet, a most important thing here to take into consideration is that he being the king had the ruling power. Such power was in fact absolute which meant that he could have done whatever he chose to do. After all, he had no authority to answer to. It would seem most probable that the official guests would have had a limited amount of influence. Most likely it is that their presence would have been concerned about whether the king would back up his word. Either way, no matter what the situation presented, it was that Herod was the King. Yet he still had to act.

He just could not dilly dally, after all, wasn't it supposed to be a party? No doubt while Herodias was impatient, all the while, the guests must have been appalled to say the least. Would not all of them being so stunned been like statues waiting for the King's decision? But then too, the king was probably extremely astonished as the whole thing must have been beyond his belief.

Poor Herod could not believe the position his wife had put him in. There can be no doubt that the incident was actually all about his wife, as the young girl at her young age would never have thought of such a gross thing. Anger must have instantly set in upon the king. Especially once he realized how his wife had played her daughter against him. Surely anger inside the king must have hit an all-time high level. And then also to be forced to do such against someone he liked, the king must have flipped his crown. If nothing else he must have been sick to his stomach.

Suddenly the time came where finally the king made his decision. Reluctantly he gave his order where such carryings on is found shown in the record of Mark. A lack of details in the description by the apostles regarding the scene as well as not noting any of the people's reaction can only suggest the distaste of the act by the apostles. As taken from his written matter, Mark in chapter 6:27 stated, "but sending an executioner, he commanded that his head be brought on a dish, then he beheaded him in the prison." Now it is that those matters also by

The Great Excitignly Holy John the Baptist

Matthew in his record, basically depicts the same thing. As taken from his written matter in 14:10 it states, "and he sent and had John beheaded in the prison".

Meanwhile could some of the guests that were having a good time possibly have thought that it was all an act of some sort? Maybe, even the guests may have thought that the whole thing was one of the king's means of trickery fun? But how sick they must have gotten when they saw what happened. When appeared the soldier with the decapitated head, how would the guests not receive the visual shock? Such disturbing feelings must have erupted, and why not after all it was supposed to be birthday party not some day of execution. Then to even bring the unsightly bloody mess in front of everyone, what a showing of what!

Wow! As described by Matthew, he concludes the sickening event with only a few but strong words. In his chapter 14:11 as taken from the written matter it states, "and his head was brought on a dish, and given to the girl, who carried it to her mother". How gross was the scene. It must be fully noted that the daughter did not give prize to the king nor run outside with it but in fact delivered it to her mother. It was precisely what the young girl was ordered to do.

Gee whiz, it was supposed to have been the king's birthday party! Do not the words as pronounce almost sound as if the girl made a procession out of it? Perhaps at first thought such would appear, however upon recollection it is that she was merely carrying out the demands of her mother. Would the guests not have been taken aback? With blood displayed in full, along the face and hair all a mess, how ugly the entire scene had to have been.

What an unwanted, sad sickening situation the guests were forced to find themselves in. Were they all not shocked or at least disappointed that the king would have done such? Especially, being the king's own birthday party, then in front of so many guests? Yet, such it is as shown in the record where Mark presents a similar attitude. As taken from his written matter in 6:28 it states, "and brought his head on a dish, and gave it to the girl, and the girl gave it to her mother". Nothing is depicted as to the girl's reaction.

Only assumptions can be made but, it seems by the way the phrase was written that the young girl had enough of the entire evening. Such may be deduced since she had not done any more dancing. She probably couldn't wait to give the heinous thing to her mother. But at her young age it is difficult to think that she enjoyed looking at what she carried. Of course, Herodias could have cared less what her daughter thought. Her emotions must have been overwhelming as the woman realized her having satisfied her hatred revenge.

But as far as the apostles' writings of what went on along with the details, perhaps it was they were too afraid to write too much detail for fear of repercussions. However, if nothing else, for sure the king's birthday party having such a prize must have given all of the people in attendance something to gossip about for an awful long time. For sure it was that Herodias had her day. Yet, it wouldn't take too much imagination to think of some quick comments that must have been spread about the king's wife among the people.

For sure it was she had her day but what would the people have remembered about her? Especially those that were in attendance having thought of being at a happy time of celebration, what would they have thought? Then what rumors would they have spread? Would there have been joyous expressions? But for the king, what? As the record indicates Herod may have lived to regret what he had done. According to the records it is able to be noted that by his actions, Herod must have believed in the Jewish God or at least in a Supreme Being, the Creator. Such is apparently shown the writings of Matthew in his chapter 14. It must be recalled how over time the king had denied his wife to satisfy her hatred. At all times he had refused to cater to his wife's efforts to do away with John.

Then also there are the various notations found in the records. Such written matter depicts where the king actually had listened to John. As the record is reviewed in indicates that Herod not only respected the preaching of the Baptist but also liked his teachings. But isn't it also found where he actually believed John to be holy? From the writings of the apostles, it can be very well determined that well after the time of John's death it is where Herod's religious feelings can also be realized.

As taken from the reliable written matter of the apostles such can be realized. True feelings it was that Herod had for the Baptist and not only did the king have such feelings but evidently even acted on them. It was the end of the mortal life of John the Baptist and regardless of how he went for sure it was he went in style. He had the last word which is proven by the ruler's actions.Since they did not wish to do what was right they eliminated that person who was their obstacle allowing them to do as they pleased.

Sure, it was that the king's wife had her way and the king showed what he was made of being without character. Yet who at the time would have guessed, but it is that both Herod and his wife eventually found their demise under no one else but Philip. Now it is in Matthew chapter 14: 1-2 it states, "at that time Herod the tetrarch heard about the fame of Jesus, and he said to his servants, this is John the Baptist, he has risen from the dead, and that is why miraculous powers are working through him". Now, what could that mean other than Herod's belief in God?

If he was an atheist or other that didn't believe in a supreme his words would have been different. Being either one, he would never have used the word, miraculous. Why? Because it is that those persons who truly do not believe in a creator don't believe in such things as miracles. To them such matters are considered freaks of nature or coincidences. Even where there are such instances that are not able to be explained by the medical or scientific community, to them there is only the same or no answer.

Now it is where Luke portrayed the same matter as Matthew but depicted he did in only a similar fashion. As taken from the written matter of Luke in chapter 9:7-8, it states, "now Herod the tetrarch heard of all that was being done by him (Jesus), and was much perplexed, because it was said by some, John has risen from the dead." Noted it should be, that Herod disagreed. Such attitude can be taken from the written matter of Luke which depicts how the king was thinking. In his chapter 9;9 it is stated what Herod's response was, "but Herod said, John I beheaded, but who is this about whom I hear such things." In combining Herod's actions before his birthday celebration along with those at the celebration plus what he said at the party clearly evidences that he was totally swayed by what his family would say.

Sure, the king listened to what other people told him but his family evidently came first. Perhaps this is shown when combining all with what the record shows in what Mark wrote. As taken from his written matter in Mark 6:14 it states, "and King Herod heard of him (Jesus) for his name had become well known." Then continuing in Mark at 6:14 it states, "and kept saying, John the Baptist has risen from the dead, and that is why miraculous powers are working through him."

Further it was where the king showed his thinking of John as a holy person. That was shown when confronted by other persons where he responded the same way. Such mind set of the king is depicted in the written matters of Mark. In his chapter 6:15 it states, "it is a prophet, like one of the prophets, but when Herod heard this he said, it is John whom I beheaded, he has risen from the dead". From the persistence of Herod saying those things of which he said, it can reasonably be taken where he truly believed that John was a holy a person. Also, some thought must be given to the king in refusing to change his attitude about John.

Upon taking into consideration the various statements in the record it becomes evident that Herod feared eventual reprisals for the gross injustice he had done to John. Of course, it is where those along with all things written in the record bring the matter back to the question of who was John? Certainly, if the king truly and fully respected him while he was alive as a just and holy man, would he not have acted differently? For sure it would have been that he would have found favor with all of the people that believed in John's holiness.

Now it is as shown from what was taken from the record, John at all times spoke and taught of Jesus being the true and only Messiah. Wherefore, it is that those words that the Baptist spoke actually preceded Jesus Christ who was in fact the Messiah. Wherefore, as shown where it is recorded where Christ being there at the same time as John the Baptist clearly manifests that both were in fact around the same parts of the country. So, what was John's mission?

Therefore, it can only be reasonably taken that the Messiah was actually in the midst of the people all of which John was advising them. Substantially such signifies that Christ was not in some distant land across the ocean or on another planet. Such matter clearly signifies that Christ was walking and teaching among the same people that John had previously already taught. Therefore, it can only be defined that

The Great Excitignly Holy John the Baptist

John was not only Holy, but of the spirit being the Holy Messenger appointed by God to walk before the face of the Lord. Thus, in fact it was that John was walking before Him, which was in fact walking before the Lord God.

No prophet, in the sense of telling the future was the Baptist, as he fulfilled his duty to his God. And it is his duty was him being the true holy messenger of the true Messiah. This matter was even pronounced by the Messiah Himself during the time when the two met at the baptism of Jesus. Of course, to understand this it takes more than just reading the words but rather giving full understanding of what Christ had said as well as the inferences. Simply it was where John the Baptist was a true messenger as spreading the word among the people of Christ already being in their midst.

Amazing it is how people have negative thoughts about everything and everyone. Even when shown documents or written matter about anything there is always doubt. Such can be thought of where Jesus speaking to the doubters even offered an opening of the minds. Did Christ not advise them how if they didn't believe Him to believe and trust the works that He did?

But even then after seeing one miracle after another such holy goodness was forgotten the next day. Sure, it was that they always remembered the action as well as even some of the words spoken. However, the sad part is where they forget the most important matter. And it is what the purpose of the action was. Then to the significance of the words which Christ spoke got lost.

As the words about the events got spoken around what were they turned into? When the gossip and twisting rumors got done with them, what remained? Most likely it is that when such statements returned to the persons who actually witnessed such miracles they were found to be partially if not totally different as omitting a lot of what was true. And so, it was about the Baptist. For sure it is even now much easier to cast doubt or twist and omit matter to please the mind of anyone who wishes not to believe what was written. Then what does that leave? It is that this leaves the most important question. Whereas, if John was not the Holy Messenger foretold by the prophets who and what was he?

Now it is by the written matter it is recorded where Jesus spoke directly to John saying that they had to fulfill all justice. And is it being that the prophets of old having spoken God's word was in fact the justice being that God is the justice. So, taking such into consideration, was Jesus then lying when he spoke to John? And then was John then also lying to the people? But there is such a question which must be asked. Who would have lived in such poor extraordinary conditions such as John the Baptist did simply to broadcast matter regarding someone else? Most important is the fact of what person in any history or religion other than Jesus Christ has worked so many miracles by the touch as well as by word?

Now it is that the same person having been written about by more than just one or two witnesses but in fact there were six written witnesses clearly establishes in credibility that Jesus Christ was the only and true Messiah. He, the Christ was in fact the only Messiah that was foretold by the prophets leaving no more to be expected. What in fact does all of this have to do with the Baptist? By those very matters it clearly, credibly establishes that John the Baptist was the true and only Holy Messenger sent by the Lord God himself to walk before Him.

John the Baptist was in fact not only human but being of the spirit returned to the spiritual existence. It seems most fitting that the exciting life of the Baptist was ended as the conclusion to the exciting party.

True it is that Herodias had her day while Herod had his fun, but then also true is that Herod and the queen's reign was stopped by none other than Philip. He called their reign to an end by having them banished to an island.

Wow! John was the only person who had been given the gift of walking before the Lord God announcing His actual presence as the Kingdom of God. Now it was that John was holy whose life experienced good and bad endings but, also it is that John the Baptist was truly the great holy exciting messenger of the true Lord God personally sent by God Himself to actually go before Him announcing the way.

Evidenced by the statements shown in the written record clearly substantiates just how excitingly holy great John the Baptist was.

EPILOGUE

Whether or not people believe in God or a Creator here makes no difference. Regarding the life and events of John the Baptist, the written records portray that the man had a singular purpose of his being. Nowhere do the accumulated facts indicate that he was a prophet talking about years to come. Plus, it was where he himself even stated so much. Yet, since he did preach of religious matter it would be most appropriate to classify him as a preacher, but not to take away from his true profession.

As shown in and by the records his profession was that of a news delivery person or a messenger of current news. There is no mystery here, for John's actions as well as his own words defined his professional duty. His was to spread the word of the Messiah having already arrived. His number one duty was to spread the message of Christ the Messiah actually being around the neighborhood. Not as one of a prophet, as he was not prophesying of people and events that were to occur years or centuries later.

Being the messenger, he was always about spreading the word of Christ the Messiah being actually present in the immediate area. At every turn John kept telling the people that their prayed for Messiah was already about them. That their hoped for had already arrived. And it was that the people heard and they listened.But then there were the civil rulers who were the human law. Amazing how their actions almost relate to how the government people in this country act. Of course, they religiously ruled themselves all the while even when in exile.

Now it was that Christ as established by the records was the Messiah that the prophets had foretold about. And it was that He had come to fulfill all justice, which was the prophesies. Such prophesies from old, that He fulfilled were those regarding of who the prophets had prophesized about. And it is that the prophets were actually telegraphers passing on the words spoken to them by the Lord God.

It is that according to the written records, the Baptist was foretold by the prophets. Easily seen it is that John had often spoken of Christ, describing Him as to what he was as well as where. Simultaneously denying of his self being the Messiah it is most important to note how he boldly advised the people often of his mission. In the records it is revealed that John was the messenger foretold by the prophets to be the one who was to go before the face of the Lord.

His primary function was simply to advertise or announce, the fact that the Messiah, who was Jesus Christ had arrived and walking in their midst. A herald and a preacher were he, but not a prophet. No, rather he was the one and only Holy Messenger of God who went before the Lord God. Proclaiming the matter of the Messiah's actual presence.

John was not about the future of the people but of their faith. In fact, he was the true holy messenger of that time period, who had been sent directly from God Himself. Being the loud speaker or host John the Baptist was all about announcing the arrived Holy One. And it was the Holy One which the people had been praying for.

There was no other, nor is there any other person that even remotely resembles what John was about or how such other person may have been foretold by the prophets. Also, there is no other praise that could be given him, which was, that he was the one and only messenger that originated as a spirit sent directly by the Lord God. Yet as was necessary, he was born of a woman who completed his purpose of being a messenger.

What else needs to be said, as the Baptist fulfilled his sacred mission? Of course, people love to debate things. Then especially when people only read part or only one of the apostles' writings they are ready to dash it around.

But why is it that when presented with other added information which may confirm what they are attempting to disprove they walk away? Is it all about having closed minds being so important? Or is it being stubborn or just selfish, as only wanting to have their own way?

Well, what about the truth or doesn't that matter? Maybe arguing then forcing their way like Herodias by being brutal is more important. Then since force does not necessarily mean truth, what can be gained except winning by denying truth?

CONCLUSION

Fiction and fantasy are so much easier. After all, why care about truth when there is the fun of Hollywood? John the Baptist as proven by the written records did not go around performing as some magician, or trickster. Nor did he perform as some fortune teller talking about things of the far distant future. Rather John the Baptist was all about the then present time.

He did in fact complete his mission being the true and only Lord God's holy messenger. And so, says the written record of the Old Testament which told of his coming, combined with the gospels of the New Testament.

All of those written documents and matters clearly and credibly attest to his holy being as the only true Holy Messenger that walked immediately before the face of the Lord God.

Sure, they killed the excitingly holy and great John the Baptist but the fact is that he did complete his mission of purpose. He did walk before the Lord God announcing His Holy presence as was so instructed by his Creator.... the End.

AUTHOR

The man never had any intention of writing the book. It just happened that way as if pushed by so many people knowing so little about so much. While attending the grade school of St. Michael's church in Chester, Penna., it was during the last years where he became a choir boy. Fascinated with the religious services he constantly inquired as to the why. Then in St. James Catholic High School it became all about the why, how and what for? Curious he was yet he didn't know it would resurface later in life.

Well mannered while respectfully enjoying people of all faiths, colors and creeds, the author was always considered just a little special welcomed into all groups. While in the U.S.A.F. the religious bug struck again where discussions erupted even during social activities of a beer bashing or card gaming time. What seemed to fascinate everyone was their selves involved where the discussions often grew into friendly, heated debates. Especially with those of other or no faiths add to by others of different colors.

Later in civilian life there was just too many people with too many versions of who the Baptist was. Always needing to know he started to do some research which developed into discussing the matters with theologians and ancient history buffs. No university of every religious denomination was spared. Wow, So much was the author learning, that it drove him needing to find more answers. There became more questions of which he had no answers. One item led into another which overlapped others. Perseverance along with inspirations helped complete the book which is not a text book.

Formatted for the general public, its content is factual matter based on and taken from the scriptures and ancient history records.. Author strained to create the book in down to earth straight talk of fact with opinions as well as questions stated stimulating the thought process. In the book he reveals many matters not necessarily mentioned in other books or left vague or even not answered.

The Great Excitignly Holy John the Baptist

Dear Reader,

While non-fiction matters the content of history is so full of life distortions the author finds it to be mind-boggling. Hope is that having purchased the book upon reading you found moments of reading pleasure along with some education. Most unfortunate for the author is that he did not know any of the Baptist's family therefore not a first person. Then also not from the time period he has written about it truly put the author in a laborious position of having to believe people of education as well as obtaining matters from various books. Difficult it was attempting to extract information from what people did not furnish and books that leave the matter in question.

Through the much research of volumes of books combined with many discussions with professors of ancient history along with those of ancient religious studies, it was like being introduced to a different world. Connecting matters already known with information received and then trying to distinguish the show of putting the matter into a written format especially to include new matter received became a huge hurdle. Too many variables from too many people with different opinions and mind settings posed a unique challenge. Amazing it was the number of people who knew what they believed yet actually knew very little with others knowing nothing about the man and his family.

It is hoped that people who have read the book may have appreciated the work that went into completing the manuscript and those that will read the book will refrain from skipping sections using the assumption of ego and those that read the book in detail truly had a reading enjoyment.

Sincerely,

Stanley E. Kornafel, author.

www.ingramcontent.com/pod-product-compliance
Lightning Source LLC
Chambersburg PA
CBHW051509120626
46551CB00012B/842